Research in the Politics of
Population

Research in the Politics of Population

Richard L. Clinton
University of North Carolina

R. Kenneth Godwin
Oregon State University

Lexington Books
D.C. Heath and Company
Lexington, Massachusetts
Toronto   London

224015

Library of Congress Cataloging in Publication Data

Clinton, Richard L.
    Research in the politics of population.

    1. Population—Addresses, essays, lectures. I. Godwin, R. Kenneth, joint
author. II. Title.
HB871.C6   301.32   72-7117
ISBN 0-669-81901-8

Published simultaneously in Canada.

Printed in the United States of America.

International Standard Book Number: 0-669-81901-8

Library of Congress Catalog Card Number: 72-7117

Contents

List of Figures

List of Tables

Foreword

The reader should view this book in a context with its predecessor volume, POLITICAL SCIENCE IN POPULATION STUDIES, and an expected successor on new directions for political science research. They emerge from a commitment by the Department of Political Science and the Carolina Population Center at the University of North Carolina at Chapel Hill to help systematically to develop this frontier of knowledge. Annual conferences at Chapel Hill on population and political science will continue to seek to help in mapping and mining this terrain.

The present book especially emphasizes studies related to population policy development. This subject can usefully be analyzed along at least three dimensions: overall population goals, substantive content of policies supporting such goals, and the process of formulating, implementing, and readjusting such policies at different levels. In the identification of overall goals, authors of this book add a most welcome emphasis on the need now for much more explicit attention to fundamental human value factors. Regarding policy content, the papers reflect needs for more knowledge of the implications of various proposed policy measures, for a broader view of policy alternatives, and for comparative studies. As for policy process, the authors advance concepts and cases to illuminate the complexities of what has been termed "participatory demography."

Population scientists already in this field should welcome these observations and their further pursuit. Demographers often demonstrate innocence about the political realities of population policy and program development. For example, a classic demographic study of India in 1950 included the prediction that a strong birth control policy by that government was only remotely possible. More recently, some able scholars have been diverted by debates between the extremes of, on the one hand, a definition of "family planning" which is far narrower than that actually used by concerned administrators and political leaders and, on the other hand, proposals for coercive population policies which could cause a nation's government to fall much faster than its birth rate. Meanwhile, many other questions of more immediate salience go ignored. Responsible policymakers must also welcome steps to build a stronger base for their art and to facilitate more systematic learning from experience around the world. In such matters, political scientists should be able to contribute.

A warning is due, however, not to expect too much. Political scientists entering this field will need help in assimilating the knowledge of population dynamics already produced from other sources. They need encouragement to concentrate now on building a sounder scientific base and to resist the pressures to start prescribing too soon. Political science is also preoccupied with building up its own body of research methods and theory, and its links with other disciplines. At this stage, political science itself may gain the most from interaction with the population field. Increasingly, however, the broader field of population studies stands to be enriched by this fusion.

Other important areas also call for more attention by political science and population research, which are distinct from but also basic to the policy studies area. A key one is the subject of governance. Obviously the institutional means suitable for facilitating freedom, distributive justice, and resource conservation among a group of people will profoundly interact with such factors as population size, composition, spatial distribution, and rates of change. The Commission on Population Growth and the American Future has helped to highlight needs for more scientific knowledge of these relationships. Another crucial area is international relations, where the population components of global relationships and conflict have been sadly neglected. Azar and others at North Carolina are now exploring aspects of research on population, peace, and international organization. And the basic need remains to advance normative political theory. In this area, modern developments in the population field force us to face issues and integrate concepts, and can help move us toward what we avoid so well: clarifying where we really want to go.

Moye W. Freymann

September 28, 1972

1 Introduction: The Study of Population by Political Scientists

Richard L. Clinton and
R. Kenneth Godwin

I. The Development of Interest in Population Variables

What is meant by "the study of population"? For demographers the answer is straightforward, the study of the demographic variables: fertility, mortality, and migration. From the standpoint of demography, then, the interesting questions include such things as how these variables can be precisely defined and measured, how their effects on future population size and growth rates under differing assumptions can be calculated, and how ever more reliable data on these variables can be gathered. Since demography is a field of sociology, many demographers are interested in exploring the determinants of variations in these variables, particularly insofar as these determinants originate in or are influenced by the family, the class system, or other elements of the social structure.

When the study of population is approached from the perspective of political science, naturally the interesting questions will involve political considerations. For political scientists, then, the study of population is the study of the interactions between demographic and political variables. As the following quotation makes clear, both dependent and independent variables can be selected from either the demographic or the political sets, depending on the particular focus of the analysis being performed:

Political demography is the study of the size, composition, and distribution of population in relation to both government and politics. It is concerned with *the political consequences of population change*, especially the effects of population change on the demands made upon governments, on the performance of governments, and on the distribution of political power. It also considers *the political determinants of population change*, especially the political causes of the movement of people, the relationship of various population configurations to the structures and functions of government, and the public policy directed at affecting the size, composition, and distribution of populations. Finally, in the study of political demography it is not enough to know the facts and figures of populations—that is, the fertility, mortality, and migration rates; it is also necessary to consider the knowledge and attitudes that people have toward population issues.[1]

1

To reflect but a moment on this comprehensive definition of political demography is to realize that the interactions between demographic and political variables are doubtless many, complex, and important. If the person coming to this realization were unacquainted with the literature of modern political science, he or she would probably assume that political demography must be a standard subfield of the discipline or at the very least one of its most thoroughly exploited areas of research. How would it affect his or her assessment of political science, one wonders, to learn that not only are neither of these assumptions correct but that only this year (1972) has the first book-length treatment of population questions by political scientists appeared?[2]

The editors of the present volume have attempted elsewhere[3] to explain this anomaly on the basis of the generalized lack of awareness of population-related problems within society at large and in terms of the concept of mobilization of bias[4] within the university and the political science profession. Briefly, as regards the former, we argued that up until the post-World War II period political scientists could not very well have been expected to have incorporated demographic variables and population issues into their research, given the fact that hardly any other social scientists were doing so. Even demographers had a rather dim and imperfect understanding of some of the fundamental aspects of population dynamics at that time, and the overall state of knowledgeability regarding population matters was low indeed.[5] Perhaps equally as important, the overall state of public concern was also low. This low level of concern for population matters is easily accounted for. In the first place, population changes are by their nature gradual, hence not easily identified as "causing" other more obvious phenomena which themselves become defined as problems.[6] Secondly, the trend in fertility was sharply downward in the more developed countries during the difficult decade of the thirties, and little was known of the trends in the less developed countries. Thus what little concern was voiced came largely from economists who foresaw in a declining population the potential for serious economic dislocations.[7] Finally, a historical perspective reminds us that people, including political scientists, had other more serious problems to worry about during these decades of the twentieth century, e.g., getting out of the depression, defeating the fascists, and adjusting to the Cold War conditions of the fatuous fifties. Thus if population issues were not generally perceived as problems and certainly not as political problems, it is neither surprising nor particularly damning that political science was not involved in the study of population.

As the decade of the sixties unfolded, however, these extenuating circumstances could no longer be pleaded in defense of the discipline. By that time techniques of demographic analysis had become highly sophisticated, and better data were available than ever before. Consequently the existence of the worldwide population explosion had become common knowledge, and the wide-ranging implications of both rapid population growth and the increasing absolute size of populations were being discussed by thoughtful individuals of widely diverse professional backgrounds.[8] Something beyond the generalized unawareness of the population components of current problems was apparently involved in the continued neglect by political scientists of population as a relevant area for research.

The concept of mobilization of bias provided us with a clue to understanding why political science was slow to join in the study of population. There was, first of all, the overcompartmentalization of knowledge characteristic of the modern university and the increasingly narrow specialization within each discipline—indeed, as a result of the "knowledge explosion," the proliferation of new and ever more specialized disciplines. Thus both the structure of the university and of the professions responsible for furthering understanding tended to obstruct communication across disciplinary boundaries. This combination of circumstances, in our view, was particularly important in inhibiting wider awareness of and more diversified research in the population area:

This lack of interdisciplinary cross-fertilization seems to have been of consider-able significance in the unresponsiveness of political scientists in recognizing the relevance of population variables, for the questions posed by population change are exceptionally interdisciplinary in nature. Particularly as regards population policy, it is all but impossible to separate the psychological, sociological, and philosophical, to say nothing of the economic ramifications of any measure contemplated.[9]

Within the political science profession itself, moreover, a mobilization of bias was equally evident. During the strife which accompanied "the behavioral revolution" the emphasis within the discipline shifted disproportionately from political to science. The preoccupation with adapting the quantitative methodol-ogies of economics and sociology for use in the analysis of political phenomena consumed the energies of most of the leaders of the discipline for a considerable period, roughly from 1950 to 1965. As a consequence, many important political issues escaped the attention of political science until they announced themselves on the evening news. To point out that the drive toward quantification and the use of ever more elaborate statistical techniques resulted in a tendency toward the rigorous analysis of often irrelevant data is not, however, to impugn the contribution of the behavioral movement in placing the discipline on a more empirical footing; it is merely to state one of the initial costs of that achievement. In a certain sense, moreover, that very achievement may have contributed to a further postponement of the study of population by political scientists, for the reorientation of the discipline toward empirical research had the effect of making investigations with explicit normative aspects seem old-fashioned and outside the mainstream of political science. Although there are many intersections between population and politics which can be investi-gated empirically and even quantitatively, it is uncommonly difficult in dealing with this combination of topics to avoid confronting ethical issues at some point. Yet by both training and socialization—and perhaps by inclination, given the self-selection involved—political scientists have become increasingly loath to tread the uncertain ground of ethical analysis.

A certain disciplinary parochialism was also adduced as helping to mobilize the agenda of political science in such a way that population questions have not been included. The inertia of the standard subdivisions of the discipline, for instance, hampers the introduction of unorthodox courses, the funding of novel research, and the publication of materials for which no accepted rubric exists. One wonders, as a matter of fact, under what heading the present volume could be reviewed in the *American Political Science Review*: Political Theory, History of Political Thought, and Methodology? American Government and Politics? Comparative Government and Politics? International Politics, Law, and Organization? Or will the book review editor despair of fitting it under any heading and resolve his problem by not assigning it for review?

Thus the neglect of population studies by political scientists can be explained and up until the early 1960s perhaps excused. More than a decade has passed since the early '60s, however, during which time the world's population has grown by a thousand million. Yet where is the research by political scientists into "the effects of population change on the demands made upon governments, on the performance of governments, and on the distribution of power"? The absence of such research throughout the '60s was made all the more notable by the fact that a demographer and a political scientist in the field of international relations jointly published a book in 1961 calling attention to questions of this sort.[10] Moreover, during the '60s a rich literature developed as population policy issues were discussed and debated by demographers, sociologists, economists, public health experts, and nutritionists.[11] None of this literature appeared in political science journals,[12] however, nor were any political scientists among its authors. By default, as it were, non-political scientists began to deal with the various interfaces of population and politics.[13]

Finally, during the late '60s, a congeries of circumstances began to bring about a change in this situation,[14] and a growing number of political scientists— ourselves among them—at last began to "discover" population studies. Among the background conditions precedent to this change two would seem to have been of special importance: the programs and financing provided by the Ford Foundation, other private foundations, and by various agencies of the U.S. government, and the promotion of cross-disciplinary communication specifically focused on demographic questions by population centers located at a number of the nation's leading universities. To a very large extent, of course, the second condition was an outgrowth of the first. More immediate causes of the change would include the rising public consciousness of the existence of a population problem;[15] the sharply increased publicity about and concern for pollution of the environment, with its frequent but sometimes incorrect nexus with population growth; and, finally, the president's request in July of 1969 that Congress set up a Commission on Population Growth and the American Future.[16]

By the early 1970s, then, given the existence of active and well-financed pressure groups,[17] heated public controversies over abortion law reform, the rapidly increasing importance of population activities within our foreign assistance program, the unprecedented appearance in some states of official propaganda aimed at discouraging in-migration, and proposed legislation before Congress to use taxation to influence fertility decisions, there was no longer any question of a place for political science in the study of population.

Indeed, the present volume and such events as the Political Science/Population Workshop held at the University of North Carolina's Chapel Hill campus in May, 1972,[18] demonstrate that an important group of political scientists representing the entire spectrum of the discipline's approaches and subject specialties is already involved in the study of population.

Not surprisingly, in view of the unparalleled rates of population growth throughout the Third World,[19] most of the political scientists whose research interests have led them to the study of population are specialists in the related subfields of comparative politics/political development. Among the topics of greatest interest for these investigators are how rapid population growth and the hypertrophy of urban areas affect the functioning of different political systems; how elites and masses, both within and between countries, differ in their views of the probable effects of demographic changes; and to what extent different types of governments seem capable of effectively accommodating and ameliorating population pressures. The last question is giving rise to what promises to be a particularly important area which might be called comparative population policy research.

The next largest contingent of political scientists involved in the study of population is made up of specialists in international relations. Far removed from the simplistic *Lebensraum* approach, this perspective focuses on the whole range of demographic variables and their potential influence not only on international conflict but on international cooperation. In terms of the latter the development of international law and the expanding role of international organizations and their specialized agencies are of interest. Some of the political scientists in this group, somewhat in the tradition of geopolitics, are combining technological, resource, and population considerations in a sophisticated attempt to predict areas of potential scarcity. Others are employing a global ecological outlook to try to discern needed modifications in the centuries-old system of sovereign nation-states.

A smaller group is investigating the population policy formation process and the administration of population programs, seeking answers to such questions as who is involved in the policy decisions and their implementation and for what reasons, upon what sort of information are these persons basing their decisions, within what constraints or parameters are population policies formulated and what is the origin of these constraints or parameters, which groups are principally affected by these policies and how are they affected, what are the unintended effects of population policies and what implications for population change do non-population policies have, what are the major obstacles to population policies in different areas of the world, and among the potential policy measures available which are preferable in terms of what values?

Several other political scientists are attempting to deal with the thorny ethical issues which invariably accompany the combination of population and politics. A few are daring to allow themselves to look ahead in order to provide as well-reasoned and informed a level of speculation as possible as regards the future political implications of present population trends. One or two others are approaching fertility questions from the point of view of women's roles and the political environment within which these roles are defined.

Clearly an exponential increase is occurring in the questions being asked by political scientists about population. Undoubtedly the number will continue to increase as further research undermines what were thought to be eternal verities and thus opens up new areas to be explored. This is, of course, all to the good, since questions must be asked before they can be answered. That political science is capable of asking new questions augurs well for the renewed vigor of the discipline in this post-behavioral stage of its development. In this sense, regardless of the contributions which political demography will make to society, it is already paying its way within political science, for until population issues began to be studied by political scientists, demographic variables were seldom included in the analysis of political phenomena. Both the theoretical import of recognizing demographic factors as variables and of taking them into account and the methodological refinement offered by such techniques of demography as cohort analysis have already begun to enhance the explanatory power of political analyses.[20]

One of the most experienced and insightful analysts of population questions, Bernard Berelson, recently noted that there seems "to be around the world a growing debate on population policy. In its magnitude and purpose the debate may turn out to be a truly historic event for mankind, with consequences far beyond the latter decades of the twentieth century in which it may work itself out."[21] Implicit in this restrained observation is the somewhat startling fact that in today's world of unprecedented population expansion population policies are among the most critical actions which governments can undertake. If this is true, and we are convinced that it is, then it is reasonable to assume that governments should be, and increasingly will be, concerned with the demographic effects of their policies. It is significant in this regard that in the past decade an increasing number of governments have attempted to alter the rate of growth of their population as well as to influence its distribution within their boundaries.

Obviously official programs of fertility regulation are fraught with danger for the individual. For governments to attempt to change the most intimate behavior of their citizens is, it would seem, an alarming extension of political power. Whether such actions would in fact be an extension of power of the state over the individual, however, is an empirical question. A great deal more work along the lines of Murray Edelman's *The Symbolic Uses of Politics* is needed before this question can be answered properly. Moreover, from the individual's point of view, even were the attempts by government to influence his or her fertility behavior to be an extension of the state's power, it might well be merely the substitution of one type of influence for another, that of society itself. Only further research into the determinants of family size norms can provide insight into the terms of this "tradeoff." And, finally, in a world where population will certainly not be stabilized before the present population has doubled, and resource depletion and environmental pollution will be continuing threats to the quality of human life, governmental intervention to limit the size and distribution of population may well prove to be by far the least of the evils among which mankind must choose.

We believe it would be one of the greatest crimes in academic history if persons who have studied the process of public policy making and the consequences of policy outcomes do not use their knowledge to help make this choice and to protect to whatever extent possible the quality of human life by contributing to the design of effective and noncoercive population policies. The articles which are included in this volume represent some of the first efforts by political scientists to understand the effects of policies which change or are designed to change population growth rates.

II. A Partial Guide to the Study of Population Policies

Population policies, like almost all other policies, result from a blend of three interrelated factors: (1) elite attitudes, (2) mass attitudes, and (3) governmental capacities. These three sets of variables determine not only the features of a given policy but also the success or failure of the policy. If we are to accurately analyze the politics of population we cannot omit any of these factors.

Perhaps the variables which most directly influence the structure of population policies are the attitudes and values of the relevant elites and the elites' perception of the existing contextual situation. Population policies are not divorced from dominant political ideologies or the current demands upon the policymakers. Therefore there will develop a "mobilization of bias"[22] for one set of policies and against other sets.

Assuming that population policies are reached in a rational manner, we must suppose that the decision makers weigh their expected gains against their expected losses for each policy alternative and then choose among the possible policies. Obviously an individual who believes that a higher growth rate is preferable to a lower rate will be less likely to approve of a policy which would reduce the fertility rate. Thus for elites who view a larger population as the principal means for increasing their national power and prestige and settling the frontier lands of their countries, the benefits to the economy outweigh the costs of feeding, clothing, and educating a rapidly increasing population—particularly since most of that population will be so poorly fed, clothed, and educated. In such a pronatal setting the elites effectively mobilize a strong bias against even a voluntary contraceptive program for the masses.

An example of the mobilization of bias in the United States is the almost exclusive emphasis on family planning programs as the most desirable policy alternative.[23] The chapters in the present volume by Elihu Bergman and Keir Nash reveal many of the causes and possible effects of this limitation on the scope of considered alternatives. These two chapters demonstrate that several sets of elites can become involved in determining that a certain type of program will be the chosen policy.

Bergman's chapter discusses how the "Fortune 500" profile of the Commission on Population Growth and the American Future and the "American Population Movement" has focused research on the problem of how to improve contraceptive techniques rather than how social and economic structures in the society can be changed to improve the probability that persons will use the contraceptives already available. Because research costs money and only members of the "American Population Movement" are presently supporting extensive population research, most of the existing explorations in the population field are related to how family planning programs can be made more effective. This research bias has the effect of insuring that the social and economic status quo will not be questioned.

In his chapter, Nash examines how the family planning bias has been further extended by the epistemological biases of demographers. Nash hypothesizes that many of the difficulties in the field of population policy have resulted from the fact that demographers have too often overlooked, minimized, or approached with simplistic tools the inherent political components of population growth rates. Unfortunately, political scientists have not attempted to correct this problem.

In addition to the importance of elite attitudes and values in the choice of policy alternatives, their attitudes and values are also among the primary determinants of how the chosen policy will be administered and what priority it will have vis-à-vis other policies. In the determination of the program's method of administration and its priority, political elites can be expected to attempt to maximize their political benefits. The low interest in population programs among the majority of citizens in the United States and the fact that benefits from population control policies are not immediately visible have prompted political elites to give these programs a low priority on the domestic agenda. This low priority has allowed program administrators to use population funds in ways designed to fit elite interests rather than the interests of the users of the family planning services. These programs, because they are directed toward the poor, have tended to fall into the familiar pattern of "poor services for the poor," while the administrative agencies have been able to use "excess" family planning resources to maintain other programs of higher priority to the administrators.

Once policy statements are translated into programs mass attitudes become a dominant factor in the success of the policy. Although the elites attempt to predict the desires and needs of the people who are to participate in the population program, only rarely are members of the "user population" encouraged to make substantial inputs into the policy-making process. Thus when the program is actually implemented, it is often found that the elites have misinterpreted the desires of the masses. Such misinterpretations can be particularly disastrous for population policies. As one of our colleagues quipped, "population policies are participatory demography." The truth of this pun is all too real. A successful population policy is dependent upon the decisions of millions of individuals, and, except in cases of permanent sterilization, these decisions must be made again and again and again. Because of their participatory nature, population policies must be designed to consider closely the decision-making patterns of the people they are intended to benefit.

The chapters by Bergman, Nash, and Clinton all demonstrate the virtual exclusion of members of the mass population from the process of formulating population policies both in the United States and abroad. In Chapters 6 and 7 Kenneth Godwin and Gerald Wright examine the attitude and value patterns of mass populations and discuss the implications of these patterns for present and future policies. Godwin examines the question: "Are the factors which are important in the decision to have a child the same factors which elites have identified as important?" Obviously if the policymakers believe that one set of factors determines the decision to have a child while, in fact, another set of influences is more important, then the population policy is likely to be unsuccessful. Godwin's analysis finds that the assumptions which elites make about mass attitudes are frequently in error. Because of this error it appears that the policy alternatives which have been suggested are based on questionable foundations.

One of the more important conclusions which Godwin derives from his analysis of his own data and the data of previous Knowledge, Attitudes, and Practice (KAP) studies is that family planning programs alone cannot adequately reduce fertility rates. He bases this conclusion on findings which lead him to believe that policies confined to family planning approaches contain two erroneous assumptions: (1) that fertility attitudes are well structured and will determine how many children a woman will think is ideal, and, (2) that the number of children considered ideal would be the crucial consideration in the determination of actual family size if contraceptives were readily available.

In Chapter 7 Gerald Wright applies the hypotheses derived in the previous chapter to the specific situation of the rural poor in the southern United States. He attempts to discern both the need of these people for contraceptives and the adequacy of existing programs to meet this need. The study concludes that the use of contraceptives by these people is simply not a part of their relevant subculture. Because of the lack of salience of attitudes concerning contraceptives, a program designed solely to make contraceptives available to the rural poor will find only a small percentage of the potential clientele participating in the program. A successful contraceptive program would first need to make birth limitation a salient and a positive value.

The last sets of variables which determine the type and effectiveness of population policies are the capacities of the government and the society. As Berelson has so clearly demonstrated, if a population policy is to be viable it must be feasible in its economic, administrative, technical, and political aspects.[24] "In other words, the key questions are: is the scientific/medical/technological base available or likely? Will the governments approve? Can the proposal be administered? Can the society afford the proposal"?[25] To insure the viability of any contraceptive program two technological and medical questions must be answered affirmatively: (1) is the needed technology available? and (2) are the requisite medical facilities and personnel available now or in the near future?[26] For example, both fertility control agents[27] and temporary sterilants[28] have been suggested as possible answers to the world's rapid population growth. Such materials, however, are not available now and are not on the immediate technological horizon.[29] In addition to technological limitations there are also those of inadequate scientific and medical personnel. In the less developed countries of the world an adequate supply of surgeons or other medical personnel is not available to perform compulsory sterilization, even if a policy involving mandatory sterilization for large sectors of the population were adopted by the governments.

Potential policy alternatives are also limited by the economic capabilities of the society. As Berelson has shown, a policy alternative must pass two requirements: (1) it must be worthwhile when measured against the criterion of economic return, and, (2) the country's budget must be able to afford it.[30] The United States and most of the other so-called developed countries can afford programs such as the institutionalization of maternal and child care, social security benefits to elderly couples who have had fewer than X children, national education programs through the use of television, and direct cash incentives for sterilization or contraceptive adoption, but these policies would be beyond the financial capabilities of many less developed countries.[31] Although foreign aid, were it accepted, might supply some of the financing for these types of policies, it is unlikely that the amount of aid would be sufficient. In India alone it has been estimated that each of the above named policies would cost over $200 million, not including administrative costs.[32]

Another difficult set of restrictions on a country's choice of policy alternatives is the society's administrative capabilities. As we discussed above, both elite and mass values limit the effectiveness of policy administration. Even beyond these limitations, however, is the limitation of the capability of the government's administrative agencies. For example, any policy which either taxes persons with many children or offers cash incentives to persons with fewer children would be difficult to administer in less developed countries. In these societies taxes are already difficult to collect and are subject to many errors—both intentional and unintentional. It is quite probable that given the low capacity of the administrative agencies, such tax programs would be highly inefficient. Similarly, incentive systems would be difficult to administer honestly in bureaucracies which have often depended on the bribe and have never extended very far into the rural areas of the country. Very probably under either tax or incentive programs many citizens of less developed countries would find it to their advantage to hide the births of their children, hence the already difficult job of keeping demographic records would become close to impossible. More coercive policies such as licenses for children or compulsory sterilization after the third child would obviously be impossible to administer in these countries.

The final and possibly most difficult limitation on policy alternatives is the political viability of population policies. Certain policies, even though technologically, economically, and administratively feasible, would not be politically feasible. Every government has only a limited amount of legitimacy and coercive power. This means that policies which major segments of a society see as ethically unacceptable or biased against their group may not be effective because these people will simply disobey the laws. Highly coercive policies such as compulsory sterilization or abortion certainly belong in this group of politically unacceptable programs. Politically unacceptable programs are not, however, limited to highly coercive policies. Even family planning or incentive programs may be unacceptable in countries where there are strong tribal, racial, or religious cleavages, for these programs may be perceived as attempts by one group to improve its position vis-à-vis other groups in society.

From his examination of population policy alternatives Berelson concludes that family planning and policies such as population education and better research into contraceptive technologies are the most viable by economic, technological, administrative, and political standards. This conclusion, however, "sustains and strengthens, subtly yet forcefully, the dominant family planning philosophy while refuting challenging positions. The consequence could be to discourage consideration and review of proposals beyond family planning that are not adaptable to existing social structures in a majority of countries."[33] In Chapters 8 and 9 Robert McIntyre and Pi-chao Chen call many of Berelson's findings into question by showing that family planning and allied policies are not the only viable alternatives. In these two chapters the authors examine policies in Eastern Europe and China which were not implemented as strictly population policies; rather the policies were designed to meet ideological requirements of

Communist doctrines and to aid in the modernization of the country. Although partially indirect and unintentional in their population effects, these policies were successful in reducing fertility rates. Such policies (in Eastern Europe the major policy was abortion on demand, while in China policies included the expansion of the public health network, changes in familial relationships, improvements in the status and opportunities of women, and the expansion of mass communications), by their success, show the limitations of looking at only those policies which appear viable under the *existing* social structures in a society.

If China has been as successful in its reduction of fertility rates as Chen believes it to have been, then it would seem logical for other countries to begin looking at means of indirectly reducing fertility while modernizing their social structures. To spend millions on a communications network, maternal-child health facilities, or on the creation of new jobs for women may not appear economically feasible if their sole purpose is to reduce births, but if the same programs can be used to mobilize the society politically and economically, the justification for the expenditure is much stronger. Similar rationales can be given for the adoption of other policies which benefit the development of the country at the same time they directly or indirectly contribute to a reduction of the birth rate.

The final issue which we must discuss in this introductory chapter is the normative position of the contributors to this volume. We hope that our research will prove important in the battle to effectively reduce population growth rates. More importantly, though, we would like for our research to contribute to increasing the freedom of people from both governmental interference and the ultimately more oppressive interference of environmental pressures on the quality of life. All contributors to this volume have endeavored to remain aware of the potential harm which could result from research into the politics of population. Hopefully our awareness of the ethical issues will alert the reader to the normative assumptions we have made. To insure that the normative issue is joined and this all-important dialogue initiated, the chapter which follows is a critique of present population policy research and an attempt to outline an alternative. In this chapter Steven Garland and Robert Trudeau emphasize the difficulties involved when coercion is studied. It should be instructive to test the applicability of their comments to the research which is reported in the remainder of the book.

Notes

1. Myron Weiner, "Political Demography: An Inquiry into the Political Consequences of Population Change," pp. 567-617 of National Academy of Sciences, *Rapid Population Growth: Consequences and Policy Implications*

(Baltimore and London: The Johns Hopkins Press, 1971): 567, emphases added.

2. Richard L. Clinton, William S. Flash, and R. Kenneth Godwin, eds., *Political Science in Population Studies* (Lexington, Mass.: D.C. Heath & Co., 1972).

3. Richard L. Clinton and R. Kenneth Godwin, "Political Science in Population Studies: Reasons for the Late Start," Chapter 8, ibid.

4. See Chapter 4, "The Displacement of Conflicts," in E.E. Schattschneider, *The Semisovereign People: A Realist's View of Democracy in America* (New York: Holt, Rinehart and Winston, 1960). Admittedly, we were broadening the concept somewhat in order to include the value structure of what might be called the discipline's subculture.

5. As basic a theory as that of the demographic transition only gained currency in the decade of the forties. See Warren C. Robinson, "The Development of Modern Population Theory," *American Journal of Economics and Sociology* 23, 4 (October 1964): 375-392.

6. We are indebted to Professor Jason Finkle for having stimulated our thinking on this point.

7. See, for example, Alvin Hansen, "Economic Progress and Declining Population Growth," *American Economic Review* 29, 1, Part 1 (March 1939): 1-15; or Joseph J. Spengler, "The Social and Economic Consequences of Cessation in Population Growth," *Proceedings of the Congresso International Per Gli Studi Sulla Popolazione* (Rome) 9 (1933): 33-60.

8. Fairfield Osborn, *The Limits of the Earth* (Boston: Little, Brown, 1953); John Boyd Orr and David Lubbock, *The White Man's Dilemma* (New York: Barnes and Noble, 1953); Harrison Brown, *The Challenge of Man's Future* (New York: The Viking Press, 1954); Marston Bates, *The Prevalence of People* (New York: Scribner, 1955); Sir Charles G. Darwin, *The Problems of World Population* (Cambridge: Cambridge University Press, 1958); Arnold J. Toynbee, "The Menace of Overpopulation," pp. 135-141 of Fairfield Osborn, ed., *Our Crowded Planet: Essays on the Pressures of Population* (Garden City, N.Y.: Doubleday, 1962).

9. Clinton and Godwin (n. 3): 144.

10. Katherine Organski and A.F.K. Organski, *Population and World Power* (New York: Alfred A. Knopf, 1961).

11. A sampling of this literature would include James W. Brackett and Earl Huyck, "The Objectives of Government Policies on Fertility Control in Eastern Europe," *Population Studies* (London) 16, 2 (November 1962): 134-146; J. Mayone Stycos, "Problems of Fertility Control in Underdeveloped Areas," *Marriage and Family Living* [now *Journal of Marriage and the Family*] 25, 1 (February 1963): 5-13; Dorothy Nortman, "Population Policies in Developing Countries and Related International Attitudes," *Eugenics Quarterly* 11, 1 (March 1964): 11-29; David Heer, "Abortion, Contraception, and Population

Policy in the Soviet Union," *Demography* 2 (1965): 531-539; Judith Blake, "Demographic Science and the Redirection of Population Policy," *Journal of Chronic Diseases* (1965): 1181-1200; Kingsley Davis, "Population Policy: Will Current Programs Succeed?" *Science* 158 (10 November 1967): 730-739; Carl Taylor, "Five Stages in a Practical Population Policy," *International Development Review* 10 (December 1968): 2-7; Judith Blake, "Population Policy for Americans: Is the Government Being Misled?" *Science* 164 (2 May 1969): 522-529; Oscar Harkavy, Frederick S. Jaffee, and Samuel M. Wishik, "Family Planning and Public Policy: Who Is Misleading Whom?" *Science* 165 (25 July 1969); Jean Mayer, "Toward a Non-Malthusian Population Policy," *Milbank Memorial Fund Quarterly* 47, 3 (July 1969); and Bernard Berelson, "Population Policy: Personal Notes," *Population Studies* 25, 2 (July 1971): 173-182.

12. So states A.E. Keir Nash, "Pollution, Population, and the Cowboy Economy," *Journal of Comparative Administration* 2, 1 (May 1970): 119-120.

13. A few citations from this genre follow: Philip Hauser, ed., *Population and World Politics* (Glencoe, Ill.: The Free Press, 1958); William Petersen, *The Politics of Population* (Garden City, N.Y.: Doubleday, 1964); Richard N. Gardner, "The Politics of Population: Blueprint for International Cooperation," pp. 285-297 of Larry K.Y. Ng and Stuart Mudd, eds., *The Population Crisis: Implications and Plans for Action* (Bloomington and London: Indiana University Press, 1965); and Colin Clark, "World Power and Population," *National Review* (20 May 1969): 687-697.

14. So far as we have been able to determine, only two political scientists could be said to have made a professional commitment to population studies before the mid-60s: A.F.K. Organski and Jason L. Finkle. They were followed during the 1966-68 period by Aaron Segal and Myron Weiner.

15. While the various conferences held throughout the world under the auspices of organizations such as the International Planned Parenthood Federation, Planned Parenthood-World Population, the Population Reference Bureau, the Smithsonian Institution, and the United Nations and its various agencies doubtless had significant multiplier effects, credit should also be given to such "clanging bells" as Paul Ehrlich and Garrett Hardin, who sacrificed much of their standing among their professional colleagues in order to bring the urgency of population challenges to the attention of the public.

16. An advance copy of the Commission's report appeared in March, 1972, published by The New American Library, Inc., in its Signet paperback series.

17. See the detailed discussion of these groups in Elihu Bergman, *The Politics of Population USA: A Critique of the Policy Process* (Chapel Hill: Carolina Population Center, Population Program and Policy Design Series, no. 5, 1971): 92-102.

18. Sixteen of the participants in this workshop will contribute chapters to a forthcoming volume entitled *Population and Politics: New Directions for Political Science Research* (Lexington, Mass.: D.C. Heath, 1973).

19. As Daly has pointed out, "a frequency distribution of countries by gross reproduction rate (GRR) is strikingly bimodal. Developed countries have a GRR of less than 2.0, while underdeveloped countries have a GRR greater than 2.0, with almost no countries falling in the dividing range around 2.0. For high-fertility countries the unweighted mean GRR was 2.94, while for the low-fertility countries it was 1.41, or less than half as large." Herman E. Daly, "A Marxian-Malthusian View of Poverty and Development," *Population Studies* 25, 1 (March 1971): 32. The appalling significance of these fertility differentials can be seen in the fact that the average completed family size for a population with a GRR of 1.41 is under three children as compared to nearly six for a population with a GRR of 2.94.

20. See the insightful use of cohort analysis and of differential fertility and mortality rates by David Butler and Donald Stokes, *Political Change in Britain: Forces Shaping Electoral Choice* (New York: St. Martin's Press, 1969): 50, 56, 62-64, 263-274, and passim.

21. Berelson (n. 11): 174.

22. For a full discussion of this concept in the area of population policy see: Peter Bachrach, "The Scholar and Political Strategy: The Population Case," in Clinton, Flash, and Godwin (n. 2): Chapter 3.

23. The most obvious example of the bias toward family planning programs is *The Report of the Commission on Population Growth and the American Future* (n. 16). Also see Bernard Berelson, "Beyond Family Planning," *Studies in Family Planning* no. 38 (February 1969): 1-16.

24. Much of this section will rely heavily on Berelson's classic article, "Beyond Family Planning," (n. 23).

25. Berelson (n. 23): 3.

26. Ibid.

27. The famous—or infamous—suggestion of adding fertility reducing agents to the water supply was made by Melvin M. Ketchel, "Fertility Control Agents as a Possible Solution to the World Population Problem," *Perspectives in Biology and Medicine* 11, 4 (Summer 1968): 687-703.

28. Paul R. Ehrlich, *The Population Bomb* (New York: Ballantine Books, 1968): 135-136.

29. Berelson (n. 23): 3.

30. Ibid., 6.

31. Ibid., 7

32. Ibid.

33. Peter Bachrach and Elihu Bergman, "Participation and Conflict in Making American Population Policy: A Critical Analysis," a paper prepared for the Commission on Population Growth and the American Future, December, 1971, p. 50 of the manuscript.

2

Population Policy Research:
A Critique and an Alternative

Steven Garland and
Robert Trudeau

When reporting on the results of empirical research, scholars often give short shrift to the theoretical concerns that initially inspired the research in favor of the theoretical implications of the findings. When population policy research is conducted in what might be called the Third World, the political implications of social science activities are usually ignored altogether. And though social science research is rarely conducted in laboratory situations, "paradigm" and "laboratory" seem to be used synonymously at times.

Nevertheless, when scholars do research or make policy recommendations, they become involved in politics. This is so whether the involvement is intended or not, for it results from the very nature of their endeavors. Consequently researchers should be conscious of the political environment in which they are conducting their research and which they are affecting.

We would define political demographers as those individuals who are studying or acting on what are commonly accepted as being demographic questions; and who are also involved in making decisions on these questions, decisions that affect power relationships in society. In addition to researchers who place themselves within the discipline of political science, our somewhat eclectic definition could also include, on occasion, people who would normally be classified, for example, as anthropologists, public health specialists, or ethicists. Our definition seeks to be cross-disciplinary and focuses on a goal (population policy) and a means to achieve it ("political process").

Population policy research is a rather recent innovation within the discipline of political science.[1] Population variables are coming to be seen as important in the social science disciplines, which have traditionally taken these data as "given." By adding new variables to its analysis, political science has broadened its perspective. But although demographic data are now accepted as variable, another whole series of assumptions preserve their status as "given." Many political demographers have ignored certain kinds of questions. These omissions reveal normative biases and, in some cases, the possible irrelevance and harmfulness of social science research.

We propose both to illustrate these allegations by means of references to portions of the available literature and also to suggest alternative research strategies and paradigms. Our citations are not meant to be an exhaustive review

17

of the literature—this paper is not a bibliographical essay. For more complete reviews, see Berelson[2] and "Population."[3] Our citations *could* be described as "selective." We have grouped the issues into three components of the policy process: the levels of analysis, the applications, and the consequences. The first of these include topics such as the focus on societal level analysis; the assumptions concerning social stability as a desirable goal; and the maddening use of phrases such as "national interest" without any questioning as to whether or not any identifiable sector of the society gains or losses as a result of the quest for society's goals.

The second category includes topics such as the clear distinction between ends and means, a distinction not usually made by most political demographers, and the question of coercion in policy implementation. We are suggesting that population policies ought to be evaluated on grounds that include the effects of the means used to implement them.

In our third category we discuss several issues taken from the literature of political demography, including the distinction between substantive and symbolic effects of policies; the nature of the assumed relationship between demographic variables and other socioeconomic indicators such as poverty; and the kinds of unintended and unexpected results (to political scientists, at least) emanating from population policies.

Though we will introduce these topics and their normative implications with references to the literature, we have no desire to generalize to all political demographers on the basis of our citations. We are purposefully choosing examples that will best serve as contrasts to alternatives, which will be presented throughout this paper. The reader can decide how closely his or her research, or research with which he or she is familiar, fits our examples or our alternatives.

Our purpose is to illustrate the kinds of normative and policy implications we think political demographers should recognize. We are emphatically not urging the adoption of one set of norms over another nor one research approach over another. Rather, we wish to point out that any research approach, including our own, has normative implications, and to some degree, effects on population policy processes. Our goal in this paper is to increase awareness of these potential implications and effects.

I. Societal Level Analysis

Societal level analysis has long been with us and is a useful way to pursue some of the objectives of social science. On the use of aggregate data as a tool, Quandt suggests that, "[s]ome hypothesized relationships . . . may be shown *not* to exist on the macrolevel, which may help to direct future research toward areas of particular relevance . . . ."[4] But these kind of data carry certain limitations on inference, notably the "ecological fallacy," referring to inferences about individual people on the basis of aggregate data. Researchers involved in societal level analysis generalize about polities or societies rather than about individuals within the larger unit. So we have a body of literature which studies aggregate birth rates, national levels of economic development, and so on.

Two concomitants tend to appear. The first is symbolized by phrases such as the "national interest." The second is the usually implied but sometimes quite explicit normative bias toward social order and system stability. That these concomitants should exist is perhaps understandable, for scholars focusing on the societal level have a vested interest in preserving the unit they are studying.[5] To feel otherwise would be to reduce their value as "scientists." As one example, we are told in *The International Encyclopedia of Social Sciences* that population policy involves the examination of demographic trends "in the perspective of what is regarded as the national interest."[6]

In contrast to this, the most liberally minded researchers see the goals of population policy making in terms of effects on individual people, i.e., improved health care or education. Skinner, although not a demographer, provides us with a good example in *Walden Two,*[7] where we find the philosophy of social engineering. In this approach, "good" individuals, or a good quality of life for them, will be produced when the proper social structures are imposed on or provided for a society. Without discussing at this point the normative considerations involved or even the degree of effectiveness social engineering might enjoy, we wish to point to one aspect of the approach most relevant here. That is that the state, or the government—whoever "creates" or "imposes" the proper social structures—tends to take on paramount importance. Once the process of social engineering is set in motion, deviant individuals tend to be seen as threats to the smooth functioning of the system, as indeed they are. The bias leans toward the system's side, even though it is recognized that the engineer's intentions are to help individuals. It is this subtle but nonetheless real partiality towards systemic analysis (and in some cases towards system survival) that we wish to suggest is a principle characteristic of the research undertaken by most political demographers. In the following paragraphs we will cite some examples of this "bias" and will begin to discuss some of the normative implications involved.

In some cases, the consequences of population growth are spelled out in aggregate terms as *social* problems. When effects on individuals are described, the individuals in question seem to be those whose lives will be negatively altered by preserving a population status quo or by a reduction in population pressure. We read of possible consequences such as "sharply increased juvenile delinquency, armed robbery, organized banditry, and outright insurrection."[8]

It appears that social scientists are aware of individual humans and ther needs, but rarely focus their efforts thereon. Fawcett suggests that "there are two conceptual levels at which population policy is generally discussed: global and national."[9] A fine example is a paper by Colin Clark,[10] wherein both of these levels are used. In the global analysis, comparisons are made between and among individual nations so as to suggest remedies for overpopulation. These remedies could be summarized, in an oversimplified way, as a reordering of global resources and interactions between units (nations).[11] But at the national level—in the Puerto Rican case, for example—this analysis immediately becomes aggregate, and we read of the island's level of economic development and industrial productivity.[12] An individualistic approach is used to suggest a redistribution of income between nations to relieve demographic pressure, but there is no parallel suggestion of redistribution *within* a nation to relieve the individual's plight.

Further illustrations of the aggregate-individual dichotomy can be presented. It has been suggested, for example, that population policies need to be planned, administered, and coordinated so as to "maximize their contribution to the national goal of fertility reduction."[13] National goals often leave little room for personal goals, since the ensuing inefficiency would inhibit the maximum contribution urged here.

Davis, in a way that is both insightful and revealing, complains about "liberal intellectuals" who condone governmental planning and compulsion in many areas but oppose it in fertility control. His is a call for consistency, but also a call for viewing population questions (like others) in a societal way: compulsory restraints on individuals are tolerable if the community will thereby profit.[14]

The response to this argument for increased control is a good example of the "liberal, intellectual" approach to which Davis refers. Harkavy and his colleagues object to this new level of societal control, not primarily because it is unethical or inconsistent with individual rights, but because such control has not yet been the subject of "thoughtful examination as to its feasibility and the costs and benefits to society."[15] This sort of response not only reveals a negative position on the development of non-familial roles for women (one of the measures called for by Davis in the paper cited above), but it also ignores the effects on, as well as the rights of, individual humans.

To focus exclusively on this aggregate, collective level, therefore, is to assure that rational, cost-benefit analyses can be applied to the population "problem."[16] It becomes simple to see that a collective restraint is necessary because individuals pursuing their own rational interests would prevent the achievement of the community's rational goals. Hardin has made this explicit, almost seeming to raise the suggestion to the level of law.[17]

Beyond this, the tendency to focus on aggregate societal level analysis seems to have precluded sub-societal study to determine who gains and who loses when population policies are implemented.[18] Instead, the emphasis seems to have been on either "national interest" or, when individuals are discussed, on individuals in the abstract. Viewed abstractly, all individuals appear to take on the characteristics of those most experientially visible to political demographers.[19] But in the context of who is gaining and who is losing by social unrest or rebellion, for example, the assumed desirability of system stability, and even of "Western values,"[20] can be questioned. (Questioning *per se* does not imply a particular answer or set of answers though to *not* question does.)

The societal approach has left little room for the consideration of the possible beneficial effects of social unrest on an entire society, much less on individuals within the society. Clearly, it is empirically accurate that social unrest *is* a danger to the national interest. What is not clear is the relationship between social unrest and individual interests, especially the interests of those presently being hurt, while societal goals are pursued by elites and studied by political demographers.

We do not wish to suggest that a population explosion is a good thing, but only that up until now, the explosion may have been seen as a problem primarily because of the danger it creates for elite or "national" interests. Political demographers play a major role here, for it is no longer necessary to determine who is gaining and who is losing once population has been intellectually defined as a "problem." The who-gains-who-loses approach could well lead to political conflict, which is to be avoided. Instead, political demographers suggest that it is the population problem that must be solved first, in order to then solve the distributive problems of equality, justice, or personal growth.

It is at least logically possible that solving the distributive problems first would result in the resolution of the problem of excessive population growth. To us, this is a preferable approach. Those researchers who have focused on the primacy of the population problem are reinforcing the notion that the population problem is *the* problem. They may be right, but they tend to ignore alternate approaches. Because the population question seems best studied in an aggregate, statistical way (and because research tools are available), the distributive problems, more phenomenological and personal in nature, tend to be relegated to ethicists, polemicists, or "naive utopians."

Politically, the societal level approach is a good deal harder to justify than the social science disciplines seem to think. Within the framework of university or elite sponsored research and within intellectual discourse in general, it is reasonable to speak of rational, aggregate approaches to social problems. But it is at least possible that different, equally valid, directions exist.

One alternate approach is to consider questions of the "quality of life" of individual people. This is an elusive concept, but we can probably agree that it consists of two kinds of components: empirically verifiable *needs*, such as food and water, and socially inspired (and subjectively perceived) *wants*, such as consumer goods or luxuries and amenities, wants often artificially created by elites. Somewhere along that continuum, we need to locate less precisely pigeonholed components of the concept of quality of life, components like freedom, absence of coercion, psychological development, love, self-esteem, and others. These need to be located on the continuum because this alternative approach is individualistic rather than systemic. Consequently, we focus on the quality of life of individual people and need to know not only where each individual is likely to be located on the continuum of quality of life but also, and first, what the continuum looks like.

We therefore would study policy processes in terms of their effects on individuals. Political structures and processes would be seen as "utilitarian," and policies would be evaluated or prescribed in individual terms. This contrasts to policy evaluation in terms of the effects on system stability or the maintenance of democratic structures, neither of which have been shown empirically to be more important for individual humans than the other components on our continuum.[21]

At this point, it would be useful to briefly clarify our concept of the continuum of quality of life. We base our approach on the work of Abraham Maslow and Christian Bay. From Maslow, we take the concept of an empirically derived hierarchy of values. His thesis is that certain needs can be shown empirically to exist for all humans, in spite of the fact that some individuals do not recognize or perceive their own needs in these terms. Additionally, these needs can, at least potentially, be ranked in order of prepotence.[22]

To evaluate whether or not policies are helping the members of a society achieve individual human goals, we would turn to Bay's "underdog" approach and an assessment of "who gains and who loses."

Bay's position implies policy evaluation by means of studying the individuals to whom policies are applied. This approach would evaluate policies favorably if they provide or satisfy the more basic human needs for *everyone* in a polity, no matter how small the deprived proportion of society may be.[23] In Maslowian language, policies should be aimed at meeting the basic needs for all the people before turning to the satisfaction of higher needs for some of the population. Additionally, the criteria for determining the level of importance of a particular need could be empirical or mystical but should not be based on political power. Hence, policies should be aimed at removing the heaviest or most serious obstacles to freedom for everyone in a society before becoming concerned with less serious impediments. For Bay ". . . a society is free only to the extent that its least privileged and its least tolerated members are free."[24]

The second tool mentioned above was the consequences approach.[25] Here, consistent with our earlier arguments, empirical data would be used to establish which individuals, groups, or interests gain from the implementation of a policy and which lose. Gain and loss can be operationalized in terms of prestige, finances, coercion levels, or need satisfaction. Whatever the operationalization, care must be taken to distinguish and show the relationship between substantive gains and losses and symbolic gains and losses. Discernible patterns in gain-loss relationships can just as justifiably form the basis for the overall evaluation of a policy process as the achievement of stated policy goals, which is commonly used as the basis for evaluation. We have characterized the latter as an aggregated or societal-level approach to policy evaluation, even when individual needs are mentioned. Our alternate approach requires a focus on sub-societal sectors and, hopefully, on individuals.

Can population policies be evaluated in this framework? Are these kinds of policies related to quality of life? It has become part of the current socio-demographic folk wisdom that zero population growth is necessary if society as a whole is to achieve equilibrium between population and resources, an acceptable level of quality of life.[26] We wish neither to confirm nor refute this hypothetical relationship between aggregate population growth rates and aggregate quality of life. But we do note that the relationship says little, if anything, about the conditions that obtain for the individual people within the society. Population policies can be shown to promote zero population growth at the societal level, and this can presumably be evaluated as "good." At the same time, if a Maslow-Bay approach is followed, these policies might be shown to be detrimental to the quality of life for some of the individuals within the society, especially when "quality of life" includes concepts like personal self-development, freedom from coercion, and the like. Contrasting evaluations might be sharper still, if researchers were to focus on the quality of life among the most deprived individuals in a society, comparing fluctuations in their living standards with those of the least deprived individuals. In other words, though zero population growth is—or will be—an empirical necessity, it is entirely possible that a focus on individuals within a society and on their basic needs may suggest more acceptable ways of achieving zero population growth for a society.

Population policies in Puerto Rico on sterilization or migration could be evaluated in these terms. Are these policies aimed at maintaining national indicators of system stability and economic growth? If so, how are individuals in Puerto Rico affected by these policies? What is the significance of the fact that some groups of individuals bear the brunt of policy implementation, i.e., the poor or women?[27]

We believe that the questions suggested in this example need to be asked. We contend that they usually remain unasked because of the aspects of the model of social science analysis that we have been discussing. We will now turn our attention to still other aspects of population policy research, notably questions of coercion, the distinction between ends and means, and policy implications.

II. Ends and Means, and Coercion

In this section we will deal directly with two issues, the distinction between ends and means and the question of coercion in implementing population policies. These two issues lead to an alternative approach, in which it is suggested that the evaluation of a population policy should be based on as many actual policy effects or outcomes as possible. This contrasts with the usual practice of evaluating population policies almost exclusively in terms of the *stated* substantive goals of the policy, whether societal or individual.

The first question inquires about the means used to implement policy. Although the process may be unintentional, by not dealing with the effects of the means used to implement a policy, social scientists are in effect holding that the ends justify the means.

The question of means used to implement a policy is important, because means frequently provide the policymakers' rationale for supporting the policy. Moreover, it is valid to investigate the motives and attitudes of policymakers, since these will have repercussions on the choice of means and hence on the total policy outcome picture.[28]

Yet another kind of questioning is relevant to political demographers: does the choice of means predetermine the nature of the ends? Or does the implementation of population policies have effects that can be analyzed separately from the effects of the stated goals of the policy? In this sense, an ends-means distinction may prove *analytically* useful. If the distinction is analytically useful, then political demographers should delve into both sides rather than focusing exclusively on the ends of the policy alone. If, for instance, in implementing the policy the recipients are manipulated, then, perhaps unwittingly, the results involve a great deal more than the announced substantive goal of the policy. Instead of merely low fertility, perhaps a nation of sheep with low fertility would result.

In Puerto Rico, research on sterilization focuses mostly on sterilization rates among various groups of women.[29] These rates are the substantive goals of a population policy, even if the policy results from non-activity on the part of the government. The psychological effects of sterilization on women are studied much less frequently. The question of the internal conflict between Catholicism and a desire for birth control, for example, has been studied only in terms of its effect on sterilization rates. Within such a framework, the significance of Catholicism in these women's lives is not acknowledged. Indeed, their religious beliefs are subordinated to the goals of population control. Since sterilization gives these women an option of only "sinning" once, it can be rationalized as preferable to mechanical means of birth control. The woman need go to confession only once, and then quietly live with her guilt. Hence, Catholicism is made to seem supportive of the policy goal of sterilization; the psychological dissonance created in these women is not discussed, much less studied.[30]

This Puerto Rican example has led us into a more specific approach to the question of implementing policies, that is, the question of coercion and compulsion. Coercion is clearly visible in schemes to restrict childbearing to adults with licenses or to enforce compulsory sterilization. But coercion need not be open and direct, and coerced individuals do not need to feel coerced in order to actually be coerced, behavioral engineering being developed as it is.

Though complex, the question of coercion is an important and a threatening one, even if it is sometimes unclear whether the proponents of coercive measures really mean what they say. Nevertheless, as Seltzer has remarked:

. . . it is reasonable to worry that those supporting fertility control for a specific race or class out of a belief that such people are "undesirables" or are "breeding like rats" will ignore reductions in individual human welfare that may be associated with proposals designed to achieve desired fertility levels by coercive means.[31]

In some cases, the vagueness of the proposals can lead to uneasiness: "If excessive population growth is to be prevented, the obvious requirement is somehow to impose restraints on the family."[32] In other cases, the concreteness is disturbing: "Also necessary is going to be a much more militant, high-powered, and even coercive attitude on the part of political officials with respect to family limitation ... Governments could, for example, attempt to exert pressure. . . ."[33] Finally, Spengler explicitly calls for increased control over individual conscience via "the carrot and the stick."[34]

In the first section of this paper, we discussed the tendency to focus on societal level evaluation, which leads with little difficulty to the acceptance of restraints on individuals in favor of societal goals. There is an abundance of literature urging or condoning coercive measures for population control, though of course to varying degrees.[35] We cite only a few to illustrate the variety.

Godwin's analysis of fertility attitudes explicitly rejects using high levels of coercion, judges those who favor low coercion levels as "incorrect," and favors medium levels of coercion because it appears that at this level, the costs and the benefits to the community are most balanced.[36] But the more subtle coercive methods of implementing policies usually go unnoticed or are adjudged acceptable by political demographers. It is our contention that "voluntary" programs can be just as effectively coercive in a more subtle way. By urging one sort of activity or another, authoritative sources such as government or leading elite organizations can in fact be quite coercive if only because of the institutional prestige these groups command, if only because the masses have come to "depend" on elites for leadership. To promote limited family size by offering bounties for sterilization appears to be a policy that coerces economically deprived individuals. As Callahan notes, " . . . if the poor desperately need the money or goods offered by the incentive plan, it is questionable whether, in any real sense, they have a free choice."[37] Any law or policy can be thought of as the use, at least potentially, of coercive power,[38] and government has been described as the sole legitimate wielder of coercive power by a generation of political scientists. In the face of this, almost all political demographers, as opposed to ethicists, ignore this aspect of the question of coercion. Generally, it is rare to find a political demographer opposing the use of governmental coercion on normative grounds. More common is the high value placed on efficiency.[39]

To educate—propagandize is too value-laden, though perhaps more accurate—the populace towards family planning by emphasizing the economic liabilities associated with large families is to trade on fear. Bay comments on one result of this kind of approach:

Social institutions require conformity to certain kinds of behavior patterns and strongly encourage conformity to the corresponding thought and evaluation patterns as well. Resistance to social pressures easily gives rise to anxieties about one's own values and about oneself, especially if resistance is followed by a measure of social rejection. The safe course of conduct in order to reduce this kind of anxiety is to become a strict conformist—again at the price of giving up the chance of developing individual potentialities.[40]

That is to say, social pressure is especially effective on people lacking in self-confidence and results in continued lack of self-confidence and greater conformity to norms from without. In a society which values conspicuous consumption and prestigious occupations, poor people are especially vulnerable.

Furthermore, this approach ignores the more fundamental causes for poverty, resulting in a subtle form of coercion that leads to continuing non-opposition by poor people to the institutions that are causing them to be poor in the first place. Rather than being encouraged to search for the social and institutional causes for their poverty, poor people are made to feel inferior for not being able to provide for a large family and irresponsible when they produce one anyhow. We are suggesting, however, that this may be only *part* of the problem. As Burch has noted: "The poor are emphatically told that they have too many children and should do something about it. The other part of the equation—that the rich get richer—is seldom mentioned."[41]

In the area of population policy, susceptibility to influence in the target group is a particularly relevant issue. Reflecting limitations in technology and motivation, women are the primary focus of these policies. Psychological studies have substantiated what lay observation reveals: that women exhibit lower degrees of self-confidence and are more susceptible to the influence of others.[42] This "feminine vulnerability" is elevated to a virtue in traditional sex role definitions, even though independence of judgment is considered the more socially desirable and healthy trait.[43] As might be anticipated, this lack of self-confidence is associated with greater conformity and intolerance toward deviance among women.[44] Consequently, in the area of population policy, the potential for coercion is exacerbated by the vulnerability of the target group. However, we must emphasize that this willingness to *be* coerced does not provide an acceptable justification for governmental coercion of the individual.

It should be noted that there are other individually important needs and values in addition to the number of children in her family. (The use of the feminine here reflects first the notion that females, more than males, have been the objects of population policies and second, that language is not apolitical.[45]) We might cite the capacity for the individual to make decisions that fundamentally affect her life as an example.[46] The prerequisite of this position is that there be some choices from which the capable individual can choose.[47] Bay speaks of the individual in terms of the realization of her "potential freedom" and the exercise of her "psychological freedom," that is, realizing that she *has* choices and having the personal strength to make a choice herself.[48] Finally, Apter has characterized "development" at least in part as the increase in available choice.[49]

Some scholars suggest that it becomes "reasonable" to coerce individuals once a distinction is made between public interests and private, individual interests.[50] However, such a distinction need not imply inevitable conflict between these interests nor precedence of the public interest over the individual. The possibility that proper and complete information will lead to lower fertility rates and enhanced human dignity[51] is worth incorporating into research paradigms.

There are, therefore, many different kinds of policy outcomes, at least for analytic purposes. Many behavioralist scholars tend to focus on aggregated analytic units such as polities or nations, and therefore will frequently include in their analysis only the aggregated effects of a policy as measured against the announced purpose of the policy. The other effects of policies, especially those attributable to implementation, seem to be thought of as being beyond the perspective of the political demographer; yet these effects are in reality no less important, especially to the individuals who are policy recipients. These effects may be ignored partly because they are less subject to empirical qualification, and partly because these questions are simply not considered eligible for the political science agenda.

As an alternative, we would suggest attempts to enhance individual decision-making capability along the lines suggested earlier. This probably means complete information as well as dispassionate discussion of as many real alternatives on as many real issues as exist. To suggest that the government's role in population policy making be coercive—even in subtle ways—because the masses are incapable of making "rational" decisions is a self-fulfilling prophecy. Policies aimed at the economic and social liberation of groups such as women, for example, will result in the creation of a group of individuals better able to see that their personal interest lies in limiting families—assuming it does—and better able to make the appropriate choices, if the choices are there.[52]

When the approach that we are recommending is used to study policy outcomes, several directions for inquiry become apparent. Are elite or governmental policies satisfying individual needs or ignoring them? Do individuals feel they have power over their own lives, or are they fooled by the "symbolic uses of politics"? Can an analysis of aggregate or budgetary data provide an objective analysis of these relationships beyond the self-perceived attitudes of elites or masses? Are policies exploitative by preserving continued dependence on elite manipulation? Or do policies promote the individual's capacity for personal decision making by creating socioeconomic conditions more conducive to this increased self-reliance? What is the validity of the genocide and imperialism arguments?

We are not questioning the desirability of any particular population policy.

We are suggesting additional perspectives that need to be taken into account *before* desirability can be established. These additional perspectives include: (1) the broad effects of the means chosen to implement a policy, and (2) the effects of both means and ends on the individuals who are recipients. It is our hope that these perspectives will not be ignored by political demographers.

It seems clear that the evaluation of policy ought to be based on more than one facet of the process, and that a more rigorous analysis of means and the effects of means ought to be automatically included along with analysis of substantive policy goals. For ethical reasons, if not for practical reasons of keeping the peace in the long run, the use of coercion should be subjected to very tight scrutiny.

III. End Results of Policy

In this section, we return to a discussion of ends. Earlier we talked about policy goals by distinguishing between societal effects and personal effects, suggesting that both need to be considered. Now we would like to examine the nature of policy goals more closely, for it appears possible that regardless of the level of analysis—personal or societal—population policies can lead to unexpected, unintended, or additional consequences beyond those presented as official or stated goals.

In other words, a policy can have many effects. These can also be projected as separate policy outcomes, at least for analytic purposes. Of this complex policy reality, most political scientists engaged in demographic research emphasize only a single aspect, for example, population growth rates or the effects of these on the "political system." This is not surprising given the importance of systems-level analysis in contemporary, behavioral political science. If other aspects of this policy reality are perceived, they are left as unresearched ancillary issues, beyond the scope of the political science paradigm.

A major thrust of this approach is the oft-assumed relationship, with causality a big part of the assumption, between demographic indicators and other socioeconomic conditions such as poverty or pollution.[53]

The intended goals of population policy usually involve some sort of relationship between a demographic variable and some other socioeconomic indicator such as poverty or pollution. Lorimer, for example, modifies the strict Malthusian position, claiming a "mutually dependent" relationship between population growth and "advances in economic productivity, health, and education . . . ."[54] Taylor and Hall also associate economic development and family planning, through health programs. It is asserted that even the "most nationalistic leaders" will sooner or later be convinced by "the inevitability of demographic trends."[55] Other sources reflect this view:

Control of population growth is one of the instruments available to governments to accomplish other objectives: economic growth and social development of the nation; improvement of the health and welfare of the people,. . .; and conservation and improvement of the environment. . . . .[56]

Population growth is clearly impeding economic development in many poor countries, rather than itself being reduced through the modernization process.[57]

Finally, Clark very clearly posits a relationship between population pressures and a nation's ability to industrialize: within each national unit, the principle obstacle to industrialization in the Third World is population growth. On the international level, these pressures could be relieved if the more developed nations would realistically deal with these problems. Puerto Rico, for example, is said to have no population problems any longer because the United States has allowed immigration of Puerto Ricans and has included Puerto Rico within the North American tariff walls. The result has been a "rate of development of real income since 1939."[58] "The American conscience can now be at rest."[59]

Stycos suggests a conceptual scheme categorizing elitist opinion on family planning and on population control in terms of (1) whether the elite group favors or opposes the policy, and why; and (2) whether the group is left, center, or right.[60] Of interest to us here are the reasons behind support or opposition, for these reasons are not so much based on the questions of freedom or coercion as they are based on the perceived consequences of the policy on the various groups represented in the schema. Of the ten group-positions presented (two cells are blank) only one deals with coercion; this position reflects the opposition of "liberal intellectuals" to the coercion they associate with population control.[61] The "liberal intellectuals" are located as centrists, reflecting their association with the kinds of policy outcomes pursued by other groups of the center, notably the "economic planners" pursuing economic development and the "physicians (and) social workers" pursuing family health and welfare. Occasionally, the social scientists delve into those consequences Stycos sees as rightist, especially policy outcomes related to political and economic stability and welfare costs, which Stycos associates most closely with "Politicians."[62]

We suggest that a review of the literature of political demography substantiates the description of the interests we have outlined in the previous paragraphs. Political demographers are simply *not* concerned with many of the other possible policy outcomes that Stycos presents.

Our point is not to deny that there is a relationship between policies and the sorts of socioeconomic factors discussed in these citations. Within the positivistic, rational paradigm most social scientists use, it is clearly logical to assume that these relationships exist. And, thanks to refined statistical and analytic tools, such relationships can be verified empirically—so we are told.

Yet it is possible that political demographers are leaving out some intervening variables. One area that comes to mind is the question of symbolic rewards and sanctions as distinguished from the more substantive outputs of the policy process. Social scientists, using their own values and intellectual ability, often ascribe behavior to the masses for reasons that simply may not exist: a family planning clinic in a ghetto may be seen by a political demographer as a substantive benefit for the masses of the ghetto. Viewed from another perspective, the same clinic might be seen by ghetto residents in several ways:[63] as an employment opportunity for elites who are not of the ghetto community; as a bandaid approach, that is, a symbolic gesture aimed at diverting attention from the ghetto's more serious problems; as genocide or racism, and hypocritical at that; and as still another attempt to make ghetto residents dependent on an alien (read: white elite) society. A review of the literature will, we believe, substantiate the assertion that few political demographers have seriously dealt with questions such as genocide or colonialism arising out of population policies.

It is possible that political demographers *do* have special expertise and that these questions can be "proven" to be irrelevant. It is also possible, however, that ghetto residents might be correct in their perceptions, correct in their assessment of the consequences, if not the motivations behind these policies. But in spite of this latter possibility, the social scientist who studies these questions "objectively" tends to see these alternate views of the clinic as problem attitudes. These problems are to be "solved" by either coercive policies (advocated by "realists" using the "culture of poverty" as their rationale,[64]) or by voluntary family planning programs, accompanied by public relations, usually called education.

But the ghetto residents who are the policy objects may have, as Callahan notes, "a very different set of ethical priorities, which the 'common-sense' rebuttals of whites simply do not touch."[65] The point is not to ascribe malevolence to the political demographers who have here been characterized as "liberal intellectuals." Rather, we wish to emphasize that some of the relevant phenomena that form a part of the policy reality are simply beyond their (and our) experience. Further, the paradigm used by most political demographers not only cannot deal with these phenomena, but also excludes them in what will someday surely be recognized as a futile attempt to make the real world fit the model rather than vice-versa.

To get back to our example, what if the ghetto residents are correct in their assessments of governmental outputs? No political demographer would, we presume, consciously support a population policy that results in genocide. But it is also true that few political demographers attempt to rigorously investigate the unintended or unexpected results of the population policies they are studying.[66] And it is at least possible, we must all admit, that some unintended and unexpected results may exist, even *if* the nature of these results is such that they exist only existentially in the minds of the policy recipient.

Consequently, we suggest that it is important that all possible consequences of population policies be studied rigorously, as opposed to focusing primarily or exclusively on those consequences that are stated by governments or other elite representatives as intended consequences of a policy. This appears to be a more objective approach, since: "the actual determinants of population trends in society are largely unintended and since the consequences of the adoption of population policies are so largely unknown."[67]

To help the researcher pursue this approach, there are guidelines available in the literature, largely discoverable in ethical arguments. Dyck discusses what might be ethically acceptable and suggests a framework for making evaluation of population policy proposals.[68] Callahan also treats these questions, going so far as to deal with specific criteria and specific issues.[69] Little of this seems to be explicitly integrated into political research on demographic questions, though these sources clearly and explicitly deal with the multiple effects of population policies.

Recent and earlier analyses of political systems have illustrated the distinction between substantive and symbolic outputs.[70] The distinction between the two is clear enough so that it has even been suggested there are actually two distinct political systems, one substantive and one symbolic.[71] Interestingly enough, policymakers themselves seem to be able to see beyond the narrow limits imposed by the social scientist's positivist paradigm. Political demographers might do well to examine additional kinds of activities in which politicians and bureaucrats engage, as opposed to the rhetoric or intentions they espouse.

One way of seeing this is to focus on the distinction between real and false issues,[72] which of course suggests some standard by which to make the distinction. If scholars are to define real issues as those that are declared to be such by funding agencies, then there are no grounds for using the alternative we are suggesting. If on the other hand, some standard can be applied, such as the Maslow-Bay approach we suggested earlier, then scholars could in fact make the distinction between issues that are related to real human needs and those that are not.

We have the impression that most social scientists see "law and order" as a false issue. Is it possible, we would like social scientists to ask, that the current turmoil on population pressures is also a false issue? To some sectors of society it is, and we hear of genocide, racism, and imperialism. In evaluating population policies and processes, we contend that it is important to ask these questions, lest we unwittingly do irreparable damage to the social environment we purport to be helping.

A surfeit of Machiavellian examples suggests that policymakers do engage in symbolic activities and do raise false issues. This is done to enhance their re-election or some other aspect of system and personal survival, whenever substantive activities might upset the equilibrium of the ship of state.[73] Might not the evidence that this symbolic activity exists suggest a more critical examination of the motives and intentions of population policy elites? Furthermore, might this evidence not inspire political demographers to deal more directly with policy recipients as individual people?

In this section, we have discussed the question of unintended and unexpected consequences of population policies, aside from those effects of the implementation process. We approached this set of policy implications from two directions. The first was semi-observational and somewhat deductive: some sectors of society not normally listened to seem to be raising ugly issues political demographers would rather not hear of, issues like imperialism and genocide. At the same time, from our logical perspective, it seems to us fallacious to assume a one to one relationship between population growth and such conditions as poverty. Rather, it appears at least logically possible that both sides of the relationship might be expanded: we would suggest, without going into the necessary details in this paper, that two additional kinds of causal variables related to poverty would be socioeconomic structures and the artificial creation of scarcity by economic elites.[74]

To suggest additional variables is not to minimize the ultimate importance (assuming a finite-energy ecosystem) of the population question. Rather, we wish to emphasize that other intervening variables and causal variables may be as important as population growth or density in understanding distributive problems related to poverty, justice, dignity, and so on. Additonally, we would emphasize that to base one's evaluation of population policies on stated goals alone would be unduly restrictive. For political demographers to achieve a better grasp of the importance of additional policy results that ought to be included as bases for policy evaluation, it may be necessary to broaden the research paradigm, to use empathy rather than objectivity, and to become involved rather than detached, even though these characteristics might reduce one's ability to predict (or to reduce uncertainty).

III. Conclusion

In this chapter, we have discussed the normative and research implications of three kinds of questions. The first focused on the distinction between aggregate analysis at the societal level and analysis that explicitly and directly studies individuals within a collectivity. The second issue we raised had to do with the effects—the additional policy outcomes—of the means used to implement population policies. We focused on coercion as one example. The final section discussed possible unintended or unexpected results of population policies, results which we feel ought to be part of our research agenda in political demography.

Clearly, we are neither unique nor pioneering in raising these issues. Our point is that reliance on the positivist model tends to preclude incorporation of such questions into research on population policy. These questions can be asked, but not answered within the current paradigm. The answers would necessitate openly normative approaches in a discipline pursuing "objectivity." Our own alternative employs concepts difficult if not impossible to measure systematically in a discipline pursuing quantification. We believe that these limitations are built into the positivist model and are not the result of malicious intentions on the part of political demographers.

To illustrate another aspect of the normative implications of the positivist model, we refer to the Maslow-Bay approach that was discussed earlier. Reliance on a positivist model (and the resulting policy implications of that reliance) imply a ranking of human needs and capabilities. The positivist model, as we have noted, relegates concepts such as freedom and dignity to the status of dependent variables. The model therefore suggests that the way to human dignity is ecological, in the sense that it is first necessary to create the proper social environment, through coercive measures if necessary, though this should be avoided. Once the "proper" social environment is created with the help of scholars and experts, then individuals will be able to function in a way that bespeaks of human dignity and freedom.

As we noted earlier, this sort of "social engineering" approach tends to regard the control mechanism (government) as more important than particular individuals who might deviate, although the "engineers" are engaged in their projects for the good of the individual. The paradox is supposedly circumvented by the practice of focusing on entire societies as the analytic unit, or by focusing on "individuals" in the abstract. This rests on an assumption of hierarchical ranking of human needs. In the continuum of "quality of life" implied by this positivist model, social order is ranked higher than individual choice. That is, if there is conflict between "freedom" and "order," it is more important to the individual that she be in a "stable" or "good" environment (we do not intend for these terms to be synonymous) than it is for her to have free choice.

Among the literature cited in this paper, Hardin's "The Tragedy of the Commons" provides a good example of this rank ordering of human needs.[75] One of Hardin's assumptions is that "rational" equals "competitive." That is, humans see other humans as competitors for scarce resources and act accordingly. It is true that in some final sense the fact of too many people will sooner or later mean that resources are scarce. At that point, people will compete for scarce resources to survive. In the meantime, it may not be valid to assume that it is in human nature to be competitive at society's expense, even though this may be a valid description of many observable social settings. It may be the artificial creation of scarcity by economic and social elites for profit maximization that has caused competitiveness to be so characteristic of social existence. Were scarcity to be eliminated—i.e., equality increased—we might discover that cooperation would replace competition as the norm. (Though we have no procedural blueprint for doing this, we would note that the sentence captures a good deal of the essence of communalist efforts.)

To ignore the logical possibility of this alternative view of human beings, as the reliance on a positivist model tends to have us do, helps guarantee that the competitive view will continue to prevail. We have sought to show that population policies and population research help produce or maintain—as unintended results—a competitive, coercive status quo. In this case, reliance on a model that assumes rational self-seeking and the necessity of restraints helps to guarantee the outcome: restraint on individual freedom. Rather than counteracting aggressive self-assertion, coercive population policies produce the opposite effect: greater conformity to external constraints and reduced self-assertion. One pathological extreme is used to justify creation of the other.

What we are suggesting is a cooperative alternative. One that is neither selfishly competitive nor self-destructively acquiescent. We are not claiming that it is possible to immediately eliminate scarcity, nor that researchers must adopt our norms. We only urge that political demographers be aware of potential human policy outcomes, and that they make their own decisions about the matter. We urge that this awareness include an honest assessment of our personal role in population policy and of our methodology's role in helping to predetermine research outcomes. Finally, we urge that any suggested alternatives be subjected to the same sort of scrutiny here presented.

We propose that human dignity, freedom, and equality be used as variables in population policy-making equations.[76] If these terms appear vague to the reader, we suggest that research in ways to validly operationalize these concepts is one of the more valuable pursuits presently available to social scientists. It is clear, however, that these three concepts are individualistic: nations and systems are neither free nor equal, except in the symbolic rhetoric of mass politics. To the contrary, *individuals* are free or equal to each other—or they are not. Nations and politics are thought of as politically "developed" only by social scientists who operationalize the definitions of nation and polity in terms of the structures and functions of government. To the contrary, *individuals* are developed—or not. The levels of equality, freedom, and development of an aggregate collection of individuals should be a reflection of the conditions of the individuals and not vice-versa.

By suggesting a series of alternate and additional questions for political demographers, we run the risk of being viewed as nonobjective, perhaps even nonrationalistic in our approach. By now it should be clear that this is precisely what we mean to be, for, as we have attempted to show, the rational objective road leads right back to the ivory tower.

In the final analysis, population questions are basically questions of ethics, of values, or norms.[77] By using paradigms that incorporate as many competing ethical positions as possible, political demographers may become more capable of dealing with the real, non-symbolic, non-intellectual world. As Dreitzel notes: ". . . the development of technological reality can itself become irrational when the political and moral dimensions lag behind."[78]

Only by becoming more self-consciously normative and only by eschewing the narrow limits of current rationalism, do political demographers stand a chance of becoming as objective as they now claim to be.

Notes

1. Richard L. Clinton and R. Kenneth Godwin, "Political Science in Population Studies: Reasons for the Late Start," in Richard L. Clinton, William S. Flash, and R. Kenneth Godwin, eds., *Political Science in Population Studies* (Lexington, Mass.: D.C. Heath & Co., 1972): 141-149.

2. Bernard Berelson, "Beyond Family Planning," *Studies in Family Planning* no. 38 (February 1969): 1-16.

3. Population Education Staff Committee, "Population Growth and Family Planning: A Review of the Literature" (New York: Planned Parenthood-World Population, mimeo, 1970).

4. William B. Quandt, "The Comparative Study of Political Elites," *Sage Professional Papers in Political Science* 1 (1970): 191, emphasis added.

5. Christian Bay, "The Cheerful Science of Dismal Politics," in Theodore Roszak, ed., *The Dissenting Academy* (New York: Random House, 1968): 208-209.

6. Hope T. Eldridge, "Population Policies," *International Encyclopedia of the Social Sciences* vol. 12 (New York: MacMillan, 1968): 383.

7. B.F. Skinner, *Walden Two* (New York: MacMillan, 1972).

8. Philander P. Claxton, Jr., "United States Population Policy—Origins and Development," *Department of State Bulletin* 63 (September 21, 1970): 325.

9. James T. Fawcett, *Psychology and Population: Behavioral Research Issues in Fertility and Family Planning* (New York: The Population Council, 1970): 23.

10. Colin Clark, "Population Growth and Living Standards," in A.N. Agarwala and S.P. Singh, eds., *The Economics of Underdevelopment* (New York: Oxford University Press, 1963): 32-53.

11. Ibid., 52-53.

12. Ibid., 51.

13. National Academy of Sciences, *Rapid Population Growth: Consequences and Policy Implications* (Baltimore: Johns Hopkins Press, 1971): 90.

14. Kingsley Davis, "Population Policy: Will Current Programs Succeed?" *Science* 158 (November 10, 1967): 737.

15. Oscar Harkavy, Frederick S. Jaffee, and Samuel M. Wishik, "Family Planning and Public Policy: Who Is Misleading Whom?" *Science* 165 (July 25, 1969): 373, emphasis added.

16. Throughout this paper, we will refer to "rational" analysis or to the "positivist paradigm." By this we mean both a research approach and a way of

thinking. To that paradigm we would attribute characteristics such as the desirability of prediction (and control); an emphasis on quantification ("a computational concept of rationality") (Hans Peter Dreitzel, "Social Science and the Problem of Rationality: Notes on the Sociology of Technocrats," *Politics and Society* 2 [Winter 1970] : 170); claims of objectivity and detachment; and the overall penchant toward "science." These characteristics are not mutually exclusive, nor do they apply to all of the "behavioralists" all of the time. But the positivist model makes no provisions for such non-rational or phenomenological concepts as projected psychic health, para-psychology, mysticism, or souls. As one example of an alternate approach, we offer R.D. Laing, *The Politics of Experience* (New York: Ballantine Books, 1967).

17. Garrett Hardin, "The Tragedy of the Commons," *Science* 162 (December 13, 1968): 1243-1248.

18. Bernard Berelson, "Population Policy: Personal Notes," *Population Studies* 25 (July 1971): 178, n. 14.

19. "Too often missionaries condescendingly see their own idiosyncracies as other people's natures." Ivan D. Illich, *Celebration of Awareness: A Call for Institutional Revolution* (New York: Anchor Books, 1971): 141.

20. Richard L. Clinton, "Portents for Politics in Latin American Population Expansion," *Inter-American Economic Affairs* 25, 2 (Autumn 1971): 45.

21. Christian Bay, "Behavioral Research and the Theory of Democracy," in Henry Kariel, ed., *Frontiers of Democratic Theory* (New York: Random House, 1970): 351.

22. Abraham Maslow, *Motivation and Personality* (New York: Harper and Row, 1954). For an analysis and a bibliography of Maslow's work, see Frank Gobel, *The Third Force: The Psychology of Abraham Maslow* (New York: Pocket Books, 1971): especially Chapter 4 and the table on page 52.

23. Christian Bay, *The Structure of Freedom* (New York: Atheneum, 1965): 7.

24. Ibid.

25. This approach underlies the analysis of the North American political system in Kenneth M. Dolbeare and Murray J. Edelman, *American Politics: Policies, Power, and Change* (Lexington, Mass.: D.C. Heath, 1971): especially pages 51-66.

26. William Barclay, Joseph Enright, and Reid T. Reynolds, "Population Control in the Third World," *NACLA Newsletter* 4, 8 (December 1970): 1-18. This source suggests that the political implications of the zero-population-growth hypothesis are tied more to the desire of a North American elite to maintain its presently acceptable level of quality of life at the expense of the Third World, rather than to an altruistic desire to achieve an acceptable level of quality of life for these "underdeveloped" areas.

27. Harriett Presser, *Reports on Population/Family Planning* no. 5 (July 1970), and Clarence Senior, "An Approach to Research in Overcoming Cultural

Barriers to Family Limitation," in George F. Mair, ed., *Studies in Population* (Princeton: Princeton University Press, 1949): 148-152.

28. William Seltzer, "Environmental Issues," *Concerned Demography* 2, 4 (March 1971): 55.

29. Presser (n. 27) and Senior (n. 27).

30. Senior (n. 27): 150.

31. Seltzer (n. 28): 56 and n. 6.

32. Davis (n. 14): 737.

33. Charles H. Anderson, *Toward A New Sociology: A Critical Review* (Homewood, Illinois: Dorsey Press, 1971): 308.

34. Joseph J. Spengler, "Population: Problem: In Search of a Solution," *Science* 166 (December 5, 1969): 1236.

35. For example: "If. . . relatively uncoercive laws should fail to bring the brith rate under control, laws could be written that would make the bearing of a third child illegal and that would require an abortion to terminate all such pregnancies." This is taken from Paul R. Ehrlich and Anne R. Ehrlich, *Population, Resources, and Environment* (San Francisco: W.H. Freeman and Co., 1970): 274.

36. R. Kenneth Godwin, "The Structure of Mass Attitudes in the United States and Latin America: Implications for Policy," Chapter 6 in this volume.

37. Daniel Callahan, *Ethics and Population Limitation* (New York: The Population Council, 1971): 27.

38. Theodore J. Lowi, "Population Policies and the American Political System," in Clinton, Flash, and Godwin (n. 1): 28.

39. William V. D'Antonio "Birth Control and Coercion: The Bishop's Statement," *Commonweal* 85 (December 2, 1966): 249.

40. Bay (n. 23): 182.

41. William R. Burch, Jr., *Daydreams and Nightmares, A Sociological Essay on the American Environment* (New York: Harper and Row, 1971): 22.

42. Josef E. Garai and Amran Scheinfeld, "Sex Differences in Mental and Behavioral Traits," *Genetic Psychology Monographs* 77 (1968): 162-299.

43. Inge K. Broverman et. al., "Sex-Role Stereotypes and Clinical Judgments of Mental Health," *Journal of Consulting and Clinical Psychology* 34 (1970): 1-7, and P. Rosenkrantz et. al., "Sex-Role Stereotypes and Self Concepts in College Students," *Journal of Consulting and Clinical Psychology* 32 (1968): 287-295.

44. Samuel A. Stouffer, *Communism, Conformity and Civil Liberties: A Cross-Section of the Nation Speaks its Mind* (Gloucester, Mass.: Peter Smith, 1963): Chapter 6.

45. Lynne B. Iglitzin, "Political Education and Sexual Liberation," *Politics and Society* 2, (Winter 1972): 241.

46. Robert J. Pranger, *The Eclipse of Citizenship: Power and Participation in Contemporary Politics* (New York: Holt, Rinehart and Winston, 1968).

47. D'Antonio (n. 39): 247.

48. Bay (n. 23): 99.

49. David E. Apter, *Choice and the Politics of Allocation* (New Haven: Yale University Press, 1971): 10.

50. Davis (n. 14): 737, and Arthur J. Dyck, "Population Policies and Ethical Acceptability," in National Academy of Sciences (n. 13): 626-627.

51. Dyck (n. 50): 628-629.

52. Han Suyin, "Family Planning in China," *Japan Quarterly* 17 (October-December 1970): 433-442.

53. Barclay, Enright, and Reynolds (n. 26): 17.

54. Frank Lorimer, "Issues in Population Policy," in Philip M. Hauser, ed., *The Population Dilemma,* 2nd ed. (Englewood Cliffs: Prentice Hall, 1969): 145. 145.

55. Carl E. Taylor and Marie-Francoise Hall, "Health, Population, and Economic Development," *Science* 57 (August 11, 1967): 655.

56. National Academy of Sciences (n. 13): 77.

57. Judith Blake, "Demographic Science and the Redirection of Population Policy," *Journal of Chronic Disease* 18 (1965), in Kenneth C.W. Kammeyer, ed., *Population Studies: Selected Essays and Research* (Chicago: Rand McNally & Co., 1969): 396.

58. Clark (n. 10): 51.

59. Ibid, 52.

60. J. Mayone Stycos, "Opinion, Ideology, and Population Problems—Some Sources of Domestic and Foreign Opposition to Birth Control," in National Academy of Science (n. 13): 544-545.

61. Ibid.: 545-546.

62. Ibid.

63. Dyck (n. 51): 623.

64. Frederick S. Jaffee and Steven Polgar, "Family Planning and Public Policy: Is the 'Culture of Poverty' the New Cop-Out?" *Journal of Marriage and the Family* 30 (May 1968): 228-235. When a "culture of poverty" is assumed (which Jaffee and Polgar do *not*), it then becomes more easily acceptable to coerce people into "proper" attitudes or behavior, without seriously facing the important questions of coercion and ethics. It is in this sense that the authors refer to the "culture of poverty" explanation as a "cop-out."

65. Daniel Callahan, "Ethical Issues," *Concerned Demography* 2 (March 1971): 46.

66. As an example of one who *does* deal with this, see David L. Sills, "Unanticipated Consequences of Population Policies," *Concerned Demography* 2 (March 1971): 61-69.

67. Ibid.: 63.

68. Dyck (n. 51).

69. Callahan (n. 65): 45-47.

70. Murray J. Edelman, *The Symbolic Uses of Politics* (Champaign-Urbana: University of Illinois Press, 1964), and *Politics as Symbolic Action: Mass Arousal and Quiescence* (Chicago: Markham, 1971).

71. Michael Parenti, "The Possibilities for Political Change," *Politics and Society* 1 (November 1970): 79-90.

72. "Family Planning Programs: Who Benefits," *Concerned Demography* 1 (February 1970): 17.

73. Ibid.: 18.

74. Henry Steck, "Power and the Liberation of Nature: The Politics of Ecology," *Alternatives* 1 (Summer 1971): 4-12. On page 8, the following appears: "To focus only on the growing population as the chief villain as many are inclined to do is to ignore the impact of an economic system where both consumer wants and economic incentives for the producer create a combined drive for production at the lowest cost and for higher consumption . . . . And so to focus on birthrates alone is to ignore the complex social, economic, technological, medical, and cultural variables involved and to lead also to proposals for harsh coercive death-rate solutions. While the problem may eventually require drastic solutions, these solutions must embrace not simply birth control or fanciful green revolutions, but quite far-reaching social, economic, and political changes. The consumption of at least 40 percent of the world's scarce or non-replaceable resources and of energy out-put by that 6% of the world population living in the United States gives one pause for thought: it underlines a distinctly political dimension to the question. Even should a stationary state or zero population growth be achieved, therefore, the question of the distribution of resources would remain on the agenda of uncompleted business between have and have-not nations internationally and have and have-not social strata within nations."

75. Hardin (n. 17).

76. The literature on these three concepts is abundant. In our thinking, we are indebted mostly to the works of Doris Lessing, Erich Fromm, Alan Watts, Ray Mungo, Herbert Marcuse, Christian Bay, Robert Paul Wolff, Paul Goodman, Norman O. Brown, and R.D. Laing.

77. Callahan (n. 65): 46.

78. Dreitzel (n. 16): 175.

3

American Population Policy Making: The Politics of Do Good, But Don't Rock the Boat!

Elihu Bergman

I. The Creation of a Policy Area

Among its diverse landmarks, the decade of the sixties witnessed the "population problem" catapulted from the marriage bed into the realm of American public policy. This transition was symbolized on March 16, 1970, when President Nixon signed legislation creating a Commission on Population Growth and the American Future to ". . . provide information and education to all levels of government in the United States, and to our people, regarding a broad range of problems associated with population growth and their implications for America's future."[1]

The celebrated political leprechaun Daniel Patrick Moynihan was on hand for the signing, whose significance he characterized: "Or to put it another way, how long do we want to stand in line to go to a movie?"[2]

At the same time, and also symbolic of the transition, a piece of legislation was under consideration in the Congress to ". . . promote public health and welfare by expanding, improving, and better coordinating the family planning services and population research activities of the Federal Government. . . ."[3]

From bed to cinema queue—this ambitious trajectory might well depict the distance the "population problem" has traversed since its discovery as a problem little more than a decade ago. And the leap further symbolizes two distinct sets of issues that comprise the "problem"—from those clustered around individual choices and actions to those clustered around group choices and actions. The first has to do with private decisions on matters such as the number and quality of individuals that should be added to the group, and when. The first set of issues are commonly grouped under the heading of "family planning," while those in the second set are increasingly labeled as issues of "population planning." The first cluster takes on an individual focus; the second, a societal focus.

These clusters—individual and societal—are manifest in the respective objectives of the Commission and the Tydings Bill. The Commission assumes a societal perspective, with a charter to inquire into

. . . aspects of population growth in the United States and its foreseeable social consequences:

41

(1) the probable course of population growth, internal migration, and related demographic developments between now and the year 2000;
(2) the resources in the public sector of the economy that will be required to deal with the anticipated growth in population;
(3) the ways in which population growth may affect the activities of federal, state, and local government;
(4) the impact of population growth on environmental pollution and on the depletion of natural resources; and
(5) the various means appropriate to the ethical values and principles of this society by which our Nation can achieve a population level properly suited for its environmental, natural resources, and other needs.[4]

The Tydings Bill took on more limited scope in addressing the issues of individual opportunity, and providing a rationale for handling them:

. . . unwanted births impair the stability and well-being of the individual family and severely limit the opportunity of each child within the family . . .

. . . over five million American women are denied access to modern, effective, medically safe family planning services due to financial need . . .

. . . family planning has been recognized nationally and internationally as a universal human right . . .

. . . it is the policy of Congress to foster the integrity of the family and the opportunity for each child; to guarantee the right of the family to freely determine the number and spacing of its children within the dictates of its individual conscience; to extend family planning services, on a voluntary basis, to all who desire such services . . . [5]

Taken together, the Commission and the Bill reflect an emerging policy agenda. The Commission is interested in what is good for the American community in the way of a population—the first time this issue has been posed outside the confines of immigration legislation. And the sponsors of the Tydings Bill were interested in what is good for the American individual in the way of a family—and for the first time would have Congress open the public purse to provide the related opportunity to choose for all American individuals. The charter of the Commission legitimizes a linkage between population growth and communal well-being. And the Tydings Bill legitimizes the inclusion of the right to plan families in the opportunity structure that the policy guarantees its individual members. Thus the societal and individual clusters were openly surfaced to comprise a discrete policy area in the American political system.

II. Issues, Concerns, and Institutions

Before 1960, population concerns were sounded in muted tones and within boundaries that enclosed a discreet dialogue on the knowledge and use of contraceptive technology by individuals who might be interested. By 1970 the dialogue was no longer muted, and its traditional constraints had disappeared. In addition to its earlier mix of individual choice and contraceptive technology, it now extends to how individuals might be manipulated by society to employ contraceptive technology.

Prior to 1960, population concerns were expressed in terms of family planning and legitimized in terms of maternal and child health and welfare. The norm of individual welfare inspired the activities of the planned parenthood movement, which for nearly five decades had been the locomotive force behind the message and substance of family planning in the United States.[6] The movement comprises a nationwide network of private local affiliates, whose membership of middle-class women and physicians was dedicated to doing good works among the needy—both the economically deprived, and those bereft of the knowledge that they could plan families. Planned parenthood existed to serve the individual mother and child and their families. This objective provided the traditional microcosmic focus—and normative baseline—for population-related concerns in the United States, and a rationale for the movement that evolved.

During the sixties, the population calculus was expanded by the entry of new ingredients, which underlined the role of society as a party of interest. One dimension suggested the obligation of society to broaden the opportunity base for mothers, children, and their families by guaranteeing the means for planned parenthood to all who might want them, including those who hitherto were denied it for social, economic, and cultural reasons.[7] Another dimension suggested the obligation of society to conserve itself by protecting its members and resources from potentially harmful consequences of population growth.[8] And the third dimension suggested an obligation of the individual to society— one which would associate his reproductive behavior with some norm of communal well-being.[9]

Thus the dialogue of population concerns, and their related activities, added a macrocosmic focus—society—and a new normative baseline, which would place planned parenthood at the service of society. New parties of interest entered the dialogue and action, as an expanded profile was grafted on to the traditional planned parenthood movement.

The concept of "family planning" or "planned parenthood" remained as the first stage in an augmented dialogue that focused on the consequences of aggregate population growth in society and on the individual. Because of its aggregate nature and remedial propositions, the expanded version is character-ized as "population planning." It reflects a different agenda of concerns and normative priorities. While "family planning" aims at the maximization of individual welfare, "population planning" takes its cues from requirements for societal welfare. Family planning has enshrined individual freedom of choice as its controlling norm. Population planning includes the interest of the community and the advantages to the individual in discharging an obligation to the collectivity. Family planning can transpire without significant intervention or coercive action by the political system; it is energized through established health systems, private as well as public. The fulfillment of population planning norms would require authoritative action by the political system—some sort of deliberate policy action.

The desired outcome of "population planning" is a population policy which would provide society with the number of children it requires to maximize communal welfare. Family planning aims at providing parents the opportunity to have the number of children they want to maximize their happiness. A leading figure in the population movement recognizes that the political dimensions of this dichotomy reflect a classic debate in political philosophy: ". . . how best to reconcile individual and collective interests."[10]

Counselor Moynihan's wait for prime time showings in the better cinemas suggests an anxiety that inspires the diverse agenda in the population planning dialogue: Are there too many people—in the world, in the United States, in less developed countries, in cities, in schools, in hospitals, and even in ballparks? As for the related, and by now well-known reactions: The world population is scheduled to double by the year 2007; and that of the United States in seventy years.[11] The density of pollutants in the atmosphere is scandalous and dangerous. Rush hour traffic is increasingly traumatic. Transfers of resources from the United States to poor countries have resulted neither in stability nor prosperity. Thirteen millions are added to the population of India each year. The Alliance for Progress has registered little impact in a region that experiences the highest population growth rate in the world. And as the demand for expenditures to finance international well-being shows no sign of abatement, the escalating demands for services and welfare expenditures at home are convulsing the American states, counties and cities.

The perception of these conditions propelled the population dialogue out of the doctor's consulting room and womens' club meeting, which together served as the principal forum for the planned parenthood movement. The anxieties about, diagnoses of, and remedies for population growth now are sounded along a global horizon of forums ranging from full-page newspaper advertisements to international conferences of scholars and public officials.[12] In between there are newly created public institutions, private associations, a new foundation, new subunits in old foundations, and new enclaves in the academic community—all preoccupied with the population problem (however visualized) and dedicated to its amelioration. Together with the older planned parenthood institutions, the new structure has come to comprise the American population movement. The major institutional components of this structure are listed in Figure 3-1.

In addition to begetting a new breed of specialist—the population professional—the population movement has developed an internal communications network, a professional jargon, a certain amount of conceptual clarity, and if not general agreement on priorities and strategies, at least a modicum of consensus

Figure 3-1.
A Profile of the American Population Movement: Major Institutional Actors

Universities: (Population Centers)

North Carolina
Michigan
Johns Hopkins
Columbia
Harvard
Princeton
Pittsburgh
Tulane
Chicago
Hawaii
California
Cornell
Wisconsin
Pennsylvania

Foundations:

Ford
Rockefeller
Population Council

Private Associations:

Planned Parenthood–World Population
Population Crisis Committee
Zero Population Growth

Government:

U.S. Congress – Senate and House of Representatives
Department of Health Education and Welfare
    Office of Population Affairs
    Center for Population Research, NICHD
    Center for Family Planning Services, HMSA
Office of Economic Opportunity
Agency for International Development

Note: These institutions were identified as the major institutional actors on the basis of several criteria, including: (1) Principal sources and recipients of funding; (2) Extent of activity as institutions and by their members in programing and funding decisions; (3) Activities as spokesmen for policy positions in legislative hearings; and (4) Membership on public commissions. (See Elihu Bergman, *The Politics of Population USA: A Critique of the Policy Process* [Chapel Hill: The Carolina Population Center, Population Program and Policy Design Series: no. 5, 1971].)

on the issues to be debated. The substance and spirit of the resulting dialogue is captured in Berelson's "Beyond Family Planning," which also expresses the guiding norm of the American population movement: ". . . everything that can properly be done to lower population growth rates should be done, now."[13]

III. A Policy Process

Public policy is visualized as the authoritative output of a political system.[14] The "policy" is the allocation or distribution; the end-product of the processing through the political system. It can assume one or a combination of incarnations. In essence it is an identifiable norm constructed in such form as to achieve an impact on the particular society or community, or on individuals or groups within it. Depending on the quality of its source political system, the public policy can be a decision, pronouncement, dictate, legislative enactment, or judicial act. It can occur as a single action, a series of related actions, or cumulatively in unrelated acts that result in an impact on an identifiable area of human behavior. A policy can emerge from a range of actions spanning all possible variations of political system behavior; for example, from a deliberate calculated pattern of activities directed toward the generation of an authoritative position on an identifiable issue, to the purposeful suppression of activities that might result in the recognition of an issue. In all this, the principal characteristic of a public policy is its authoritative quality—it is the enforceable product of an act or series of actions, or non-actions, that transpire within a political system.

A policy process is visualized as the interaction of institutions and related activities within a political system—of actors and actions—associated with an identifiable area of concern in the system.[15] The quality of the particular system determines how the concern is identified, and by whom. The players and the rules of the game involved in a policy process are determined by the quality of a system. The process can involve a limited number of actors who establish a unique set of rules to handle an issue that is the product of their particular caprice. Or it can involve a wide range of actors handling an issue resulting from widespread communal concern, and operating within norms, previously established and widely and consciously accepted, that uniformly determine the style of interaction within a particular system.

There are other variations in policy processes. For example, a process associated with an identifiable issue or area of concern can evolve as the *ad hoc* composite of several processes connected with related or peripheral concerns, the outcome of which creates a collateral though identifiable impact on the issue in question. As another variation of policy process, a series of transactions within the political system can transpire without yielding an authoritative output. The cycle need not have been completed. Thus it is possible to identify interactions within a system clustered around certain concerns, issues, demands, and the like, that have not yet resulted in authoritative outputs, and indeed may never do so. These identifiable patterns of activity, as much as those resulting in completed cycling or authoritative action, can be regarded as policy processes.

"Population policy" would be the authoritative outputs of the decisions and actions of government deliberately taken to have an impact on population characteristics. The American population policy process is the pattern of actors and interactions within the system that creates these decisions and actions. Because population size and the rate at which it grows have emerged as the major policy concerns, the policy process has tended to focus on issues related to growth.[16]

Although the American system has not yet produced an authoritative norm of population growth, the issue of population growth has produced an identifiable pattern of activity within the system that qualifies as a policy process. Whether this pattern of activity—this policy process—runs a complete cycle of the system by producing a norm—an authoritative output—is an interesting object for speculation. But even in the absence of the output, the pattern of activity exists; the process is alive and thus the legitimate object of political inquiry and analysis.

IV. A Model and a Reality

The nucleus of a policy process is best visualized as a set of actors, individual and institutional; a set of resources, of whatever character and combination might be appropriate to the process; and the linkages and interactions that evolve among these components as the actors deploy the resources. The actors both exercise the power that determines the allocation of resources and frame the issues around which the allocation evolves.

For the American population policy process, this image would be portrayed in two matrixes, one depicting the network of actors and resources involved (Figure 3-2) and the second reflecting a network of their relationships (Figure 3-3).

There are three distinctive roles in the American population policy process. The first is concerned with the illumination and conceptualization of population issues, the application of scientific methodology to the related human and social problems, and the translation of scientific findings into remedies susceptible to application. This role is performed by specialists with the requisite intellectual capacities and professional credentials. The group is accordingly characterized as the Professional/Intellectuals. Their distinctive product is a resource that is characterized as Cerebral.

The second role is concerned with legitimizing remedies to problems perceived as relating to population change, and creating conditions whereby these remedies will be accepted and applied to the problems. This role is performed by

Figure 3–2.
The American Population Policy Process: Network of Actors and Resources

| | Institutional Bases | | | |
	University	Foundation	Private Association	Government
Individual Actors				
Professional/Intellectual	X	X	X	X
Private Influential		X	X	
Public Official				X
Resources				
Influence		X	X	
Money		X		X
Authority				X

persons of stature and influence in the community, derived from their professional success, social status, wealth, and other sources of preeminence. They function in their private capacities. The group is accordingly characterized as the Private Influentials. Their product is a resource described as Influence.

The third role is concerned with authorizing the opportunities for scientific

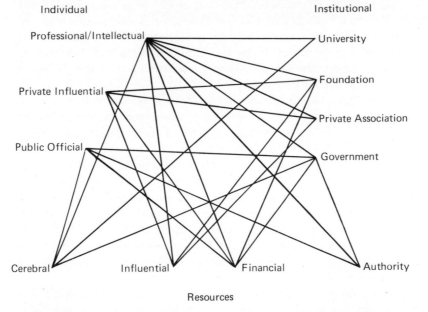

Figure 3–3. The American Population Policy Process: Network of Relationships.

processing and the application of remedies. This role is performed by officers of the government, in both the legislative and executive branches. The group is therefore described as Public Official. They dispose over two resources, a principal product which is Authority, and a collateral one which is Money.

These roles are based in four types of institutions which function as the principal suppliers of one or more of the resources. Thus the university supplies cerebral substance. The foundation supplies both a cerebral resource and money, and because of its unique quality as an institution in which people of means and preeminence dispose over cerebral and financial matter, the foundation is frequently a supplier of influence. The private association, as a grouping of individual citizens, is principally a supplier of influence, but because of the multiple roles of some associations in providing technical assistance and raising money, they can also supply cerebral substance and money. And the government, whose principal product is the combination of authority and money, also functions in a multiple role, and because of its direct participation in research is a significant cerebral supplier.

Their multiple roles as suppliers of resources determine the distribution of individual actors in institutional bases. Thus professional/intellectuals, with the widest spread, are based in all four. Private influentials operate from bases in foundations and private associations. And public officials are, naturally, based in government institutions.

The American population policy process thus is visualized as a pattern of multiple roles played by its institutional and individual actors. The roles are linked by a network of multiple relationships among the actors. And the resources over which the actors dispose are subject to multiple handling. The process transpires in a consensual setting comprised of open channels of communication among the actors, easy access to one another, general agreement on objectives and methods, and a compact structure in which to operate. Of the three groups of individual actors, the professional/intellectuals are positioned to wield the greatest influence in policy making because of their presence in all four institutional bases, and their access to all categories of resources.[17]

Missing from this picture are the policy consumers; the constituency that would benefit from the major output of the policy process—the provision of publicly supported family planning services. Or as one of their members, Mrs. Laetitia Wilson, put it while testifying on the Tydings Bill, ". . . the people who count."[18] Indeed, beyond the anonymous statistical evidence of need by these potential consumers for the policy output, the only evidence of their presence in the process of policy formation is reflected by Mrs. Wilson's appearance before the House Subcommittee considering the family planning legislation, and the appearance of another consumer, Mrs. Bobby McMahan, before the Senate Subcommittee dealing with the same legislative proposals.[19] But Mrs. Wilson and Mrs. McMahan comprised only two of the approximately fifty spokesmen who addressed the two subcommittees, and neither they nor their peers are represented in any of the institutional bases that exercise direct influence over the resources employed in the American population policy process.

It can be argued—and it has been—that the wants of these consumers are known; that they are ineffective spokesmen on their own behalf; and that their interests are effectively represented by others,[20] though there is no conclusive evidence for the credibility of this argument. It can also be argued that responsive and responsible policy making does not require the direct involvement in the policy process of the consumers of policy remedies, the beneficiaries of policy allocations, and the constituencies of policy areas. This argument similarly lacks credibility.

Allocations in particular and identifiable categories have traditionally involved participation by their potential beneficiaries in the distribution process. Thus the maritime, aviation, railroad, and trucking industries participate in federal support and regulation of transportation; electricity producers and electric cooperatives in utilities regulation; farmers in farm policy; veterans in veterans' benefits; members of trade unions in labor policy, and so forth. The inputs of these groups are made from institutional bases that have evolved as a result of opportunities for direct participation in the policy process—trade associations; farm groups; veterans' organizations; labor political actions groups; and the like.

Those who have not participated directly in policy processes directly affecting their concerns were denied the opportunity for reasons of bigotry, economic deprivation, and other forms of exclusion from the political system. But as the constraints to their involvement in the political system erode, these groups too are creating institutional bases from which to participate more directly in policy development, such as organizations of welfare recipients and minorities. Thus there is ample precedent, and increasing demonstration of value, for a direct, rather than a mere representational, access to the policy processes.[21]

Of course, there is no guarantee that more direct access of those most directly concerned with the outcome of a policy process will improve the quality of the process or of the outcome. But in the particular area of American population policy there are reasonable grounds for speculation on the quality of outcome and process, in which the quality of access could be an influential factor.

V. The Theology and the Practice

An optimistic vision of a better society and a better life for its members is the inspiration that propels the American population movement in its works. Though there are different shadings to the common vision and variations in its composition, it is a benign image based on a conviction that man and society can improve given the opportunities for doing so. As its operational route to the achievement of this norm, the American population movement has adopted the family planning formula, which would provide all members of the community the opportunity to determine the quantity and timing of their offspring. The resulting policy agenda is a derivative of the norm and the formula, and the policy process a creature of the agenda. The agenda thus is focused on concerns that would expand a particular opportunity, and the policy process involves activities that would translate the concern into a reality.

Whatever the variations in the desirable futures visualized by individual participants in the population policy process, there is little perceptible inclination among them to question each other's favorite image, or the motives for it. The reactions of some suggest a desire to preserve society as it is, while others clearly are looking for substantial changes in the status quo. But across this spectrum, the family planning formula constitutes a neutral adhesive that joins all in common cause because it is accepted as a conduit to whatever version of a better society they value.

Likewise, there are different constructions placed on the scope and content of the family planning formula. Some see a bare-bones version limited to the availability and delivery of a contraceptive technology wherever it is needed. Others suggest a requirement for supplements to contraceptive technology; for example, opportunities for the broader exercise of individual choice in matters such as education, employment, and housing, in order to render the family planning opportunity more meaningful and effective. Yet whatever the varying constructions of its ideal product, the population movement has coalesced around a narrow interpretation of the formula—a focus on fertility manipulation—as the platform from which to conduct its operations.[22]

Thus enclosed in a consensual environment, and functioning in a compact, self-contained, easily communicative structure, both of which are supportive of each other, the American population policy process is protected from influences that might deflect the principal thrust of its energies by introducing modifications in its agenda and operational platform. Greater access to the policy process, say, by groups in the community affected by the policy, could create such deflection.

In this connection, let us accept the family planning formula as a desirable and consensual core of American population policy and consider two conditions for a successful family planning enterprise in the United States, an enterprise designed to provide the opportunity to employ contraception to all Americans. The first condition is a system through which the opportunity can be effectively delivered, and the second is an environment in which the opportunity, once available, will be sought and employed in pursuit of the benefit it is supposed to yield. The absence of either of these conditions renders the opportunity elusive.

At its present stage of development, contraceptive technology is best delivered through a health care system. The quality of the product is determined by the quality of the system. To make the product universally available, the system requires universal accessibility in the community it presumes to serve. Additionally, to make the product, and thus the opportunity, complete and viable, the system requires certain structural capabilities, the most important of which is the absence of constraints to making the product universally available.

In its existing state, health care in the United States is treated as a commodity subject to trading in the market place. This condition subjects it to the elemental forces of the market place, the most important of which is a traditional method of allocation involving a pricing mechanism determined by the interplay of supply and demand. The price of the commodity and thus its availability are established by conditions of relative scarcity. The market mechanism may work well in performing a pricing function. But so long as some parties of interest are denied access to the market place because they have little or nothing to trade, the market mechanism does not work effectively in performing a distribution function.[23] In a sociological analysis of the medical profession, Freidson argues the failure of consulting professions, including the medical, to "... practice forms of regulation which assure the public that care of a uniformly high quality is available to all irrespective of their economic and social status." This failure is buttressed by a "... position of organized autonomy" which provides the profession "... its monopoly over special work ... its special place in the social order ... " and "... permits the profession to create an important segment of the socially constructed universe."[24] Here then is a fundamental constraint in the capacity of the American health care system for delivering the family planning opportunity. The population presently denied access to the opportunity is the same population whose access to the market place is limited.

The market condition of health care erodes the family planning formula, and thus the related opportunity, in several respects. Even if contraceptive technology were removed from the market and allocated by some other mechanism, as American population policy now envisions, other product components which determine the value of contraceptive technology remain in the market place. Health care facilities, for example, comprise the points-of-delivery. Yet their existence, capabilities, and geographic distribution are determined largely by the pricing mechanism. Equally critical, and related to the availability and capability of health care facilities, is the total health care product available to mothers and living children.[25] The quality of this product is a significant determinant of fertility choices, which the contraceptive technology is supposed to implement. The argument that more healthy and alive mothers and children result in the production of fewer children is made persuasively by Polgar and Kessler. They develop this position in the context of an argument that "Family planning and other health services for the family are mutually reinforcing."[26]

Taylor and Hall argue along similar lines: "Increasing evidence shows that health service may be indispensible for reducing population growth. A minimum level of health seems to be necessary for acceptance of the idea and practice of limiting or spacing births. Parents need assurance that children already born will have a reasonable chance for survival. In addition, readily accessible minimum health facilities are probably essential for providing modern contraceptive information and materials."[27]

A conference on Infant and Child Mortality and Fertility Behavior (Research Triangle Institute, February 17, 1971) produced no conclusive evidence that would support the impact of improved maternal and child health care on fertility. However, it was agreed that not all the evidence is in hand.[28]

At this conference Taylor reported that some of his work suggested the value of health system inputs: (1) In Indian Punjabi villages, the acceptance of family planning technology is directly related to the quality of maternal and child health care; and (2) A preliminary analysis of two Nigerian villages at differential stages of modernization suggests that the direct delivery of health services has a greater impact on lower family size than does a higher level of modernization.[29]

And Siegel cited the established relationship between the provision of adequate nutrition and the development of intellectual potential, which creates a development syndrome that in itself reduces fertility, i.e., a higher capacity to absorb education leads to improved employment options and opportunities.[30]

Yet the total health care product in the United States remains a commodity distributed and priced by exchanges in the market place.[31] Until the product, rationally designed to meet community needs, is allocated by a mechanism rationally designed to deliver it to the community, the family planning opportunity is devalued and its effectiveness blunted.

While individual fertility preferences are achieved by contraceptive technology, they are determined largely by conditions in the surrounding social and economic environment.[32] These are the conditions that also determine how well individuals are able to live. They comprise the opportunity structure that the community makes available to its members—the package of opportunities for expressing and achieving individual preferences in areas such as education, housing, nutrition, and employment. While these opportunities comprise ingredients of the welfare package that the family planning opportunity is intended to facilitate, they likewise determine the value of the family planning opportunity itself and, once available, how likely it is to work both in the achievement of individual fertility preferences, and as a conduit to a broader range of opportunities.

As presently employed in American population policy the family planning formula is designed to influence a single demographic condition—fertility rates. The formula envisions an allocation of opportunity to manipulate fertility. But for its optimal impact, the formula requires an ingredient that would enable it to influence another demographic condition—population distribution. Like health care, the distribution of population in the United States is not determined by conditions primarily relevant to individual and communal well-being. While the allocation of health care still is influenced by a pricing mechanism, the distribution of the American population where most of it is concentrated still is influenced in significant measure by bigotry.

At least with respect to residential segregation, however, it is not necessary to confront the socioeconomic patterns before it is possible to deal with racial residential patterns. It would be a major accomplishment indeed to reduce racial housing segregation to the level of socioeconomic segregation.[33]

Thus, individuals are prevented from achieving their preferences on where they might like to live, or where it might be most convenient or economical for them to do so.

Though it enjoys no juridical status in influencing population distribution, bigotry camouflaged in juridically acceptable forms ranging from zoning ordinances to ill-disguised manifestations of hostile sentiment, can impede a rational distribution of the American population. Accordingly, the social and economic pathologies resulting from irrational distribution such as confinement in central cities are perpetuated, while the social and economic opportunities available through rational distribution are denied. Effective access to the opportunities related to freedom of choice on where to live—better education, housing, employment opportunities and the like—would create conditions likely to affect fertility behavior by providing an environment which could facilitate the achievement of fertility preferences among the population groups where deprivation of all opportunities runs highest.

Rational policy approaches to health care and population distribution are likely to achieve multiple benefits. They would round out a limited family planning formula and open complementary channels to higher levels of individual and communal welfare which is the announced purpose of the family planning formula.

But rational approaches in these areas could require tampering with the policy process and the way it now operates by some pushing around by the political system of individuals and groups whose interests and behavior currently bar rational treatment of health care and population dispersal. Thus the instruments of political power available in the American population policy process might be employed for modified objectives, a revised agenda, and by actors in addition to or other than those now involved.

VI. A Prognosis and an Obstacle

The construction of a comprehensive as opposed to a limited family planning formula calls for changes in the established boundary and prevailing style of population policy making. As a start, there is need for the clarification of objectives. The existing opaque pattern of favored visions of the future around which the American population movement has coalesced masks a differentiated set of goals which represent potential sources of conflict within the policy process. It is not enough to lay claim to such abstract norms as "higher quality of life," "increased opportunity," and the like. For each claimant, or group of claimants, there may be a different set of goals which determine their respective agenda. Thus the reduction of fertility among the poor to lower public welfare costs would suggest quite a different set of remedies than does reduction of fertility among the poor to accelerate their access to the American opportunity structure. Likewise, the manipulation of fertility to control population growth poses a different set of concerns than does the manipulation of fertility to expand individual opportunity. The clarification of differential goals and their related agendas would permit a more systematic and open treatment of all relevant issues.

Such treatment would involve an evaluation of the alternative strategies that might be attached to each of the agendas through a determination of their differential costs and benefits among members of the society. This assessment would require a complete statement of the alternative routes through which the objective, however conceived, might be attained—an inventory of the options. Once identified, the complete range of options, whether traditional or innovative, familiar or not so familiar, would be linked to objectives in a formulation of their relative effectiveness and their differential impact on the community and its members, including both participants and non-participants in the policy process. The resulting calculus would yield a balance sheet of costs and benefits expressed not only in financial terms, but in economic, social, and political terms as well. And such a statement of potential reward and deprivation would provide the grounds for a dialogue in which all parties of interest could express their preferences, if they so desired, because there would be some clear options about which to express their preferences. The yield of such an enterprise might not be a complete family planning formula, but even if incomplete as it has been thus far, it would bring into focus the deficiencies that a complete formula would remedy and provide grounds for more effective action by all interested parties.

In all likelihood, achievement of the ultimate family planning goal which in essence aims at buttressing opportunities for individuals to improve the condition of their lives, requires a formula which moves beyond family planning. The ingredients of this formula are suggested by the body of knowledge that has evolved as a result of increasing concern with population issues over the past two decades. This body of knowledge, and its related conceptual apparatus and analytic tools, is distinguished by its focus on aggregates of individuals, and particularly on associations between the quality of the aggregates and the conditions of life experienced by members of the aggregates.

The quality of the aggregates is reflected in characteristics of size; rates of growth; composition (e.g., sex, age, and ethnic); and location. And conditions of life for the aggregates include factors such as nutrition, health, employment, education, shelter, leisure, ecological situation, civic activity, and the degree of access to and opportunity for improving all these factors. The quality of aggregates and conditions of life in this population equation exercise a reciprocal influence on one another (see Figure 3-4).

In introducing his concept of "sociological demography," Goldscheider focuses on these relationships:

. . . the cumulative processes of population events and the resultant implications for the size, distribution, and composition of populations are fundamental to the structure and functioning of human societies. People are the stuff from which families, groups, societies and nations are constructed; the processes of population are the building blocks shaping the form and content of social units. In turn, the individual and personal aspects of population phenomena are conditioned and affected by the power of social forces; what appears on the surface to represent biological and idiosyncratic events are by their nature social as well.

. . . The size, growth, density, concentration of population, birth and death rates, cityward and suburbanward migrations, have become social issues for many reasons and in various social contexts, but mainly because population processes affect and are affected by the organization and anatomy of society. The quantity of population shapes the quality of social life. The reverse is equally true; the quality and fabric of social life shape the quantity and character of population processes.[34]

Population policy consists of authoritative actions, principally by governments, designed deliberately to influence the equation. However because of the potential scope of the population policy equation, population policy concerns in reality become synonymous with social policy concerns. So long as the guiding norm of population policy is the improvement of men and societies, the policy options involved are best formulated and processed within the broader context of social policy.

Figure 3–4.
Population Policy Focus, Aggregates of Individuals

Quality of Aggregate		Conditions of Life	
Size	*Mobility (Improvement)*	Nutrition	*Opportunity (access)*
Growth		Health	
Composition		Employment	
Location		Leisure	
		Shelter	
		Education	
		Civic	
		Ecological	

Thus the population policy discourse, with its family planning emphasis, would move beyond its recent preoccupation with size and rates of growth, and begin to grapple with other issues and options suggested by a social policy focus. Such an expansion of the discourse is likely to involve not only new and more controversial substance, but new and additional participants.

Yet despite an expressed commitment to enlightened social policy goals by many individuals involved in the American population policy process, it remains more narrow and restrictive than their visions suggest it should be. There is the central focus on a fertility strategy—how best to manipulate fertility to achieve the major objectives. While there is major concern with environmental conditions that affect fertility behavior, so far it has emerged as a concern more for understanding the conditions and their impact, than for a quest of possible means to manipulate them. The differentials—the social and economic determinants of fertility behavior—tend to be accepted as given.

This fertility approach has led to a dependence on contraceptive technology—its effective development and deployment—as the principal remedial instrument. The social and economic environment accordingly is excluded as an object of population policy manipulation, and fertility behavior adopted as the prime target for manipulation through an optimal employment of contraceptive technology. Thus grounds are created for an attempt at technocratic solutions to problems equally or more susceptible to structural remedies. And with the agenda set in this framework, the quest for technocratic solutions tends to absorb fully the skills, energies, and resources that are in short supply to begin with and under considerable pressure to yield solutions on an urgent basis.

Here then is a policy ambience which discourages inclinations to invite additional complexity and conflict by confronting issues not defined as immediately relevant. Accordingly, whatever faults it reflects, there is a willingness to accept the constraints on the enterprise as they are, and "the system" as it is. Thus the suggestion by a sensitive participant in the policy process that though the system requires certain alterations for the good of the cause, the attempt to achieve them would be something of a quixotic enterprise, so in effect: let's operate with what we have. Or the arguments by others who likewise recognize systematic ills: ". . . if we want to do something about population, let's stick to population . . ."; or ". . . population is what we know best . . ." So, as a result of these and similar perceptions, the policy process tends to resist impulses for system manipulation, and accepts, though in some cases knowingly and reluctantly, a status-quo bias.[35]

But given the alliances in the American population movement it is difficult to visualize any other bias as a viable basis for the consensual platform from which it functions. We have seen the movement—the major participants in the policy process—as a compact network of actors and multiple relationships; as one of the actors described it: "an interlocking directorate." Within this complex, the significant public support is derived from an elite of influential Americans—"successful people"—as they were characterized by one of their members. These are individuals who have achieved their success within the existing system for distributing advantages among members of the community. It is a system that has served them well. And it is unlikely that they would be inclined to tamper with it in any significant degree. On the contrary, the behavior of this stratum of American society often suggests a preference to conserve the system as they know it and value it.

Some of the ingredients of a complete family planning formula might involve tampering beyond the bounds this influential group regards as legitimate or in their interest. It would be fanciful, for example, to conceive of the Hugh Moore group, which publishes the strident advertisements calling for birth control, supporting equally energetic appeals for the immediate dispersal of ghetto populations into the suburbs of metropolitan areas. And it would be unlikely to find full-page *New York Times* advertisements sponsored by this impressive group of Americans pleading for a health care system that would serve the needs of all Americans and for the immediate measures, as radical as their pleas for population control, required for the construction of such a system.

Likewise, it would not be reasonable to expect the influential Population Crisis Committee, with its "Fortune 500" profile,[36] to support a population dispersal strategy or a revised health care strategy with the same vigor and skill they have devoted to fertility manipulation strategies. Even the good citizens who have supported the voluntary family planning ideology through the national network of Planned Parenthood affiliates could not reasonably be expected to coalesce around an expanded ideology, with all its controversial implications, that would really legitimize the rights of all Americans to live where they might prefer.

Some of the most influential actors in the professional/intellectual sector of the population movement are members of the medical and public health communities. They, too, appear to prefer functioning within a familiar and limited framework. For example, the testimony of their representatives in the several population-related hearings of the 91st Congress reflected a focus on a fertility strategy.[37] If there was any conviction on their part that an effective family planning formula required inputs from an area they know best—the provision of adequate health care—they were silent on the matter in the congressional forum.[38]

The population movement is rounded out by public officials in the legislative branch and executive agencies. These actors perform their roles in accordance with the styles peculiar to their institutional bases. Thus the legislators are inclined to a less, rather than a more, controversial approach, particularly in new areas such as government intervention in population matters where the political cost-benefit calculus is not adequately determined. To the extent they are interested in population matters at all, they would tend to be more comfortable with a narrow legislative framework suggested by a limited family planning formula confined to fertility strategies, rather than a broader and more controversial one that would evolve from considerations of population dispersal and health care systems. And as for the federal bureaucracy, it is traditionally a follower—not a leader; an implementer—not an innovator; for these are the conditions of its traditional role.

Therefore a limited strategy, one that reduces the area of controversy, is likely to be more compatible with the interests and styles of the principal actors in the population policy process, as it now exists. And this is a strategy best sought within the confines of the familiar, the given, the status quo.

The converse of a limited strategy might create waves in the system requiring that its coercive power be exercised in unfamiliar ways. An effective population dispersal strategy, for example, would involve, among other things, coercive measures to provide residential opportunities in metropolitan suburbs to those now denied them.[39] The deprived group comprises the residents of central cities, principally poor and non-white. The components of the opportunity package are familiar: housing at prices within their means; transportation systems consistent with their needs; access to the necessary education, health, and recreational facilities; and a pattern of community behavior that, if not encouraging to, is not suppressive of the exercise of claims to these opportunities.

In the existing climate of suburban America, this is a controversial package. Its realization would require the compelling of some members of the community to do things they would not ordinarily do. Federal financing of construction, for example, would be employed to compel the creation of low-cost residential housing in the traditionally high-priced suburbs.[40] This would affect suburban builders and developers and their financing institutions.

The capacities for federal support and regulation of transportation might be employed to manipulate metropolitan transportation systems. This would affect the suppliers of transportation, public and private; groups interested in particular means of transport, such as the builders and users of highways; and institutions which arrange financing for the related enterprises. And the juridical system might be energetically employed to facilitate the staking of claims to new opportunities. This would affect members of the community, who if not inclined to suppress the opportunities, do not welcome their creation.

A health care system exploitive of existing resources and responsive to existing needs similarly would involve new forms and objects of coercion. Flash has speculated on where the coercion might logically be, and most likely will not be, applied:

Short of violent revolution, World War III, or some other catastrophe in the next few years . . . can it really be expected that President Nixon (or any identifiable successor) might lead the nation and the Congress into a unified, rational and substantial legislative commitment to a system of adequate health care for all Americans? . . . can it be conceived that . . . new voices will be any match for the old, those of substantial vested interest in the present health care non-system serving the American corporate state so well? . . . If any unified legislative response is in fact conceivable within the limits of 1970 establishment politics and government, it is far more likely to reflect these myths of corporate entrepreneurship and efficiency than those of American democratic populism and consumerism.[41]

A direct approach to this issue might suggest several targets for manipulation, including, for example, some of the following: the traditional ideology of health care in itself, based in part on norms which support a highly individualized role for the physician and a high degree of autonomy for the medical profession;[42] the institutional arrangements by which health care is distributed, and the actors and processes involved in making the related decisions; the existing structures and constraints that determine the development, deployment, and utilization of health manpower; and the techniques for financing the distribution of health care.[43]

Considering the existing system for providing health care in the United States, this inventory is not void of controversial substance. It suggests the potential for pushing around institutions and individuals hitherto unaccustomed to being pushed around. One might speculate, for example, on the reaction of some American physicians upon being informed that they are the servants of society, like the clergy. Or consider the institutional reaction of established Schools of Medicine and Public Health, whose institutional support from federal sources would be conditioned upon the surrender of their autonomy, followed by a merger into a single structure whose role would be determined only by requirements for the optimal production of health manpower. And how about the sentiment of students in these institutions, autonomous or merged, whose matriculation was conditioned on a commitment, additional to any military obligation, to serve the national interest, say for a period of two years, wherever the nation might determine?

These have been suggestions of some implications for a policy process that would seek a broader interpretation of the family planning strategy. So far the existing American population policy process has not demonstrated the inclination to deal with an agenda of this scope. Whatever the consciousness of an expanded agenda and its potential, the existing policy process has reflected a preference for the narrow interpretation. Thus, the policy issues are bounded within a familiar range—a manageable format—one derivative of the preferences of those whose biases impose the limitations. And within this limited range the potential scope of conflict in the policy process is narrowed. The population policy discourse which should be a social policy discourse is confined to a family planning agenda.

The result of this condition is a controlled discourse, one that automatically excludes some potentially relevant questions and issues, both because existing participants in the policy process have failed to tune them in, and because participants who might do so are presently excluded from the policy process. Here then is a mobilization of bias in a policy process, a pattern of behavior that suppresses certain types of decisions because their ingredients are effectively denied entry to the arena of decision. These related exclusionary forms of behavior in a policy process are described as follows:

"Mobilization of Bias"

All forms of political organization have a bias in favor of the exploitation of some kinds of conflict and the suppression of others because organization is the mobilization of bias. Some issues are organized into politics while others are organized out.[44]

"Non-Decision Making"

A "mobilization of bias" is a condition that is sustained by "nondecision" making. A "nondecision" is: . . . a decision that results in suppression or thwarting of a latent or manifest challenge to the values or interests of the decision-maker. . . . nondecision-making is a means by which demands for change in the existing allocation of benefits and privileges in the community can be suffocated before they are even voiced; or kept covert; or killed before they gain access to the relevant decision-making arena; or, failing all these things, maimed or destroyed in the decision-implementing stage of the policy process.[45]

The exclusion of these controversial ingredients is not a product of malevolence on the part of the policy actors involved, and in most cases, not even a conscious act. It is the product of their life style, their value system, the way they see the world, and a consequence of the world they fail to see and feel.

This particular policy style is consistent with the style of policy making common to the American system. It has been characterized as something of an interest group syndrome, where the resources over which the system presides—the advantages—are parcelled out among those who stake claim to particular categories on the basis of principal concern or interest in them.[46] As a result, there is a compartmentalization of interest, in which particular concerns are linked to particular objects. The particular concerns thus tend to be satisfied. Since everybody with the power for staking a claim tends to receive a piece of the action, and that piece which interests him most, an attitude of mutual toleration evolves among the claimants. The grounds for conflict thus are reduced. And the incentive to rock the boat—to disturb the structure that renders a mutually satisfactory allocation of advantages—is suppressed.[47]

As group interests are compartmentalized, so is the pattern for distributing the substance over which they preside. Distinctive styles for distribution evolve within each compartment, styles compatible with the substance involved and the preferences of the parties of interest to each. And where the interests of compartments collide, their respective claimants seek settlements of competing claims at the margin, in such manner that the outcome is least disturbing to the compartment of each. Participation or membership in each of the compartments meanwhile acquires a restrictive character, not by any deliberate quest of exclusivity, but because the original membership becomes accustomed to one another, and to the substance and the style of each compartment, and they like it that way.

VII. A Challenge

We have seen how membership in the population policy compartment is dominated by a professional/intellectual group. They function from all institutional bases that form the compartment and are in positions to influence all categories of resources over which the compartment disposes. In their multiple roles, and through their network of influence, they determine in significant measure the behavior of the compartment—what enters, what departs, and what happens in the interim. Given the scope of their involvement and their influence, actual and potential, they earn the distinction of being the High Priesthood of the American Population Movement.

The role of American professional/intellectuals in policy making has been subjected to critical scrutiny and continues as an object of soul-searching among members of the intellectual community.[48] The issue is posed as the extent to which professional intellectuals distort both their scientific role and the policy process by functioning as intellectual technicians in the policy process or as activists in the political system. As a formula for the maintenance of their intellectual integrity, it has been suggested that intellectuals maintain a discreet separation between their scientific and activist roles.[49] This is an ideal formulation, and for purposes of the present discussion it is enough to accept it as sound. But the reality remains that in the population policy process, intellectuals are functioning in multiple roles, and there is no perceptible inclination among them to seek a separation between their scientific and activist incarnations. Indeed, those involved display little discomfort with these multiple roles and appear to welcome them as contributing positively to one another and to the enterprise in which they are involved.

Therefore, for the High Priesthood, the issue is their success in achieving an optimal mix of their roles for the good of the enterprise. Given their influence, preeminence, special skills, and intellectual resources, their responsibility is formidable and their behavior critical to the quality of the policy process.[50]

If, for example, the quest of an expanded family planning formula is relevant to the objectives of the population movement, and indeed relevant as an ingredient in the broader fabric of American social policy, then the professional intellectuals might effectively take the lead in structuring the agenda accordingly. Or at the very least, they might take the initiative in providing the substance with which to evaluate the question of relevance. If certain irrelevant concerns, like the welfare of the blue whale and the bald eagle, are piggy-backed on the population discourse, then the Priesthood might illuminate the distortion, and resist the temptation to employ it for opportunistic reasons.[51]

And if the discourse should be opened to accommodate a more meaningful participation by such as Mesdames Wilson and McMahan and "the people who count," it is the High Priesthood who can best secure their admission. It is, after all, these people "who count" who presumably are the immediate objects of the prevailing policy discourse as well as its principal beneficiaries. The evidence suggests that their participation thus far is limited and symbolic. And though there is evidence of a feeling among the High Priests and their associates in the population movement that "their wants are known," there is no evidence to support this confident position. When they were summoned to the family planning hearings, Mesdames Wilson and McMahan were called in to respond on the narrow issue of fertility manipulation and their preference for the related opportunity. They were not asked to state their preferences for alternatives or complementary ingredients that might more effectively provide them the opportunity to achieve their fertility preferences. The issue was not posed to them to elicit their reactions on their favorite visions of American social policy. If the issue had been so structured, they might have been informed that $382 million (the amount proposed in the legislation) was being sought to purchase a package of opportunities for them, but that the same amount might purchase comparable packages of varied ingredients which would yield greater or lesser or equal advantages sooner or later. Then, given their concerns and priorities, what type of package would they prefer? Or perhaps if these particular opportunities are not supreme in their order of priorities, they might be given the chance to express their agenda of concerns and inquire of the system how it proposes to respond, whatever the price tag.

That the High Priests and their associates in the American population movement have not expanded their discourse and have failed to encourage the entry of more participants and more issues to the compartment in which it evolves is not the result of their insensitivity, lack of knowledge, or absence of idealistic bent, and certainly not of any deliberate malevolent design. In little more than a decade, all the principal actors have been swept into a pioneer enterprise which would attempt social engineering by the manipulation of population variables. There is a sense of urgency about their work, compounded by high expectations, and shortages of funds, manpower, experience, and knowledge. On balance their performance has been responsible and enlightened. Indeed, their fellow members of society who benefit from their labors might derive comfort and confidence because they are engaged in the engineering of a better society. But the particular quality of the American population policy process, its peculiarities, strengths, and deficiencies, is not explained by factors of novelty and urgency alone. It is the product of the system in which it functions and reflective of the prevailing values and styles. Likewise, its principal actors are influenced by values and styles both derived from, and which they perpetuate in, the system.

Social engineering is regarded as a worthy enterprise in American society. But a high regard for this worthy enterprise most often is accompanied by an expectation that it is most effectively accomplished with a minimum of boat-rocking.

Though traditional designs for society may be durable and functional, innovative structures often are better, even though they may require a departure from tradition that can be disturbing to those who have a stake in tradition. In any case, a determination of relative merit requires the consideration of all alternative designs, innovative and traditional, utilizing all available materials, and reflecting the preferences of all parties of interest. This would be a rational approach to designing a structure, physical or social. Sometimes the process involves a bit of boat-rocking.

The American system enjoys the resources, physical and institutional, to conduct this type of policy enterprise. To the extent these capabilities are unemployed or underemployed in discrete policy processes and in the system at large, the system departs from a distinctive norm of political participation that is supposed to be bed rock in the American political edifice.

Notes

1. Public Law 91-213, S. 2107, 91st Congress. Approved March 16, 1970.

2. *New York Times*, 17 March 1970.

3. S. 2108, 91st Congress, 2nd session. Commonly referred to as the "Tydings Bill" in recognition of its principal sponsor on the Senate side, this bill subsequently was enacted a Public Law 91-572—Family Planning Services and Population Research Act of 1970.

4. Public Law 91-213 (n. 1).

5. S. 2108 (n. 3).

6. The evolution of the planned parenthood movement in the United States is best recorded and evaluated in David M. Kennedy *Birth Control in America: The Career of Margaret Sanger* (New Haven: Yale University Press, 1970). (Note particularly the comprehensive bibliographical essay.) See also the review of this volume: Alan F. Guttmacher "Margaret Sanger's New Look," *Family Planning Perspectives* 2, 3 (June 1970): 49-51.

7. The "opportunity position" was formalized as a federal policy objective by President Nixon: ". . . we should establish as a national goal the provision of adequate family planning services with the next five years to all those who want them but cannot afford them . . . " (Presidential Message to the Congress on Population, July 18, 1969.) Though the opportunity norm had been at the core of the planned parenthood movement, it achieved considerable status as a national welfare goal as the result of the recommendations of the President's Committee on Population and Family Planning (1968). This Committee was a "blue-ribbon" collection of population experts and public officials. Though

appointed by Johnson, its recommendations provided the substance of Nixon's population message. For excerpts from the Committee report, and its composition, see "United States: Report of the President's Committee on Population and Family Planning," *Studies in Family Planning* no. 40 (April 1969).

8. The "rights of society" position comes through in the statements of Kingsley Davis and Paul Ehrlich. See, for example, Kingsley Davis, "Population Policy: Will Current Programs Succeed?," *Science* 158, 3802 (10 November 1967): 730-739. Paul R. Ehrlich "Paying the Piper," *New Scientist*, 14 December 1967. Reproduced in: Garrett J. Hardin, ed., *Population, Evolution, and Birth Control*, 2nd ed. (San Francisco: W.H. Freeman, 1969): 127-130.

9. The "obligation to society" position is put cogently by Garrett Hardin. See Garrett J. Hardin, "The Tragedy of the Commons," *Science*, 162, 3859 (13 December 1968): 1243-1248. (Also reproduced in Hardin, ibid.)

10. Bernard Berelson, "Beyond Family Planning," *Studies in Family Planning* no. 38 (February 1969).

11. There are differences of opinion among the experts on the quality and consequences of U.S. population growth. See, for example: "New U.S. Census Projections," Internal Memorandum from Frederick S. Jaffe to Selected Planned Parenthood/World Population Staff, 13 April 1970; Ben J. Wattenberg, "The Nonsense Explosion," *New Republic* (April 1970): 18-23.

12. As an example of the advertising that occasionally appears in the *New York Times*, see the two full-page versions linking population control to environmental improvement sponsored by Hugh Moore and a cross-section of American notables: *New York Times*, 26 September 1971, Section E, pp. 8-9. This group has sponsored the now-famous population time bomb version of their message as well.

Noteworthy international conferences during recent years included the U.N. World Population Conference in Belgrade, Summer 1965; International Conference on Family Planning Programs, Geneva, August 1965; University of Michigan Sesquicentennial Conference on Fertility and Family Planning, November 1967; and The Ford Foundation Population Consultants Conference, Como, April 1968.

13. Berelson (n. 10).

14. This concept of "public policy" is utilized because of its breadth and flexibility. It is based on the political systems concept developed in the work of David Easton: *The Political System* (New York: Knopf, 1953) and *A Systems Analysis of Political Life* (New York: Wiley, 1965).

15. For a comprehensive treatment of the major conceptual approaches available for the analysis of policy processing, see: Enid Schoettle, "The State of the Art in Policy Studies," in Raymond A. Bauer and K.J. Gergen, eds., *The Study of Policy Formation* (New York: The Free Press, 1968).

16. For example, see Berelson (n. 10).

17. For a detailed analysis of the spread of activities of the professional/intel-

lectuals, see Elihu Bergman, *The Politics of Population USA: A Critique of the Policy Process* (Chapel Hill: The Carolina Population Center, Population Program and Policy Design Series: no. 5, 1971).

18. U.S. Congress, House Subcommittee on Public Health and Welfare of the Committee on Interstate and Foreign Commerce, Hearings on Family Planning Services, 91st Congress, 2nd Session, pp. 425-428.

19. U.S. Congress, Senate Subcommittee on Health of the Committee on Labor and Public Welfare, Hearings on Family Planning and Population Research, 91st Congress, 1st and 2nd Sessions 1970, pp. 276-280.

20. See reactions to the absence of poor and black representation on the Commission for Population Growth and the American Future, in Bergman (n. 17): Chapter 3, "Reflections of a Movement."

21. See, for example, a recent study of the Community Action program in Baltimore: Peter Bachrach and Morton S. Baratz, *Power and Poverty: Theory and Practice* (New York: Oxford University Press, 1970).

22. This narrow interpretation most frequently leads to a preoccupation with family size and population size. Cornely deplored the tendency to talk about population in terms of numbers and suggested that the discourse should evolve around a completely different set of referants more relevant to the condition of American society: values, stratification, and racism. (Paul Cornely, The Third Annual Fred T. Foard Jr. Memorial Lecture, The School of Public Health, The University of North Carolina at Chapel Hill, February 11, 1971.) For another criticism of this limited interpretation, see Benedict J. Duffy, Jr., and Paul B. Cornely, "Beyond Birth Control to Family Services and Family Planning," paper prepared for the 12th Congress of the International Federation of Catholic Medical Associations, Shoreham Hotel, Washington, D.C., October 11-14, 1970; and R. Kenneth Godwin, Chapter 6 in this volume.

23. William S. Flash, "Political Implications of National Health Insurance Proposals" (Paper prepared for presentation at the Conference of Social Behavioral Sciences in Health and the Medical Care Section, American Public Health Association, Houston, October 25, 1970).

24. Eliot Freidson, *Profession of Medicine: A Study of the Sociology of Applied Knowledge* (New York: Dodd, Mead & Company, 1970): 378-379. In addition to a segment of the socially constructed universe, the condition of "organized autonomy" also facilitates a form of ologopolistic control over a segment of the market place, in this case, that corner where medical care is traded. This restrictive condition prevents distribution of the product without regard to economic and social status. See also an indictment of the American health care system for failing to serve its constituency, i.e., all Americans who require health care: John and Barbara Ehrenreich, *The American Health Care Empire. A Report from the Health Policy Advisory Center* (New York: Random House, 1971).

25. The requirement for an adequate health care system both to achieve

fertility reduction and better society goals is argued by, among others, Harald Frederiksen, "Feedbacks in Economic and Demographic Transition," *Science* 166, 3907 (14 November 1969): 837-847; Steven Polgar, "Population History and Population Policy From An Anthropological Perspective," *Current Anthropology* 13, 2 (April 1972): 203-211 and 263-267; Earl Siegel, "Family Planning in the Strategy of Health," *North Carolina Medical Journal* 29 (February 1968); and Carl E. Taylor, "Five Stages in a Practical Population Policy," *International Development Review* 10, 4 (December 1968): 2-7.

Though Frederiksen, Polgar, and Taylor focus on developing countries, their arguments for the multiple advantages of adequate health care are equally applicable to less developed enclaves in the United States.

26. Steven Polgar and Alexander Kessler, *An Introduction to Family Planning in the Context of Health Services* (Geneva: World Health Organization, 1968).

27. Carl E. Taylor and Marie-Françoise Hall, "Health, Population, and Economic Development," *Science* 157, 3789 (11 August 1967): 651-657.

28. "Topical Investigation and Analysis of Promoting Family Planning Through Health Services" (Research Triangle Park, N.C.: Population Planning and Statistics Series, Research Triangle Institute, 1970).

29. Ibid.

30. Ibid.

31. Boulding illustrates some of the social and economic distortions that accrue from the allocation of medical care in the market place. Though he doesn't recommend its total removal from the market place, he does suggest a more rational approach to the definition of a health care system—its scope and substance—through a multidisciplinary approach called "a social science of health." See Kenneth E. Boulding, "The Concept of Need for Health Services," in Donald Mainland, ed., *Health Services Research* (New York: Milbank Memorial Fund, 1967).

32. The social and economic correlates of fertility are treated comprehensively in the Growth of the American Family surveys and the National Fertility studies. See Ronald C. Freedman, Pascal K. Whelpton, and Arthur A. Campbell, *Family Planning, Sterility, and Population Growth* (New York: McGraw-Hill, 1959); Pascal K. Whelpton, Arthur A. Campbell, and John E. Patterson, *Fertility and Family Planning in the United States* (Princeton: Princeton University Press, 1966); Charles F. Westoff and Norman B. Ryder, "Recent Trends in Attitudes Toward Fertility Control and the Practice of Contraception in the United States," in Samuel J. Behrman et al., eds., *Fertility and Family Planning* (Ann Arbor: University of Michigan Press, 1969).

33. Karl E. Taueber, "Negro Population and Housing: Demographic Aspects of a Social Accounting Scheme," in Irwin Katz and Patricia Gurin, eds., *Race and the Social Sciences* (New York: Basic Books, 1969): 145-194. There is empirical evidence that socioeconomic factors do not explain segregation in

housing and thus the residential distribution of populations in metropolitan areas. Thus a strong justification for the inference that bigotry is a significant determinant of the distribution of the black population. See the discussion in: John F. Kain, ed., *Race and Poverty: The Economics of Discrimination* (Englewood Cliffs: Prentice-Hall, 1969): 22-27.

34. Calvin Goldscheider, *Population, Modernization, and Social Structure* (Boston: Little Brown and Company, 1971): 3-4.

35. With particular reference to developing countries, Raulet contends: "The family planning movement, in overstressing the independent contributions of fertility reduction programs, has tended to underplay conditions such as improved health, lowered mortality, and altered opportunity structure which makes these contributions possible at all." Harry M. Raulet, "Family Planning and Population Control in Developing Countries," *Demography* 7, 2 (May 1970): 211-234. Also, Hauser observes: ". . . the possible quarrel with the present family planning movement is not with what it is attempting to do or with what it is doing. It is rather with what it is failing to do. It is failing to explore or to administer longer-range as well as the short-range programs against the possibility that its fundamental assumptions and basic premise . . . may prove to be erroneous. The family planning movement is failing to insure itself against the failure of its present rationale and methods. This is dangerous because at the present time it is not known whether a birth control clinic will, in fact, bring about a more rapid decline in birth rate than improved and universal general education, or new roads facilitating communication, or improved agricultural methods, or a new industry that would increase productivity, or other types of innovations that may break the 'cake of custom' and produce social foment." Philip M. Hauser, "Family Planning and Population Programs," *Demography* 4, 1 (1967): 412.

36. This characterization of the Committee's profile emerges from an analysis of its membership. The Committee, frequently mentioned as the most effective interest group in the American population movement, is composed of officers of major corporations, prominent public officials, academic figures, members of leading law firms, and retired military officers. For further analysis of this group, see Bergman (n. 17): 93-95.

37. See the testimony of the physicians who appeared in Hearings (n. 19).

38. On the likelihood of support by the professional medical community for extensive changes in the prevailing health care system, consider among others the discussions in Friedson (n. 24) and the Ehrenreichs (n. 24).

39. For a discussion of the social and economic advantages of a population dispersal strategy in metropolitan areas, see John F. Kain and Joseph J. Persky, "Alternatives to the Gilded Ghetto," *The Public Interest* no. 14 (Winter 1969): 74-87.

40. The incumbent administration refuses to adopt this course. The *Boston Globe* reported on January 30, 1972: "In developing policies to enforce the fair

housing law, HUD Secretary George Romney has been careful to observe President Nixon's promise that federal programs would not be used to 'force economic integration' of the suburbs."

41. Flash (n. 23): 8.

42. See the illumination and analysis of these conditions in: Freidson (n. 24).

43. Duffy addresses these issues in proposing an imaginative strategy for health care reform in urban areas. See Benedict J. Duffy, Jr., M.D., *Consumers, Cities, and Health.* Statement for Boston meeting on the President's Committee on Health Education, January 6, 1972.

44. E.E. Schattschneider, *The Semisovereign People* (New York: Holt, Rinehart, and Winston, 1960).

45. Bachrach and Baratz (n. 21).

46. This is the prevailing condition of American policy making behavior argued by Lowi. See in particular the expositions in: Theodore J. Lowi, *The End of Liberalism: Ideology, Policy, and the Crisis of Public Authority* (New York: W.W. Norton, 1969); and Theodore J. Lowi, "The Public Philosophy: Interest Group Liberalism," *American Political Science Review* 61, 1 (March 1967): 5-24.

47. In his analysis of the prevailing approach to problems of deprivation at home and abroad, Montgomery cites the unwillingness of the relevant U.S. policy processes to consider the potential of radical structural change as a solution—even if it appeared the most promising route: "Neither venture . . . was prepared to tolerate revolution as a solution to poverty." John D. Montgomery, "Programs and Poverty: Federal Aid In the Domestic and International Systems," *Public Policy* 18, 4 (Summer 1970): 536.

48. The soul searching is exemplified in both international and domestic dimensions, the former in Kalman Silvert, "American Academic Ethics and Social Research Abroad: The Lesson of Project Camelot," in I. L. Horowitz, ed., *The Rise and Fall of Project Camelot: Studies in the Relationship between Social Science and Practical Politics* (Cambridge: The M.I.T. Press, 1967); and the latter in Daniel P. Moynihan, *Maximum Feasible Misunderstanding: Community Action in the War on Poverty* (New York: The Free Press, 1970). (See especially: Chapter 8—"Social Science and Social Policy.") Both dimensions are discussed in a review of recent literature on the subject: Joel J. Schwartz, "The Social Research-Social Policy Nexus," *Public Administration Review* 31, 6 (November-December 1971): 678-686.

49. Ibid.

50. Recognizing the potential leadership role of university-based professional/intellectuals in engineering a rational set of health care policies for America, Cornely challenged them to "define the unacceptable," form the health constituency, and display the requisite "enlightened and responsible guts." Cornely (n. 22).

51. Many High Priests do in fact cry "foul" on this account. See Philip

Hauser, "On Population and Environmental Policy and Problems" (paper prepared from transcription of extemporaneous talk at the First National Congress on Optimum Population and the Environment at the Pick-Congress Hotel, Chicago, June 8, 1970).

4

Demographology in U.S. Population Politics

A.E. Keir Nash

Introduction

There are at least two grounds on which political analysts might seek to criticize the politics of American population policy making. One of these—instanced by Elihu Bergman's preceding essay—is essentially *procedural* or *structural*. Such a viewpoint might, as in Dr. Bergman's analysis of the institutional affiliations and socioeconomic positions of those whom he asserts make population policy, be primarily concerned with arguing that the very structures of decision making are unsatisfactory because they are insufficiently democratic. On this showing, the procedures are deficient from the outset, and their policy making—whatever its content—is consequently suspect.

Another ground for criticism is essentially *substantive*, or *contact-oriented*. That is to say, it is primarily concerned with the questions: Is the content of population policy advice, regardless of who may be the political actors making advisory inputs into the policy-making process, adequate to produce "good population policy"? Is the substance of the policy outcome "correct," and if not, why not?

In actual practice, of course, the two modes of assessing the politics of population are not likely to be entirely separate. It is relatively unlikely that someone would raise procedural objections unless he also felt that there was something inadequate about the substantive policy results. And, it is unlikely that objections would be raised to the substance without being accompanied by at least an implicit judgment that the processes of policy making are less than optimal.

Nonetheless, a theoretical difference does remain. And, it is not devoid of practical importance in a political order characterized by a constitution which sets bounds to permissible political activity. It is, of course, the distinction between means and ends. The force of the first, or procedural, critique rests heavily upon normative prescriptions about appropriate political means for attaining desirable ends. In a democracy, the normative prescriptions are likely to be concerned with effective representation of the political wills of its citizens—as, again, Bergman's essay illustrates.

This essay, by contrast, is more directly concerned with ends—with the goal of "right population policy making." And, as will be seen, to the extent that

71

questions of political means enter in, they do so for that reason. While I would certainly not abjure a general interest in whether policy making procedures are sufficiently democratic, my central concern in this essay lies elsewhere, in the question whether the substantive inputs, the information and advice which is fed in, are in fact adequate. To anticipate, I shall argue that they are not. More specifically, I shall concentrate on what appears a dominant way of thinking about population and population policy among what (and here Bergman and I agree) seems to constitute a particularly strong group among population policy advisers—the demographic part of what Bergman calls "the cerebral core" of the population movement.

To put the matter a bit differently, my central aim is to illuminate the mode of thinking which appears to predominate among a particular part of the policy advisory process. The essay constitutes, then, if you will, a venture into what I would call "the politics of knowledge" among a particular political elite—those influential in making population policy. In that policy process, at least, it is certainly arguable that "knowledge is power." It is the knowledge of experts and the political power of social scientists advising and participating in government.

"Club" versus "Democratic" Population Politics

It is now just on two decades since the current major phase of serious concern about world population growth began in the United States. At least that is so if one considers the anxiety during the 1930s about incipient underpopulation in the industrialized west as basically different,[1] and if one dates the onset of serious concern from the time when major American foundations began to channel sizable amounts of money into population research.[2]

Depending upon how one inclines to view matters and trends in the population field, another more or less fortunate break in the course of affairs has appeared in the last half decade. I am thinking, of course, of the emergence of "population" as a general public issue. Whatever else one may think of the academic Paul Reveres of the movement such as Garrett Hardin or Paul Ehrlich, one has to credit them with greatly furthering the transformation of "population" policy making from a quiet eighteenth-century politics[3] of small groups meeting genteely together far from the vulgar crowd and agreeing on "the public interest" to a public politics wherein all can claim an equal right to speak about, if not to make, population policy.

This still continuing process of conversion from a "club-like" politics of self-co-opting elites[4] to general public politics has brought into the open a second distinctive aspect of the world population debate. It is the "Politics of U.S. Population Stabilization—How and When?" What was not seen a decade ago as proper subject for overt U.S. governmental action[5] is now distinctly so seen. No better evidence exists than the creation in 1970 of the National Commission on Population Growth and the American Future. Whatever else such a presidential or a national commission may be "for"—a way of convincing the public that something is being done about a problem when it is not, a means of co-opting distinguished business and professional leaders into supporting something the president wants to do, etc.[6]—undeniably it marks the legitimation of a social problem as a fit topic for political concern. At that point—if it has not already done so before—a stress or strain in the society or the economy clearly flows over into the political realm and becomes part of the "public agenda."[7] When President Nixon requested that Congress create a population commission—and regardless of his later reaction to its policy recommendations—the "population problem" became, even in the most circumscribed definition of the word, "political."

In fact, however, I would argue that to describe the movement of the population issue over the past few years as from the "non-political" to the "political" is to define the word "political" too narrowly. Certainly an "elite population politics" had existed before. Moreover, and this is what raises the point from one of semantics to a matter of practical significance, so narrow a definition is likely to lead to less than optimal population policy making.

Why might this be? Because to opt for a narrower definition is itself to give a definite, if inadvertent, political ruling with a distinctive policy consequence. That is to say, the effect of the definition is to separate away from the "hurly-burly" of the political arena the population experts who have long been doing research and giving advice, and at least to fortify the influence of their expertise by dubbing it "pure" of politics as against those who utilize the more public route of population agenda-building. Specifically, it preserves and strengthens the conservative "demographic-family planning" side of the American population debate relative to the "Johnny-come-lately" crowd of environmentalists. On this showing, the demographic perspective can pretend to the status of "scientific objectivity" even though, of course, the pretense may not be at all appropriate to the "academician in government." Those who are "tainted" with public politics—largely the environmentalists—cannot make this pretense. Hence they are one down in the game of elitist population politics.

Such at least is an arguable possibility, and I shall have simply to assert here my belief that I am right in thinking I have seen a sufficient number of instances of such definitional efforts which, naively or otherwise, thrust in such a direction. Quite apart from broader questions of adequate public representation, then, I believe that there is a real and disturbing phenomenon here in the politics of population advice. At least it is such, unless the nature of the policy advice thus advantaged is the "best side" of the debate. As this essay will seek to show, I do not think that it is, particularly at the present moment of the population debate. That moment, I think it fair to say, is one where there threatens a "stage of reaction"—something of a "counter-reformation" in the population movement, a counter-reformation led by a number of population experts who have been placed in something of a state of shocked resentment at the "invasion" of the gentlemen's expert-advisory club of demography and family-planning by the Ehrlichites and the Hardinians.

Recently, resentment has surfaced as counter-attack. Without wishing to deny the validity of all the criticisms made by these "demographic Catholic" counter-reformers of the "protestant environmentalists," let me suggest that it would be helpful were the pendulum not to be driven equally far in the other direction, were the *status quo ante Ehrlich* not entirely to be restored.

Why? Because it strikes me that the counter-reformers have for virtually each error to which they point in the logic of the ecological protestants at least one logical equivalent error of their own; and, not infrequently, one which portends greater political damage should it be generally accepted.

Political Values and Political Language

To ask adequately about the politics of population requires asking about the linguistic formulations characteristic of research, discussion, and advice concerning population policy. To assert this is not to deny that, as Harold Lasswell once put it, politics is concerned with "who gets what, when, and how."[8] Nor is it to take issue with David Easton's description of politics as the "authoritative allocation of values."[9] Rather, it is to assert two further points about the roles which language plays in determining "who gets what" and how values are allocated by politics. One of these is fairly obvious, the other perhaps less so.

The first stems from the observation that politics is not generally conducted openly as nothing more than dishing out the spoils. Politicians and policymakers are not wont to depict themselves as engaged in a Machiavellian game of pure force. Political language legitimizes the distribution of values and goods.

However, this is not to suggest that the language of politics is purely and simply obfuscation. The most important point about the functions of political language may not be that it camouflages base motives and justifies the perfidious ways of one politician to another or to "the people." On the contrary, it may be that such language conditions the political actor's own thinking. After all, political thinking, like any other type of thought, takes place in certain patterned modes. Political language, in other words, may suggest why patterns of value allocation are as they are.

Quite possibly, therefore, one should examine the structure of policy advisers' "linguistic habits" *less from* the perspective entailed by assuming conscious intent to "camouflage," and *more from* the perspective entailed by assuming unintended "self-conditioning" in the minds of such political actors. Such, at least, is the perspective whose implications I wish to explore here.

How do these generalities about the functions of language in politics bear upon the specifics of population politics and population policy? First, through another generality: there may be something of a Gresham's law of twentieth-century politics. "Bad language drives out good politics."[10] George Orwell once argued much the same case very plausibly.

While Orwell conceded to those dubious of attributing such political power to "mere language" that a general linguistic decline in accuracy and freshness must have underlying political and economic causes, he insisted that:

an effect can become a cause, reinforcing the original cause and producing the same effect in an intensified form, and so on indefinitely. A man may take to drink because he feels himself to be a failure, and then fail all the more completely because he drinks. It is rather the same thing that is happening to the English language. It becomes ugly and inaccurate because our thoughts are foolish, but the slovenliness of our language makes it easier for us to have foolish thoughts.[11]

Thus wrote George Orwell in 1946 as he went on to argue that an increasingly salient characteristic of twentieth-century politics was allowing hackneyed clichés or deliberate circumlocutions to justify almost any kind of despicable political act. Let me quote again from him, for what he said long before American involvement in Vietnam still seems so extraordinarily on target:

In our time political speech and writing are largely the defense of the indefensible... Thus... defenseless villages are bombarded from the air, the inhabitants driven out into the countryside, the cattle machine-gunned, the huts set on fire with incendiary bullets: this is called *pacification*. Millions of peasants are robbed of their farms and sent trudging along the roads with no more than they can carry: this is called *transfer of population* or *rectification of frontier*. People are imprisoned for years without trial, or shot in the back of the neck, or sent to die of scurvy in Arctic lumber camps: this is called *elimination of unreliable elements*. Such phraseology is needed if one wants to name things without calling up mental pictures of them.[12]

If the use of euphemisms is one characteristic of the degeneration of political language in the twentieth century, the use of stale clichés or hackneyed circumlocutions is the other. The first deceives another, the second deceives oneself. And, to conclude drawing upon Orwell, the first step toward improving matters is to seek out and identify these recurrent "ready-made phrases... which anesthetize the brain."[13]

To be specific, I would suggest that, whatever else may be the case in our highly politicized contemporary world, the politics of population policy making has been adversely conditioned by the frequent recurrence of such phrases and statements. The recurrence of these statements has tended to hem research and advice, and hence policy, into certain categories of political thought—ones that happen closely to approximate the categories of classical liberalism. And what is most extraordinary, they have continued to do so even while in other realms of politics, economy, and society, the policy prescriptions of this old-style liberalism are most clearly going by the boards.[14] Much of the language of population politics may be, then, singularly anachronistic. Quite probably it constitutes a barrier to clear and wise policy making.[15]

The existence of such a barrier is becoming more important as we begin seriously to contemplate actually doing something about the American "population problem." Above all, we need to be clear about the impact of what we are doing on the political realm. Today's political effect is tomorrow's political cause: policy output from the polity affects the society. That effect in turn creates different political conditions and hence new input into policy making.

If, to pose an increasingly talked about possible policy resolution, we resolve on population stabilization (whatever exactly that vague phrase itself may mean), then we are faced with both a certainty and an uncertainty. It is certain that from the adoption of such a national policy *there will flow at least three sets of political effects*: (1) upon citizens' political attitudes; (2) upon governmental behavior in other policy areas; (3) upon the relative power or influence of various groups among the population elite on the formulation of population policy itself. It is much less certain what the particular effects which make up membership of those sets are, and how important, both individually and collectively, they may be.

The first set of results is composed of the differences between citizens' attitudes toward the political system in the presence of—as opposed to those obtaining in the absence of—such deliberate population policy-making. If, to give an example, a population policy reduces a cohort's size by *n* percent below what it would otherwise have been, what political differences does that make? Will the members of the cohort feel more or less well-disposed toward the political system? Will they tend more or less to support the political party of their parents? Will they feel better or worse about the police?

One could go on with a list of such possible differences more or less indefinitely. The trouble is, of course, that I am not—and as far as I know no one else is—really in a position to give very many clear answers to such questions.[16]

The same difficulty obtains if we phrase the problem not in the language of recent political science but return to the ethically infused language of classical political theory. Suppose that we ask, for example: what do different population futures import for the freedom of future citizens, or for the likelihood of their achieving justice in the future legal system, or indeed for the future of almost any other abstract noun of this sort which we—like political philosophers since Plato and Aristotle—generally laud a political system for maximizing. If we ask questions of this sort, what answers can we hear? Precious few, whatever the language of inquiry, unless we are made happy by apocalyptic dichotomies—by predictions of political "being" or "not being."

Much the same may be said about *second set of political implications of population policy making. That set consists of the differences which one population future as opposed to another would make with respect to the polity's distributive and regulatory behavior.* Or to put it in Lasswell's less opaque language—the differences as to whom the political system lets get what, and how others are prevented from getting what else. Or, to use Easton's language, *the differences as to what values the political system allocates.*

Here again, in talking about futures from the standpoint of the polity, just as when we discuss the future of citizens—the answers are slim. Not, of course, that it is *impossible* to say anything. Indeed, some authors have used a species of deductive reasoning which has a surface plausibility in order to reach certain conclusions. Thus, for example, one hears from time to time a recurrent argument with respect to political freedom: population growth and freedom are said to be incompatible because, it is asserted, a larger population requires a larger government and more regulations, hence less freedom.

Just so, I imagine, one *could* argue that a population stabilization policy—if successful in significantly reducing unwanted fertility—would produce happier and hence less revolutionary children. Thus one could argue that population stabilization is good for the socioeconomic status quo and for domestic political tranquility. One *could.* Indeed it is almost the obverse of this which one hears from time to time from certain leaders of ethnic minorities—where hostility to birth control seems to stem from a sense that more young bodies and more outraged young minds are needed to bring about political justice for the particular group in question. The strength—and the weakness—of both these logically similar deductivist arguments are the same. They are hard to deal with because they start with assumptions about the empirical world which may or may not be so, but which no one has the wherewithal to refute. How is it, for instance, that the author knows that more regulation entails less freedom? Am I, to trot out an old sawhorse, made less free by a law prohibiting the driving of cars when drunk? In one sense, of course, yes; if I am enamoured of engaging in inebriated driving. On the other hand, of course, no; insofar as it keeps other drunks from running into sober—or drunk—me.

Similarly, how is it that we know that the *ceteris paribus* clause built into both of the above interpretations of the results of reducing unwanted fertility is one in which the *cetera* really are *pares*? The answer is that of course we do not.

So, too, with respect to describing the members of the second set of population implications—those bearing upon the government's distributive and regulatory behavior. How do we know whether population future *A* is likely to have a more redistributive cast to its politics than population future *B*?

The trouble with such efforts to derive political conclusions about the future is that certainty thus deductively reached is only satisfactory to those who see politics through a screen of rather careless language.

It is, however, desperately insufficient to leave matters here. For, as one of the most influential members of the population movement has said,[17] one great hindrance to wise population policy making is that demographic effects are felt so far in the future. If one accepts this point, and if one accepts that part of the demographers' critique of radical environmentalism which judges it too certain about the uncertain, then one is increasingly confronted by a basic problem: as population stabilization becomes a more and more salient political topic, it becomes—to repeat and particularize an earlier generalization—more and more important that we gain the ability to enumerate and interrelate the chief members of the first two sets of political results (those to citizens' political attitudes and to governmental behavior) flowing from stabilizing population.

It would be unfortunate in the extreme if, because of absence of proof of significant political effects, population policy decisions were made only on the basis of things known about other realms of population effect—chiefly the economic and the environmental. It might after all be that we stand in need of some vital but missing information of a political sort which, if we but knew it, would dictate another population policy course.

To say this is—because it is to raise again the question, why are we so ignorant about political effects—to lead us to a third, and narrower, set of political implications. *The third set consists of the effects of adopting a population stabilization policy upon the relative political influence of various groups concerned with population policy advice and formulation. Here my concern is particularly with effects upon a particular group of advisers—social scientists and natural scientists active in influencing population policy making.* My concern arises because our present inability to discuss intelligibly the gross political consequences to the American future of population policy-making is in at least some important measure due to the current "composition" of those academics who influence population policy-making. In brief, if there is weakness in such present advice, then *either* the attitudes and views of such advisers will change, *or* their influence will change.

Second, and to tie my earlier general point about politics and language specifically into population, if we are to gain that ability to enumerate and describe, then the political debate of population policy making must be clarified. At present (and without in any sense seeking to excuse other fields of social science such as my own [political science] where, with one or two exceptions, we have certainly been notoriously slow about getting into population matters) it is fair to assert that our inability to say more is in significant part due to the recurrent linguistic formulations among the most "policy-potent" group of social scientists, the demographers. Accordingly, it is to their linguistic, and hence political, habits of articulating "problems of population" that we now should direct our attention.

The Problem-Formulating Language of Demographology: A Phenomenon in the Politics of Policy Making

Probably the best way to get at demographers' linguistic habits when formulating "population problems" is to pursue a procedure more popular in the humanities than in the natural or social sciences *explication de texte*. As I do not wish to seem more presumptuous or unkind than necessary, however, let me make an observation and an admission before proceeding.

The observation is that when I seek to characterize a "demographic pattern of formulating policy problems," a "demographic consciousness," if you will, I do not wish to imply that by any means all who display the demographer's professional shingle think thusly. Consequently, though it is a bit more clumsy and entails not one but two rather atrocious double entendres, I find it fairer to refer henceforward not to a "demographic" but to a "demographological" consciousness. It is not of demographers functioning as the certified public accountants of the social sciences that we need be wary. It is when they attempt to divine impact of population upon the political future much as graphology seeks to define personality from penmanship that we need be cautious of their logic.

To say this is to suggest the admission. I certainly cannot prove that the triad of recent texts about to be examined point to more than a triple straw-man. I can only assert my belief that they are reasonably representative of most demographers who, in fact, now populate the "corridors of population-policy power."[18] Each piece has been written in the present decade. Each has been presented in establishment quarters (the National Commission on Population Growth, the annual meeting of the Population Association of America, and what is best described as something of a "Festschrift soirée" in honor of a leading demographic light). All have been authored by persons who, if any are to be, *should* be labeled "establishment types." If, in short, *anyone's* comments can be taken as representative of a "contemporary population establishment's" thinking, then these can.

In a sense, the political language of paper A—originally a presentation at the 1970 PAA meeting[19]—is less ingenuous than is typical of demographology. For, as is *not* the demographologic wont, it professes at the outset that it will "not try to be evenhanded." Abjuring objectivity as mythical, it instead invites itself as an "ample target(s) for everyone whether in approval or disagreement." Nonetheless, and this is important to note, what follows the invitation—an attempt to elucidate and to denigrate the purposes, means, and thinking of Zero Population Growth "hardliners"—is designed to be more than just extremist ramblings far on the "reactionary" side of the debate. The rest of the paper seeks that status of respectability which is awarded in contemporary social science generally only to the "objective" effort. In brief, one may view Paper A as almost a counter-blast on the horn to summon the gray-haired opponents of the "young ecological irresponsibles" to the fray. It is perhaps, the first blast of the counter-reformation. As such it contains a linguistic-political strategy of general and not merely particular interest.

Paper A begins with the *Multiple Straw Man Gambit*. This is not, in case anyone suspects it, using one straw man for several purposes. Rather it consists in putting up several in order to ignore (or at any rate with the result of camouflaging) the more real opponent standing behind. In this instance the counter-reformer posits three possible types of meaning for Zero Population Growth and three corresponding types of "believer": (1) ZPG as a platitude; (2) ZPG as a sales slogan; and (3) ZPG as an urgent goal to be sought by drastic means.

The platitudinist is he who is "sensible"—i.e., he who knows that in the long, long run the normal condition of mankind is ZPG. The counter-reformer has no argument with him—by virtue of having reduced him, in the act of description, to a very harmless character anyhow. The sales sloganeer is he who doesn't really believe in ZPG now, but who uses it as a battle-cry on the grounds that it is effective propaganda. Our counter-reformer dismisses this person as beneath contempt on the grounds that for a "scientist" it is difficult enough to stick to the truth anyhow. This leaves only the "true believer alarmist," he who wants ZPG if not yesterday, at least now.

It is with this third straw-man that the counter-reformer seeks to deal, not with he who might be offered as the "true man." There is after all a fourth ZPGer who is overlooked—he who might urge serious efforts now to achieve NRR of 1 or .8 in say ten years and ZPG at an appropriate time thereafter. That noted, what is said of the "true believer alarmist"? In writer A's view, he has the undesirable characteristic of wanting ZPG with an intensity which makes him "willing to accept many second and third order effects without careful examination." This is an interesting pronouncement inasmuch as it is a prevalent demographological tendency to do much the same at other points in the debate.

Writer A is rightly aware that it "is the ecologists who are taking the hardest line." And he does not like it. Hence we have the *False Modesty Chutzpah* ploy. This, which might also be labeled the *Clark-Kent-Savonarola gambit*, opens with a declaration of innocence: "On matters of resources, energy, and ecology I am outside of my professional field." One might surmise that such a declaration would be the prelude to a chary statement to the effect either that the "case was unproven" or that some caution as to the weight to be applied to the ensuing judgment would be in order on the part of the reader. In fact, however, no sooner is the statement of lack of expertise out of the author's mouth than he proceeds to the swift and confident judgment that he has read and listened to the ecologists and "found their case wholly unpersuasive." There are no substantial limits in sight either in raw materials or in energy that alterations in the price structures, product substitution, anticipated gains in technology and pollution control cannot be expected to achieve." This is subject only to the single condition that we "can only look ahead about a generation in terms of specific technology and known raw materials. . ."

This is a difficult paragraph to deal with because of its internal linguistic confusion. Apart from any doubts that the "weight of professional opinion is" quite so "overwhelming" as author A insists, a number of assertions need disentangling and comparing. First, if we can only see about a generation ahead specifically, what is it except rosy confidence based upon Western man's post-renaissance scientific and technological career which leads to his perceiving no substantial limits in sight? Obviously, there are some limits in sight with respect to some resources.[20] Therefore the only way in which this paragraph can make any sense at all is to assume that price structures, or product substitution, etc., can deal with everything. This *is* confused. How is it that price structure alterations: (a) come about in just the right fashion to deal with shortages; (b) deal with shortages at all? Surely, scarcity's running up the price of something does not create (in non-organic "natural" instances at least) more of it, *ipso facto*. An odd economics is at work here. One aspect of it is seemingly a curiously belated belief in the invisible hand of Adam Smith, although it is not altogether certain exactly what sort of an economy Smith's hand is meant to be hovering above. Possibly what is intended here is that which some contemporary economists have in mind when they call for full internalizing by industry of "the social costs of enterprise" rather than passing them "uncosted" along to the public. Even if so, however, we are not fully out of the thicket of argumentation for two reasons. First, "internalizing costs" does not change the resource limits—if by such limits one means the known world—reserves of the set of all elements and compounds in nature which man is capable of utilizing at any given time. "Internalizing costs" may reduce a given level of consumption and/or a given level of pollution: in the industrialized world it is difficult to see another dominant economic result than lower consumption per capita because, of course, internalized costs are hardly unlikely to remain internalized; they are far more likely to be passed on to the consumer in the form of higher per unit costs.

But to say this is to suggest the second reason for caution: the efficacy of an attempt to move from a fairly free economy to a "fully cost-internalized" one assumes an enormous increase in the power of the polity to dictate terms of enterprise to the economy. To generalize, the logic underlying a "loose call" to "internalize costs" may on examination rest on little more substantial than an axiom of pious faith about the political future. One might well be tempted to ask what, other than faith, can sustain a logic which argues *both* that one cannot spell out technology more than a generation or so in advance *and that* we do not perceive real resource limits in sight? The logic is not strengthened in practice by its accompanying caveat—that, "assuming an ordered world," one can "reasonably predict immensely powerful developments based on cheap and virtually unlimited energy." Unless I wholly misunderstand the arguments of some ecological hardliners, it is precisely this assumption about an ordered world which they would debate. So too, as a political scientist, I find it very hard not to say—looking about at the world of the late 1960s and early 1970s, at Biafra at Pakistan-Bengal, at Vietnam—that at the least this assumption is open to question. I would even venture the guess that political debility is as great a spectre as famine for the remainder of the century. Indeed, I would go a little farther and say that I would not be surprised if thirty years from now some of us look back upon the last three decades of the twentieth century and agree that the greatest problem intensified by population was not starvation, nor ecological peril, nor social freedom, but the inability of governments to govern without chaos.[21]

Neither of these arguments about the possible dangers of ecological chaos or political debility, closely related and important as they are, are dealt with by Paper A. Rather, on the contrary, we are treated to (shortly after the above quoted passage) two confusions. The first devolves from a play on words coupled with a failure to draw parallel inferences. The author of Paper A argues that much of the pessimistic ecological argument is based upon the prediction of non-renewable resources in a finite world. This, he argues, misses the point. Why? Because "Resources are not material. They are socially defined." But, the fact that coal did not become a resource until a few centuries ago does not (as seems to be inferred) prove that new resources will always crop up in future as needed. Why could not, logically, the longer, pre-renaissance past of mankind be the proper parallel here? Why not the eons when man without fire, or, later, without any metals harder than tin, hid fearfully from beasts of prey? Why, in brief, should the modern image of all-competent man prevail permanently? This is both in contradiction to what the ecologists are telling us about such substances as chlorinated hydrocarbons and pelicans' eggs and in contradiction to what the redoubtable Arnold Toynbee never tires of telling us about civilizations' recurrent and fatal sin of hubris. Surely we should ask for a more open, a less self-certain, case on the matter than Paper A presents.

Another analytic weakness is the paper's failure to draw parallel, second-order conclusions. It suggests that non-renewable resources generally turn out on inspection to be "materials which have declined in relative worth." As an example, we are given "land in the U.S." It is said to be "never more abundant." Unless there is some kind of odd reckoning taking place on the basis of Alaska's admission to statehood, then this sentence is literally not true. We are told that even with modern machinery it "no longer pays to clear land in the United States." Is it then, that what the author is really calling for here without quite realizing it is not more population but for economic-political revolution?[22]

Surely what Paper A offers here is a less than compelling argumentation. But, to repeat—and this is the reason for going on at length about it—is not atypical. Nor is it "below par" for the demographological course. What lies behind—what is the source of this kind of reasoning?

This is not the place to attempt to enter upon a psychological analysis in any depth of what it is about the demographologers which leads them in these curious directions. I would, however, suggest one possible candidate: what may be at work is a sort of "academic territorialism" à la Ardrey's and Lorenz's studies of animal behavior. As one who has recently passed a most interesting year spending more time with demorgaphologers than I ever would have anticipated, let me toss out one observation. There is something slightly comic about the defensiveness against "outsiders" of the very population professional group least keen upon the experiments of men such as Calhoun, on density's effects upon behavior,[23] and Lorenz, on aggression.[24] They virtually *patrol* their population territory against all others.

There is a second possibility which should be considered in seeking to account for "pugnacity" when names such as Hardin and Ehrlich begin to appear in discussion. It is closely related to "academic territoriality": The social sciences and particularly American sociology have for the past generation been largely wedded to a nineteenth-century view of natural science's and by inference social science's proper procedures, to a kind of Baconian inductivism. One characteristic aspect of this view of the scientific enterprise has been a tendency to denigrate the role of abstract concepts and deduction thought. As I have argued elsewhere,[25] this general North Atlantic tendency has dovetailed with traditional American pragmatism to produce a curious deafness to claims of the abstractly working intellect. Furthermore, it is just possible that even when the comparison is restricted to scientists of the sociological persuasion, demography tends to attract a less "airy-speculative" group than most.

Finally, it may be that the very Americanness of American demographologists leads them in this direction. The author of Paper A declares not long after the section we have been examining that he is not "one of those who share in the ocean of guilt now flooding the literature because our small fraction of the world's population consumes the lion's share of the world's resources." While willing to envisage a smaller American share of the total, he is not willing to consider an absolute decline. In other words, he is patently on the side of expanded extraction and resource utilization. While admitting that industrialized nations have engaged in "outrageous waste" of resources, he insists that, on balance, our heavy use is expanding supplies and reserves and beneficial to the world. If this strikes one as a bit insensitive, he dismisses the question of imperialism by calling it an intricate discussion about whether the developed nations have paid enough for Third-World resources and insisting that "substantial reductions of our purchases from those regions would bring them to economic chaos and in general greatly retard their own development."

Of all the passages I have read recently by social scientists of note, I find this among the most depressing. It manages to be literally right at the price of being almost wholly misleading about both present realities and future possibilities. Of course, in one sense, Western investment in the Third World has "expanded reserves"—without Standard Oil's engineers who would know of Venezuelan oil? But this is an ethically atrocious variant of Bishop Berkeley's old horse about "if a tree falls in the woods with no hearer around, is there a sound?"

Here the conclusion rests on the earlier equation of "resources" and the "human knowledge" enterprise. And it entirely misses the point of those who claim that the international order should further economic justice between nations. What many countries of the Third World object to is not that they don't have abundant resources lying in the ground, but that it is we who, armed with knowledge and money, extract them. Their position is that we put them over an oil-barrel and then say "if we let you off, you'll be worse off." Of course, in one (short-term) sense they would be worse off. But to leave the matter there overlooks the whole question of long-run political and economic justice between regions. As a political scientist, I am constrained to say that the mentality which can pen these sentences and pass them off as a satisfactory "look-see" at the relationship between population, pollution, and the economies of developed and underdeveloped regions is a mentality painfully out of tune with the political realities of the last third of the twentieth century.

To conclude, policy advice of this sort is, it seems to me, almost bound to lose its political influence in sectors of the government making decisions about implementing population policies. Or, if it does not lose out over the next few years, if a decade from now this kind of apolitical policy advice can still be successfully preferred by academics or other population professionals to governmental decision makers, then we are likely to be in even worse international political shape than we have recently been.

Demographology, Unwanted Fertility, and Voluntarism

If the preceding selection, Paper A, was an address to the "annual demographic forum," the Population Association of America, by a "dean" of population affairs, the next one, Paper B,[26] is almost the epitome of what I earlier referred to as "club" population politics. This paper was presented recently at a "Round Table" of a fund in the population business honoring another elder statesman of "human fertility."

Paper A was primarily concerned with attacking the ZPG alarmists about world and U.S. population growth and calling up the demographological troops. Paper B represents the thinking of a demographer of some considerable reputation concerning the question of population policy making in the contemporary United States. If political insensitivity to the Third World and logical confusion are the most interesting aspects of the preceding selection, selection B is perhaps most interesting for its tendency to use "Orwellian phrases" that are both "in" with, and unexamined by, the "population fraternity."

Author B begins by stating that he will focus on population growth rather than population distribution on the grounds that distribution is "more confounding" and "possibly less manipulable." The latter phrase suggests another conservative political aspect or thrust to demographology besides that with respect to resource extraction in the Third World, namely the almost fatalistic sense that matters are largely foreordained in respect to population distribution. To Author B, future U.S. metropolitan growth will "be a function of natural increase as the transition from a rural to an urban to a metropolitan to a megalopolitan society runs its course." Apparently, the drift of population into urban areas in the U.S. is as remorseless as the tied in the Bay of Fundy and only a Quixotic Canute of a population commission would seek to do much about it.

Let us examine this assumption for a moment: is it not oddly disjunctive with other assumptions not only in related realms of population but even in the author's own field? What, thus, is the reason for the demographologist thinking (as earlier with A) so "free-willy" a thought as that our resource search will always keep ahead of the consumption game and that we can almost at will re-engineer the economy, and then contrariwise, thinking so "deterministically" that megalopolitan growth has a fixed future? Are we simply seeing the manifestation of a personal urban bias which is not disturbed by the flight from rural areas? Possibly, but to stop there seems insufficient and unsatisfying. It is tempting to suggest that we are seeing the demagraphological "shuffle" wherein everyone else's professional subject matter is supposed to change its spots, while one's own leopard skin stays put. However, this interpretation won't do by itself. What of the author's policy recommendations with respect to human fertility? If anything is clear about the thrust of Paper B, it is its advocacy of an activist position—of bending the political status quo to the desired end—when it comes to unwanted fertility. Unwanted childbearing is said to be "a social problem of the first magnitude, a problem which if conceived in public health terms would be classified as one of major epidemic proportion."

I do not here dispute the problematic nature of unwanted childbearing. What I want to ask is: Why are policymakers supposed *to spare no effort* by way of governmental activity in order to eliminate unwanted childbearing, and *to make no effort* to deal with the urban tide? Is it simply a question of freedom—of letting people have their druthers? But, after all, if the best statistical evidence indicates that about one-fifth of all children born in the United States are unwanted,[27] far more than 20 percent of the population in megalopolitan areas state a preference for living elsewhere.[28] The seriousness of such expressions of opinion is often challenged. But then why not also ask about the former? If it is said that people move to cities because they "really want to," because they want the higher income, the cultural attractions, etc., despite the fact that industrial location largely determines the location of job opportunities and hence produces less than effective free choice, then why can we not also properly say, in analogous fashion, "people really want to have those kiddies. Otherwise they wouldn't have done so."

Note that I am not saying here that one position is right and the other wrong. I am merely arguing that no population policymaker of any reasonable perspicacity should find an unexplained disjunction between urged activism and urged fatalism in these two related areas entirely satisfying.

Another important demographological confusion has to do with the policy effects of accomplishing the goal of eliminating unwanted fertility. For many proponents of this goal, one of its attractions lies in its pushing the country well along toward (sometimes the speaker seems to be saying "to") a NRR of 1. Yet in the paper under scrutiny, the author—a vigorous proponent of eliminating unwanted fertility—suggests an interesting policy conundrum. "As fertility becomes increasingly a matter of choice, it becomes more sensitive to fashions and more changeable and unpredictable in the long run." Strictly speaking, one should not claim quite so much. If fertility becomes more unpredictable, then how can we predict that it will be more changeable or more sensitive to fashions? That aside, what of the assumptions to which this view is linked in order to provide the author's final policy recommendations?

One important assumption affecting policy is that ZPGers are fools because they assume that zero population is attainable soon. I don't know how often I have heard a demographer remark "How ignorant! Don't those ZPGers know that even if we reached replacement tomorrow, the population would keep on growing for another 65 years?" Surely *some* ZPGers do. And if there is something wrong with the demographic understanding of those who don't, there is also something debatable built into the demographological rejoinder. It is the assumption that no thinkable population policy could seek a growth rate lower than 0 nor an NRR lower than 1. Of course, if one did so the population might get to ZPG a good bit sooner. While I do not advocate ZPG tomorrow, because I am convinced by Thomas Frejka's elaborate projections that the difficulties would be enormous,[29] I do not see why the only goal can be, or should be, NRR=1. There is surely something between, on the one hand, "Project Constant Population" with its attendant violent swings in fertility and, on the other hand, ZPG in 2040. In brief, in the United States we may be committed to expansion to say 250-275 million. But we are not necessarily committed to 300-350 million in the lifespan of those born today, which is about where soon attaining and sticking to NRR=1 could put us then.[30]

In one important way Paper B is stronger than Paper A—it is more cognizant of the complexities of political things. Nonetheless, it is hard to avoid the conclusion that two phenomena similar to those seen before are also here at work, more or less in tandem. One is the repetitive tendency to resolve ambiguity in favor of one particular policy direction when there is really no particularly good explicit reason, or set of reasons, apparent in the text for so doing. The second is a tendency to use phrases which may "sound good" on the surface, but which paper over certain difficulties inherent in population policy making. These, since they crop up in a number of variations again and again, are what I call recurrently misleading statements.[31]

Let us examine one instance of this procedure at work. The author of Paper B recognizes the complexity of social interactions and relationships which may come about from, or in attendance upon, other changes relating to fertility. Various programs to improve the status of women may turn out ironically to have pro- rather than anti-natalist effects. And there is some evidence ·that income and family size are positively correlated among those able to control fertility. If this is so, the improvement of control and rising incomes may conceivably combine to augment fertility.

So far so good. But what are the implications drawn for policy? One, "That it should not be based in any irreversible way on aiming fertility in this or that direction." And two, that "zero growth although probably a desirable target is also probably an illusory one in any literal sense." Again, so far, so good. But then what comes? "That the population policies currently in the making should not aim only at reducing population growth—especially if that means introducing measures which are in any sense irreversible and not desirable in their own right—seems clear from the unpredictability of the future direction of fertility."

As a political scientist, I can only view this sentence as—for at least three reasons—debatable in the extreme. First, consider the phrase "measures which are in any sense irreversible." Apparently, it derives from the sense that at some point in the future we may want the birth rate to go up rather than down—or, at any rate, that we can't know that we won't want it to do so. Therefore we do not now wish to be committed as a polity to a direction we cannot alter. Sensible enough. But does it necessarily follow therefrom that each "measure" must be reversible as it applies to each individual member of the polity? Does this properly function (as apparently it functions here) as an argument against, e.g., a vasectomy in the absence of technology to reverse it in each individual case? Let me stress that I am not advocating any particular view of the matter as to the desirability of irreversible versus reversible contraceptive methods in a particular case. These are questions of freedom and governmental force which need resolution, but not in this paragraph. All I want to do is simply to point out the cloudiness of the thinking involved here. What may be an irreversible measure for an individual is not necessarily an irreversible policy direction for a society. Indeed, in the absence of positing explicitly a situation wherein the society feels it needs more births from the same cohort of "denatured" individuals, there is no logically proper inference from the "measure" to the "policy" at all.

Second, consider the phrase, "not desirable in their own right." This in my experience, is one of the favorite recurrently misleading statements in demographology. It is misleading because it cannot really mean what it says—unless we are to believe that some demographers have somehow created a viable late twentieth-century equivalent to Jefferson's self-evident principles, in this instance self-evident *desiderata.* I do not. It is, after all, almost "in the nature" of a policy measure that it is not an end but a means, that, in short, it is always desirable or undesirable in relation to something else. So too here. And the suppressed relationship is, what? I would suggest one of two things. *Either* there is some end which the author himself thinks is desirable. If so, he should be more explicit. *Or* this phrase is simply a means of avoiding some hard thinking about means, ends, goods, and "bads." The latter judgment here is probably the case.

To say this is to suggest the third, and last, relevant point here: political action upon such a position may produce a policy disaster. Why? Precisely because it leaves values unexplained. As such it makes almost fruitless an appeal to principles of political justice, leaving rather the political resolution in the realm of competing groups of self-interested persons. In brief, to speak of "desirables in their own right" is effectively to leave population policy making in the domain of "might makes right." Even if the role of population interest-groups and elites means that it is a very nice might which is making right, I am not at all convinced that that is where we would be wise to seek to place population policy decisions.

If a "cautious demographological" view leads to uncertainty about the future and predictability, it nonetheless allies itself rather easily with what I will call the fallacy of the Exterminated Middle in order to reach a "non-planning" policy terminus. Thus the following statement in Paper B is a common one: "Since . . . it is unlikely that we can fine-tune population growth anyway—probably even less than the economy can be finetuned . . . , where does that leave the policy-maker?" Not quite, I fear, where the author of Paper B would like to drop him. Who after all is seeking to "fine-tune" population growth? The most that population control advocates generally talk about is a rather gross type of tuning. Hence the economic analogy is misleading—for many modern governments do seem to think that they can "grossly tune" the economy. It exterminates the lesser, the middling, goal that lies between planning everything and planning nothing.

What causes underlie this elliptical logic anyhow? I expect that one of the most important is a sense common to demographologists that "population is their baby" and a consequent reluctance to see new fields of inquiry plowed. After all new fields require new heads, or new thinking. And genuinely new thinking is not easy. At best it is troublesome.

A second cause is almost certainly the actual unconscious political bias of demographologists' personal political views—when and if they think about it. The sentences immediately following in the text of Paper B do not prove, of course, but they do hint at, what this bias is. Thus:

The proposition that population growth aggravates social, environmental, governmental and other problems in the U.S. and makes their solution more difficult has at least strong intuitive appeal if not the force of scientific evidence. By and large it is a much more convincing proposition than the obverse would be—that the U.S. would benefit from increased growth. But it ceases to be overwhelming in its logic when compared with the *laissez faire* position of ignoring it, especially if the costs of intervention are high in terms of infringing on freedom of choice.

Like some of what we have examined before, it is not immediately easy to tell what exactly is here asserted. We are told that the view of population growth as an intensifier of "other problems" has intuitive if not scientific appeal. The next sentence seems to give a bit—"it is a much more convincing proposition than" the notion of benefits from increased growth. But convincing in what fashion—intuitively, scientifically, how? The last sentence in the paragraph, however, is where I believe the real clue lies.

"Freedom of choice"—freedom in general—that, I take it, is the crucial value underlying much of the population debate. Of course the question of choice *is* central to the future politics of population if a governmental decision in favor of an explicit and comprehensive population policy is made. But, even now—when the principal political implications of population are those which derive from the fighting of would-be population policymakers outside the population establishment with those inside—it is a strongly motivating word. To put it bluntly, this is why some biologists are so unpopular with some demographers and family planners.

It is intriguing to me that so often a chain of demographological illogic winds up at that terminus of freedom—as if there is a deep-seated anxiety about it. Thus, consider for instance, Paper C, written by a distinguished demographer whose views and research have in many respects closely paralleled those of author B. Paper C was delivered recently in a most influential population policy-making place[32] and is a frankly advocative piece for certain policies. Essentially they are those of *laissez-faire.* Thus the concluding paragraph winds up:

I recommend that we be much more trusting of individuals to recognize and seek their own welfare in this most intimate and complex sector of their lives, and much less trusting of the ability of governments to decide that welfare for them. In my view, the proper mission of governments is to ensure the fullest opportunity for individuals to decide their own futures. I see no problems in the demography of such a world. Let's give freedom a chance, and meanwhile begin to acquire the data and knowledge and talent necessary to determine population policies, if and when it becomes more evident that such are needed.

Now my point here is not to denigrate this passage. Indeed, I would rather compliment it by saying that it is the best statement of a weak policy position which I have heard. Rather the curious thing which we should note is the route taken to get to this result which is not at all the "iffy" demographological viewpoint of the Paper B that we can't predict the future, therefore let us not tamper. Rather the gist of it is: [the] "birth rate is now lower than it has ever been in American history. It declined by one-third from 1957 to 1968." This drop, the argument runs, is part of a long-term general decline. Thus:

I expect higher-parity fertility to continue downward henceforth, in line with a long-run trend, . . . which began at least as far back as the beginning of the nineteenth century. A decline in the quantitative demand for children is a universal accompaniment of the social transformation in the direction of the modern urban-industrial society—associated with the growing ascendancy of individualism over familialism, a reversal of the direction of normative obligations between the generations, and a growth in the competence with which unwanted children can be prevented, because of improved contraceptive technology, higher education, freer communication about fertility regulation, and especially the declining weight of legal impediments and religio-moral objections.

To be sure the author is by no means so incautious as to conclude that we will actually get all the way to ZPG by eliminating unwanted fertility alone—a position which I have sometimes heard inferred. Nonetheless, he seems to think that we have a good chance of getting close enough to it not to worry. My purpose here is not to dispute this, it is rather, and only, to note the curious similarity to the outcome of Paper B. It is in this demographologic geography as if "all roads lead to liberal voluntarism." Sometimes it is hard to avoid the conclusion that the logic of demographology constitutes a closed system of reasoning.

Conclusion: Whither Population Politics?

In drawing this examination of some aspects of population politics to a close, it remains to ask what is the moral for future population policy making to be derived from our explication of these representative demographological texts? Obviously, no single practical moral—no one guide for action among those concerned with population growth—can be delineated.

Let me suggest, however, certain salient points about the "success" of future population analysis and policy which can be reasonably inferred from what has been, in effect, an exercise in the "politics of knowledge."

First, the indifferent success of the population movement in the last two decades *has not been only due* to the "objective difficulties" of the circumstances within which population experts have had to work. Without for one moment denying these awesome difficulties, let me be so bold as to hazard the guess that the difficulties "in the field" have appeared so intractable in substantial measure because demographers, and their close "allies" the family planners, have too often overlooked, minimized, or approached with simplistic tools the field's inherent political components. To put it a bit differently, their counting-capacity has hypertrophied while their broad-scale socio-political analysis has remained anemic.

Second, almost certainly this anemia has been a derivative both of influential demographers' extra-academic policy-desserts and of the powerful reinforcement of the "counting house" mentality represented by established journals in the field such as *Demography*. One of the most neglected areas of social science study is framed by the question of how a particular discipline's "leading outlets"—and their associated rewards for professors publishing in them—press toward intellectual conformity? Journals in the population field would be a first-class candidate for study for an analyst embarking upon this sub-area within the politics of knowledge.

Third, this establishment network of population journals and experts tends to a "conservative policy output" on several counts. *One* of these we have seen typified in the language patterns of one of our authors concerning the role of U.S. investment abroad. *A second* conservative thrust consists in whatever push demographological views give to the middle-class, nuclear-family norm underlying the family planners' "vision." *A third* is perhaps only conservative in the short run—because it may in the long run backfire. It is essentially composed of two parts: (a) a lack of understanding as to why it is important—and a resulting failure—to take seriously the pressure of minority groups (who historically have been the "targets" of upper and middle class family planners) to get in on the population decision-making action; and (b) a lack of understanding as to why minority groups, once informed of, and given free access to, contraceptive techniques may still not rush whole-heartedly to adopt a small-family norm. Even if, *and this is important to note*, minority-group mothers answer opinion surveys to the effect that they did not "want" one or more of their children—even if they do so answer in numbers which suggest that "unwanted fertility" is a prime social problem—it is not impossible that they will continue to have such children. Why? Not because of "lower class moral frailty." Quite the contrary. Speaking as a political scientist again, trying to perceive, if dimly, the shape of politics in the 1970s, it is hardly inconceivable to me that "child-bearing beyond the number wanted" could become a minority norm—if indeed it is not already—under the influence of black power and the like. If so, it would be one impelled by a very different sense of right from that which seems to underlie and to condition the disguised ethical thinking of demographology's policy recommendations, where the mores of a latter-day atomistic individualism seem to determine "proper policy goals."

The above comments will, I imagine, seem virtually unintelligible to those demographers whose problem-formulating language bears great likeness to that we have discussed. If so, that is what I meant by saying a bit earlier that their socio-political analysis is afflicted with anemia. It is an anemia, I must observe, of a most suburban sort, certainly not the sickle-celled variety.

Until, I would urge, the point of such remarks is far more obvious to the demographologists, I am not terribly optimistic about the quality of population planning in this country. Or at least I am not as long as they are the most influential group of policy advisers drawn from academe. Until then it strikes me that a most important task for those of us who are not of this persuasion is to push. I think that the best that we, not in this establishment, can do is to try to further either its conversion or displacement. I do not mind which happens. Nor will I venture to predict which will occur. I would, however, argue that both on humanitarian grounds and if policy is to be efficacious we are in great need of policy advisers in academia who are neither deaf to this nation's and this world's social ills nor unable to link their academic profession closely with a sense of compassion.

Notes

2. The early 1950s.

3. For a good description of this in the larger political system, see Samuel Beer, *British Politics in the Collectivist Age* (New York: Alfred A. Knopf, 1966), particularly Chapters 1-3.

4. See Elihu Bergman, Chapter 3 in this volume.

5. Recall Eisenhower's 1959 statement abjuring federal activity in the field.

6. A good if ironic analysis is Elizabeth B. Drew, "On Giving Oneself a Hotfoot: Government by Commission," *The Atlantic Monthly* (May 1968).

7. See Roger W. Cobb and Charles D. Elder, *Participation in American Politics: the Dynamics of Agenda-Building* (Boston: Allyn and Bacon, 1972).

8. See Harold Lasswell, *Politics: Who Gets What, When, How* (New York: Meridian Books, 1958—reissue).

9. See David Easton, *The Political System*, 2nd ed. (New York: Alfred A. Knopf, 1971).

10. George Orwell does not use this phrase. But that is the essence of his brilliant essay "Politics and the English Language," published first in 1946 and reprinted in George Orwell, *Collection of Essays* (New York: Doubleday Anchor, 1954): 162-177.

11. Ibid., 163.

12. Ibid., 173.

13. Ibid., 174.

14. For a discussion of this, see Theodore Lowi, *The End of Liberalism* (New York: W.W. Norton & Co., 1969).

15. See ibid., and also A.E. Keir Nash, "Pollution, Population, and the Cowboy Economy," *Journal of Comparative Administration* (May 1971): 109-128.

16. However, for a preliminary collection of essays along these lines, see A.E. Keir Nash, ed., for National Commission on Population Growth and the American Future), *Governance and Population* (Washington, D.C.: G.P.O., 1972).

17. Bernard Berelson, president of the Population Council, at the Third Smithsonian Conference on Population, Belmont, Maryland, November 8-11, 1970.

18. See Bergman's chapter (supra).

19. Paper A is by Frank Notestein and appeared as "Zero Population Growth: What Is It?", *Family Planning Perspectives* 2, 3 (June 1970): 20-24.

20. Even "conservative" non-alarmist individuals such as those to whom the Population Commission "let" most of its related research would not, I expect, be quite so optimistic as this re all resources.

21. Note I am not so confident as to say this will be our judgment—merely that I will not be bowled over if it is.

22. One of the recurrent curiosities of the demographological persuasion is the way in which—in order to avoid "change in the demographic bailiwick," in the absolutizing of the "right to have umpteen babies"—demographological prescriptions for change elsewhere may unwittingly (it seems) entail extraordinary upheavals in other domains. One which comes up with fascinating frequency is what amounts to an unconscious call for overhauling the economy. Sometimes, in following the "Don't Touch My Baby" tendency, a demographological analysis of "what's wrong" may involve a critique of the capitalist system's day to day operations without quite understanding that each single criticism, each "day" may add up to rather more than the demographologer is bargaining for. For an interesting exploration of the tendency of diverse groups engaged in arguing about population as a problem, see the interesting (as yet) unpublished paper by Ralph Potter, Harvard Divinity School, "The Simple Structure of the Population Debate."

23. See, e.g., John B. Calhoun, "Population Density and Social Pathology," *Scientific American* vol. 206 (February 1962): 139-148.

24. See, e.g., Konrad Lorenz, *On Aggression* (New York: Harcourt, Brace & World, 1966).

25. In Nash (n. 15).

26. By Charles F. Westoff, entitled "Some Reflections on Population Policy in the United States," Milbank Memorial Fund Round Table Dinner honoring Clyde Kiser, May 5-6, 1971.

27. See Larry Bumpass and Charles F. Westoff, "The 'Perfect Contraceptive' Population," *Science* 169, 3951 (18 September 1970): 1177-1182. But contra, see Judith Blake, "Population Policy for Americans, Is the Government Being Misled?" *Science* 164, 3879 (2 May 1969): 522-528.

28. See numerous Gallup and Harris polls on the subject.

29. Tomas Frejka, "Reflections on the Demographic Conditions Needed to Establish a U.S. Stationary Population Growth," *Population Studies* vol. 22 (November 1968): 379-397. Frejka's intriguing article is concerned, *inter alia,* with what changes would be necessary (because of the irregularity of the present age pyramid in the United States) in the crude birth rate between now and the

year 2365—if we were to make a decision to keep U.S. births constantly equalling U.S. deaths. The crude birth rate would have to fluctuate drastically between 8.27 and 16.36, slowly being dampened down over the next several hundred years.

30. The growth becomes inevitable for the next sixty-five years or so only if one fixes NRR = 1 as the minimum. One might choose a middle course, say, permitting the birth rate to swing down as low as 9.0 and as high as 1.3. One would, thus, buy less drastic changes at the price of lengthening the time before a non-fluctuating (though not a "zero-growth") population would be reached. The point here is, again, to avoid stumbling through the Exterminated Middle, or all-or-nothing, Fallacy.

31. Borrowing of course from Gilbert Ryle's famous article in philosophy, "Systematically Misleading Expressions."

32. Testimony by Norman Ryder before the National Commission on Population Growth and the American Future, May 28, 1971.

5

Opposition to Population Limitation in Latin America: Some Implications for U.S. Policy

Richard Lee Clinton

Introduction

Some recent research in Peru on elite attitudes toward population questions revealed that, among the best informed segment of the sample studied, two obstacles to the formation of an explicit population policy were perceived as most serious: general non-recognition of the problems posed by current population trends in Latin America and reaction to the involvement of the United States in programs to limit population growth.[1] The task assumed in this chapter is to inquire into the underlying determinants and interrelationships of these obstacles and the extent to which they might spring from factors common to Latin America as a whole. Based on this inquiry I will then address the policy issue of what an understanding of the origins and interconnections of these obstacles suggests as regards the approach which should be taken by those who wish to see population matters treated in a manner consonant with the improvement of the quality of human life.

Fundamental to the investigation to be attempted here are two basic questions: Why does the United States seem to favor programs of population limitation over other forms of foreign assistance to developing countries? And why are Latin Americans seemingly oblivious to the existence of a severe and possibly catastrophic population problem?[2]

The United States and Population Control

In approaching the first of these questions, it might properly be noted that much of the U.S. government's notoriety for having forced population limitation on unwilling underdeveloped nations seems exaggerated. It is, of course, quite likely that some official representatives of the United States, smitten by a missionary zeal as regards the impressive results to be achieved through population limitation, have given undue emphasis to "selling" family planning programs. Doubtless a few such zealots have tried to "push" the acceptance of such programs. But the fact remains that only very recently have population activities begun to receive really significant attention within U.S. foreign assistance policy. The first population unit was established in AID in 1964,[3] but it was not until

1968 that funds really began to flow to this new activity. The amount allotted by Congress for fiscal 1968—$34.8 million—was eight times the amount for the preceding year and more than three times the total allotted up to that time.[4] It is true that the level of funding for population activities has risen dramatically since 1968—$45.4 million in 1969, $74.6 million in 1970, $95.9 million in 1971,[5] and $125 million in 1972[6]—but even these more significant amounts represent a minuscule proportion of total U.S. official development assistance to less developed countries.[7] While these dollar outlays may occasionally be supplemented by local currencies generated by U.S. food aid, their order of magnitude makes clear the relatively modest commitment to population limitation as an element of U.S. foreign assistance.

It remains to be explained, however, why the tendency to emphasize population limitation has become increasingly pronounced in recent years. There are, as might be expected, two competing explanations for this tendency. According to the one current in the Third World and in Communist areas, the United States seeks to limit both the population and the industrial growth of underdeveloped countries because it depends on their resources to support its own inflated level of consumption.[8] A corollary to this explanation is the argument that the United States favors birth control in developing areas because it recognizes that population pressures contribute to revolution, and it knows that revolutionary governments would be harder to manipulate.[9]

The opposing interpretation of U.S. motives in promoting family planning programs is premised both on the moral obligation incumbent upon the rich nations to assist the poor nations and on the concept of enlightened self-interest. There are a number of variations on these themes. One would be the reminder that today's developed nations owe much of their present good fortune to the impetus they received in the past from the underdeveloped countries' resources and markets. Another would emphasize the need for reducing the unconscionable disparities in living standards among nations as a prerequisite for world peace. Still another would stress the growing interdependence of all the passengers on "spaceship Earth" and the consequent need to lower reproduction rates as one of the several steps in fighting depletion of resources, pollution, and ecological imbalance.

Without disputing any of the reasons offered in support of either explanation, I would include along with them several other considerations to which I would attribute equal or greater importance. In the first place, there is simply no denying *the fact* of a worldwide population explosion which, in a finite world, must eventually be contained. It is becoming increasingly obvious, moreover, that the technologies necessary for maintaining the standards of living prevalent in the most developed (or overdeveloped!) countries entail very high costs in terms of environmental quality and ecological balance. While there is every reason to believe that highly efficient recycling processes and more ingenious ways of utilizing waste heat energy will be devised in future years, it remains a virtual certainty that consumption patterns, living styles, and many other aspects of the behavior of human populations in the developed countries will have to be very substantially modified as well. The functional relationship, in a mathematical sense, between population size, standards of living, and ecological problems is becoming as apparent in the modern milieu of global interconnectedness as it has always been in situations of primitive technology and limited resources. Thus it is more accurate than ever to assert that if man does not control his numbers—and by extension his profligate dissipation of nature's "capital"—by conscious means, controls by dreadful natural mechanisms will inevitably be applied. I see nothing surprising or sinister in the fact that this phenomenon has been discerned initially in the developed world, where relative abundance has contributed not only to increasing levels of pollution, but also to the growth of universities, research centers, and of both the natural and the social sciences. Nor, once the alarming findings of biologists, oceanographers, demographers, and other scientists have been disseminated, is it in any way unusual that they should be acted upon, even acted upon precipitously and without sufficient reflection as to how such acts might be interpreted by those who are not yet aware of the seriousness of the menace which threatens.

Secondly, the appeal of population limitation to those engaged in developmental assistance must inevitably be immense, for much of the frustrating sense of running just to stay where you are would be removed if population growth rates ceased to wipe out the advances which under present conditions are so laboriously yet ephemerally achieved. To the legislators and governments which finance the bulk of developmental assistance, the idea of lowering population growth rates in recipient countries must also have great attraction. Not only has the ultimate futility of developmental efforts unaccompanied by reductions in the rate of population growth become increasingly apparent in the light of recent experience, but the relatively lower cost of providing fertility control assistance as compared to other types of aid has become a major consideration as domestic demands on government revenues are more violently pushed. In this regard, the apparently growing negativeness of the American public toward the whole foreign aid program should be recalled. This is not the place to discuss the various circumstances to which this is largely a reaction; suffice it to say that the net effect is congressional reluctance to contribute further to a possible taxpayers' revolt.

Finally, there is the all-important matter of the framework of ideas and values within which U.S. developmental assistance programs are conceived. Unquestionably, as Louis Hartz has so ably shown,[10] the impact of liberalism on North American values has been decisive. For present purposes only two aspects of the liberal-democratic ideology need be mentioned: its aversion to drastic change and its humanistic-individualistic emphasis. The former largely accounts for the North American's almost automatic rejection of radical alternatives and his distaste for—even fear of—revolutionary upheaval. The humanistic-individualistic values of the North American, on the other hand, determine his focus on the basic welfare of the individual and on the opportunity structure within which that individual operates. These two traits act in tandem to enhance the allure for North Americans of population planning in developing areas.

In all fairness, it should also be admitted that the leftist critics of the U.S. population "establishment" have a point.[11] The "interlocking directorate" of the population movement in the United States does indeed contain a disproportionately heavy representation of corporate wealth.[12] Doubtless it is true that these persons are far more prone to lend their support to programs such as family planning than they are to efforts at more basic structural changes in the interest of greater social justice. Is this really to be wondered at, however? As Parenti has remarked ". . . it is in the nature of social elites that they show little inclination to commit class suicide."[13] To concede this rather obvious point is not, therefore, to subscribe to the conspiratorial view of capitalist cabals concertedly attempting to quash pressures for fundamental readjustments in the distribution of the social advantage.[14] Nor is it to repudiate the efforts made by these sectors, as some would have us do, for as Chaplin has argued "motives for, and consequences of, actions need have little relationship."[15]

Viewing the Latin American response, or lack of response, to demographic realities from the vantage point of liberal democracy, with what many consider its reprehensible moral relativism, creates another serious problem, for it becomes difficult not to class as a fanatic anyone who objects to programs which would make possible the voluntary limitation of the number of every family's children in accordance with its ability to provide for them. From this point of view it seems impossible that the unmistakably pernicious effects of unregulated human fertility could be unrecognized. As I have shown elsewhere, however, the situation is much too complicated to permit such simplistic judgments, for the detrimental results of rapid population growth do not go unperceived, at least not by the better educated Peruvians whom I have studied in depth.[16] Nevertheless, there is a wide gulf separating the perception of deleterious effects and ascription of blame for their causes. It is here that a far greater recognition of differing values and peculiar cultural biases is needed, for only such recognition can provide a viable basis for cooperation and mutual respect between inhabitants of different cultural areas.

Nowhere perhaps is this caveat more warranted than as regards Latin and Anglo-Americans, for the similarities of their cultural heritages often conceal the profound differences which separate them.[17] This matter is of such importance that it merits examining in considerable detail, for so long as either party to the dispute over the pressing need for making family planning programs available to all is under the impression that the other party harbors malevolent intentions or is hopelessly irrational, there can be little progress in this or any other important area of mutual endeavor.

The Psychology of Underpopulation and
the Force of Nationalism

If the "hopelessly irrational" assumption is discarded in approaching the question of why so many Latin Americans intransigently refuse to admit the existence of a fast-worsening population problem in their area, one is forced to ask: To what, then, do they attribute the widespread suffering and want which, in spite of all their efforts, continue to afflict the masses of their people? The answer is prompt in coming: to underdevelopment. Nor can this answer be quarreled with. As the theory of demographic transition suggests, it is pervasive underdevelopment which is at the heart of the problem of high fertility as well as, by definition, of the undernourishment, disease, low productivity, and early death which are the lot of the masses in underdeveloped countries.

Granted the rationality of this response, it could still be asked why Latin Americans so often fail to perceive the connection between rapid population growth and the persistence of underdevelopment. Again the answer is quickly supplied: because the real problem is not the high fertility rates but the dependence of the area, i.e., its semi-colonial status, which exposes it to domination and exploitation by foreign states, multinational corporations, and native elites. According to this analysis, foreign capitalists and their local accomplices, the oligarchy, control investments, financial institutions, the major extractive industries, and increasingly, consumer goods industries as well.[18] As if this did not assure them of sufficient power to manipulate the national economy in their own interests, they also wield disproportionate influence over their respective countries' foreign policy and, in addition, they fix the prices which will be paid for Latin American products and those which will be charged for the capital goods and other items imported into Latin America. Freed from the debilitating state of dependence in which it finds itself, the proponents of this view insist, Latin America could easily assimilate its fast-growing population and become self-sustaining.

It should be clear by this point that the educated Latin American, although perhaps somewhat simplistic, is far from irrational in his view of underdevelopment and the role of population growth therein. He is, however, also far from unbiased in his assessment of these matters. With the doubts as to his rationality behind us, though, we can more profitably explore his bias. This bias depends largely on the deeply embedded belief that Latin America is chronically *under*populated—that its vast uninhabited areas offer limitless opportunities for colonization, that its natural resources are virtually inexhaustible, and that one of the major obstacles to taking advantage of these conditions is the shortage of people. Alberdi's nineteenth century dictum "Gobernar es poblar" still echoes throughout the region.

That the "fact" of Latin America's underpopulation is so often advanced by

Latin Americans as proof that the population explosion is somebody else's problem evidences a crucial confusion, current throughout Latin America as well as elsewhere, between the very different matters of population density and *the rate of population expansion*. In other words, to say that a country has the space and other resources to accommodate a population twice or three times its present size is not to say that it can do so within the next twenty to thirty years. That this vital distinction is so seldom drawn in Latin America indicates the generally low level of discourse which prevails there when population matters are discussed.[19] Certainly educated Latin Americans are not incapable of dealing in more sophisticated terms where population is concerned; they are merely indisposed to do so by what might be called an entrenched psychology of underpopulation. The extraordinary hold of this outlook on the Latin American mind is attributable to the intricate web of reinforcements which sustain it.

Unquestionably a prominent strand in this web is nationalism, one of the most powerful forces abroad in the developing areas.[20] In Latin America, nationalism is frequently manifested in friction between contiguous states, usually in the form of boundary disputes and arms races. These conflicts and rivalries have proven immensely useful to politicians, militarists, and certain segments of the financial and commercial communities of the states involved and consequently have seldom been allowed to drop from public view. Thus in Latin America relations between neighboring nations are normally tainted by past hostilities and suspiciousness of future intentions, as is the case, for instance, between Argentina and Brazil, Argentina and Chile, Bolivia and Chile, Bolivia and Paraguay, Peru and Chile, Ecuador and Peru, Venezuela and Colombia, Costa Rica and Nicaragua, the Dominican Republic and Haiti, and El Salvador and Honduras, to name only the most serious examples. Strained international relations are invariably conducive to pronatalist influences, but even in peaceful circumstances nationalism feeds the feeling that only populous nations can become rich, powerful, and respected members of the international community.

Another aspect of the problem of Latin American reluctance to recognize the immediacy and seriousness of the population explosion also draws in part on the force of nationalism. Latin Americans do not want to believe that they have a population problem precisely because the United States is foremost in insisting that they have one. The origins of this seeming recalcitrance are to be found both in the long and understandable tradition of anti-Americanism in Latin America and in the distrust syndrome which displays itself so prominently in Latin American culture.[21] The combination of these traits makes it improbable that the professions of altruism which accompany North American efforts to encourage the spread of family planning programs will be accepted as genuine, even to the extent that they may be. As Sanders has observed in reference to the reaction of the leftist intellectual in Latin America to the millions of dollars spent by the Ford Foundation for population research in underdeveloped areas:

In his own experience individuals and institutions do not dedicate large sums of money without concrete selfish objectives. He doubts its claims of disinterestedness in promoting human well-being; it must function in terms of some interests, which he suspects are those of powerful business groups in the United States.[22]

Given this bias, the frequent demonstration of the interlocking relationships which exist among the different organizations with involvement in the population field and between these organizations and business leaders[23] is taken as prima facie evidence of their fundamental community of interest. And the nature of these interests is deemed self-evident in view of the significant contributions from families such as the Fords and the Rockefellers.

Buttressing the conviction of Latin Americans that the United States can only be acting in its own narrow interests, moreover, is the widely shared belief that the richest nation in the world would be unable to maintain its present standard of living if it could no longer import vast quantities of resources from the rest of the world. The argument is frequently made that the United States is trying to convince the less developed countries to curtail their population growth, since the more of their resources which are consumed locally, the less will remain for export. When it is pointed out that "with approximately eight percent of the non-communist world population, the United States is presently planning to reserve for her own industries and her own consumption between 50 percent and 100 percent of the world's mineral resources,"[24] such reasoning can hardly be dismissed as totally lacking in plausibility.

The Church and the Left

Firmly aligned with the two mutually supporting obstacles just discussed are two other potent forces which, although opposed to one another in almost every other respect, make common cause in their opposition to programs which would facilitate the limiting of births. These two forces are the Roman Catholic Church and the political left. In spite of the divergent origins of the opposition from these quarters, their combined resistance to the idea of official programs of family planning has a profound impact on the climate of opinion in Latin America.

The various factors influencing the Catholic position on contraception have been dealt with by others.[25] Here it need only be pointed out that the Church's stance on the whole matter of contraception and family planning is congruent with certain metaphysical assumptions which can perhaps be summarized by the Biblical query "For what shall it profit a man, if he shall gain the world, and lose his own soul?" [Mark 8:36.] This is simply to say that, ultimately, in keeping with its fundamental *raison d'être*, the Church places a higher priority on man's spiritual than on his material well-being. Moreover, the Catholic intellectual tradition, with its exceptional emphasis on holistic interpretations, demands that no sphere of human activity be considered in separation from all other spheres, with which it is inevitably connected. Thus, the Catholic mind is repelled by the simplistic suggestion that human sexuality be manipulated for the purpose of facilitating economic development; the ethical implications of such a measure must first be thoroughly explored and reconciled with man's overall nature.[26]

The political left in all its forms, albeit for differing reasons, also rebels at the idea of reducing population pressures as a means of contributing to economic and social development. There is, in the first place, a tendency among many leftists similar to that just described in reference to the Church, to seek holistic interpretations in conformity with a given ideology. Thus, for instance, have Marxists tenaciously adhered to Marx's unsatisfactory rejection of Malthus, even at the cost of thereby understating "in one important respect the true extent of class exploitation under capitalism," *viz*, the differential access to safe, effective means to limit family size.[27] In the second place, radical leftists are, by definition, convinced of the absolute necessity for revolutionary transformation of society. In their view, a gradualistic reformist approach, no matter how sweeping, could never succeed in eliminating societal structures which are inherently inimical to the full development of man's human potential. Thus to postpone the revolution is to prolong man's bondage, and to argue that this bondage could be rendered more agreeable by family planning programs is, from their perspective, a weak plea indeed. Neither are they moved by the charge that they would be sacrificing whole generations for an ill-defined and possibly unattainable future, for to them nothing could be worse than the hopelessness and squalor in which so many millions of peasants and slumdwellers now eke out their miserable existence. These leftists would argue, with Heilbroner, that

... the way in which we ordinarily keep the books of history is wrong. No one is now toting up the balance of the wretches who starve in India, or the peasants of Northeastern Brazil who live in the swamps on crabs, or the undernourished and permanently stunted children of Hong Kong or Honduras. Their sufferings go unrecorded, and are not present to counterbalance the scales when the furies of revolution strike down their victims.[28]

Finally, there is the rejection of family planning programs emanating from the non-Marxist left. For these less doctrinaire, more pragmatic leftists the repudiation of family planning programs is to a considerable extent a vexed overreaction arising from a varying mix of factors discussed earlier under other headings—nationalism, anti-Americanism, and distrust. Their attack on family planning derives not from opposition in principle but primarily from their disgust and chagrin at the way it seems to be increasingly thrust upon them as the panacea for all their developmental ills.[29] They resent pressures, however indirect, from countries in more favored positions to adopt measures which these more developed nations have not been willing to apply to themselves. If the population explosion is indeed everybody's problem, they ask, then why do most of the industrialized nations, most conspicuously the United States, not have positive population policies? Why should the struggling nations-in-formation bear a disproportionate share of the burden of reducing population growth rates *after* the industrialized nations have already enjoyed long periods of population expansion? When the importance of manual labor as an energy source in the less developed nations is considered, particularly in the light of the Chinese experience, one can better comprehend the pervasive Third World feeling that perhaps they are being held back more than they are being helped by the industrialized nations. It is also impossible to deny the validity of the complaint that the increasing availability of funds directed exclusively at research projects or action prógrams involving fertility control is syphoning scarce talent away from other development activities which might be more productive.[30]

The Hispano-Catholic Cultural Tradition

Another important contributor to the Latin American outlook toward population matters is the fact that there are a number of strongly pronatalist tendencies inherent in the Hispano-Catholic cultural tradition. Fundamentally these tendencies derive from the undisguised patterns of male dominance within the Hispano-Catholic ethos. For example, the culturally and religiously sanctioned superiority of the male over the female implicitly sustains a double standard in sexual mores which serves, if not to encourage, at least to lessen the inhibition of males to indulge in premarital and extramarital sexual relations.[31] The well-known, albeit often exaggerated, *machismo* syndrome further contributes to the frequency of multiple households, illegitimate children, and large family size norms. The preference for male offspring is yet another male-dominant factor resulting in large families. Finally the male dominance of Hispano-Catholic culture has pronatalist consequences by severely restricting the range of educational and employment opportunities for women and by discouraging easy and open discussion between husband and wife and mutual consultation on important family decisions.

An additional pronatalist influence with roots deep in the Hispano-Catholic tradition might derive from Hispanic law. Unfortunately the present writer's competence does not extend to this area, but his limited acquaintance with some of the legal regulations governing inheritance and adoption suggests that the role of Hispanic law might prove to be an important topic for population policy research.

The Environment of Underdevelopment

Another source of pervasive pronatalist influences in Latin America is what might be described as the environment of underdevelopment. Not only in backward agricultural areas, where children can perform work of value to the family unit almost as soon as they can walk, but even in urban settings there is often a tendency to feel that numerous children are an economic asset. In part, particularly in the mushrooming slum areas surrounding Latin American capitals, this is a persisting agricultural attitude, but to a considerable extent it prevails even among many within the urban middle classes.[32] This can be explained to some degree by these classes' vulnerability to the inflationary spirals and monetary instability which plague developing economies. In the absence of adequate retirement plans and systems of social security and in an inflation-ridden atmosphere, these sectors, in spite of their affluence relative to the majority of their countrymen, are unable to provide for their later years. In such a situation, children constitute the only available form of old age insurance.

The economic upheavals endemic to developing areas also enhance the precariousness of conducting business there by, *inter alia*, making credit scarce, interest rates high, and long-range planning impossible. In turn, the greater likelihood of business failure contributes to the usefulness of large and extended families as a surrogate form of unemployment compensation. Thus, if one's enterprise or that of one's employer should founder, one can usually find employment with a brother or an uncle or a cousin until a fresh start can be made.

The dangers and uncertainties involved in doing business in an underdeveloped economy combine with the distrust syndrome described earlier to make family connections essential for accumulating sufficient capital to begin a new enterprise. And if the concern prospers, the need for delegating responsibilities again underlines the importance of family ties, for the limited trust that does exist in Latin American culture is largely reserved for members of one's own family.[33] Large families are not, therefore, by any means an altogether irrational response for the middle classes, given the context of distrust and unpredictability in which they live.

In explaining the large family size norms of the rural masses of Latin America and other areas of the underdeveloped world, rationality unquestionably plays an important role. Not only are the reasons just discussed in regard to the middle classes largely applicable to the marginalized masses, but, in addition, the substantially higher infant mortality rates prevailing amongst the more disadvantaged sectors make lower fertility seem of particularly dubious benefit to them. Given the importance of the assistance provided by children and the likelihood that only a few of those born will survive to provide that assistance, the impoverished masses of the Third World can hardly be said to be irrational in refusing to limit their fertility. On the contrary, the basic rationality of their position simply underscores the need for improving the conditions under which they live as a prerequisite to their acceptance of such ideas as family planning and family limitation.[34]

Although of less importance than the basic rationality of pronatalist attitudes in a situation of great uncertainty and scarcity, another aspect of the environment of underdevelopment should also be mentioned. This aspect refers to a set of conditions which are normally a concomitant of underdevelopment: isolation and monotony. In the isolated villages where most of the population of the Third World can be found, diversions are few and the nights are long. Ignorance of the precautions that might be taken, combined with a high frequency of intercourse, provides a far more appealing explanation of the high birth rates among poor peasants than does the spurious correlation between undernourishment and enhanced fecundity posited by Josué de Castro.[35]

The Role of Race

Yet another of the determinants of the Latin American outlook toward population matters involves race. In spite of their insistence that racial prejudice does not exist among them, Latin Americans are a peculiarly color-conscious people, as evidenced by the richness of their vocabulary where subtle variations in racial mixtures are concerned. In addition, I know of nowhere else where actual certificates of whiteness (*gracias a sacar*) have been issued by the government as was done, for a fee of course, during the colonial period in Spanish America.[36] The classic statement of the potential greatness of Latin America's hybrid race, *La raza cósmica*, by the Mexican intellectual, José Vasconcelos, seems, moreover, to be as much a hopeful prophecy—and perhaps even a displacement of anxieties stemming from lingering doubts—as it is a tribute to the new race. That the *potential* of the *evolving* new race is *to be* realized in some glowing *future*[37] in itself seems to imply something of an apology for the present state of the race.

At any rate, sensitivity regarding their mixed racial composition is a widely shared trait among Latin Americans in those areas where miscegenation has been extensively practiced. This sensitivity heightens their awareness of the growing polarization of the world into white and colored nations. The unhappy state of race relations in the United States receives wide and uniformly critical coverage by the media in Latin America and serves to reinforce the already existing animus toward the crass, materialistic, and overweening Anglo-Saxons, a stereotyped image which the antics of the omnipresent "Ugly American" do little to dispel. In this setting, many take seriously the claims such as those of the Brazilian intellectuals, Rachel de Queiroz and Darcy Ribeiro,[38] that U.S. sponsorship of population control in the less developed countries is motivated by racist designs to prevent the darker peoples from outnumbering and eventually overpowering the whiter ones. Although the charges of genocide usually rely on simpleminded caricatures for support, such arguments are occasionally couched in idealistic terms of considerable sophistication and appeal, as when Ribeiro foresees miscegenation resulting in

a more homogeneous type of human being, who will possess a greater aptitude for living with and identifying with all peoples. . . . If the Anglo Americans succeed in their proposition of reducing Black populations and the mixed contingents of Latin America by imposing a policy of demographic containment, the result will be a fortification of heterogeneity and racism.[39]

Implications for U.S. Policy

It should be clear by now that Latin American opposition to national programs of family planning, let alone to anything which could realistically be called population control, is no hastily erected barricade. On the contrary, the elaborateness and extensiveness of this opposition make it more readily comparable to an emotional-intellectual Great Wall. Reports of how family planning programs have been introduced in other areas of the world[40] serve to heighten the contrast between the sort of obstacles faced there and the type confronting present efforts in Latin America. Nowhere, it seems, has there been such a multifaceted and pervasive opposition as is found in Latin America.

For policy considerations the preceding discussion can be summarized as follows: The basic values and overall Weltanschauung of Latin Americans produce an intellectual and emotional matrix which is singularly hostile to suggestions emanating from the United States that measures be introduced for lowering birth rates in order to facilitate the task of development.

What, then, can the United States do to persuade Latin Americans of the fast-approaching disaster imminent in undiminished human fertility? While measures such as raising the level of foreign aid to one or two percent of our GNP and eliminating activities which lend substance to charges of imperialism would, of course, pay huge dividends in terms of increased trust in our motives, I will limit my policy advice to, alas, more realistic and direct suggestions.

In the first place, all efforts should be bent toward convincing Congress and the American people that this country urgently requires an explicit, positive population policy. Until we have an enlightened population policy of our own, we are not only handicapped in our efforts to alert others to the need for population limitation and improvement in the quality of human life, we are in a morally untenable position in even making the attempt.

Simultaneously, Congress and the American people must be made aware of the profoundly counterproductive consequences of overemphasizing the role of population limitation within our foreign aid program.[41] Such measures will never be truly effective until hospitable conditions for them exist. Rather than insisting on the need for family planning programs in nations which do not yet really want them, our foreign aid agencies should provide assistance in developing the infrastructure for such programs, e.g., maternal-child health clinics; training facilities for medical and especially paramedical personnel; improved transportation, communication, and administration; and education of every type. Within government-sponsored research, moreover, although far greater support should be made available for basic research in reproductive physiology and for the development of safer, cheaper, more effective, and easier-to-use means of contraception, the tendency to give top priority to projects which focus narrowly on fertility regulation must be reversed. Instead, studies of all aspects and ramifications of population, preferably by or in collaboration with foreign researchers, should be promoted.

Finally, if none of the above can be accomplished, at the very least let it be made known to people in responsible positions the harm they do the humble cause of family planning when they make thoughtless statements about the relative cheapness of limiting population growth as a means for increasing per capita GNP in developing areas,[42] or the possibility of requiring population limitation programs to be in effect in developing nations before they could qualify for developmental loans,[43] or the advisability of mixing contraceptives into the powdered milk and other foods we distribute abroad.[44]

Given the tensions and distrust which divide the world today, it is difficult to imagine a more volatile topic than that of foreign-sponsored population limitation. The sensitivity surrounding this matter is such that the very terms "population control" and even "birth control" carry ugly connotations for many of the inhabitants of the Third World and should be eschewed in favor of more positive expressions—euphemisms, if you like—such as "family planning," "responsible parenthood," and "population planning."

Unless the sensitivity and frequently the rationality of Third World peoples in regard to population limitation are recognized, understood, and respected, the prospects for alleviating human suffering on a massive scale are far from encouraging.

Notes

1. Richard Lee Clinton, *Problems of Population Policy Formation in Peru* (Chapel Hill: Carolina Population Center, Population Program and Policy Design Series: no. 4, 1971), especially pp. 125-131.

2. Both of these questions were implicit in the remarks of the distinguished Mexican economist, Víctor Urquidi, in a lengthy impromptu rebuttal to a paper delivered by J. Mayone Stycos at the International Conference on Population and Urbanization Problems in Latin America held at the University of Houston

on April 2 and 3, 1971. See Philip B. Taylor, Jr. and Sam Schulman, eds., *Population and Urbanization Problems of Latin America* (Houston: University of Houston, Office of International Affairs, 1971): 28-32.

3. Agency for International Development, *Population Program Assistance* (October, 1969): 11.

4. Agency for International Development, *Population Program Assistance* (December, 1971): 23-24.

5. Ibid., 23.

6. Population Crisis Committee, *Population Crisis* 8, no. 1 (February 1972): 1.

7. In 1970, for instance, the funds for population/family planning activities made up only some 2.3 percent of total U.S. official development assistance. Moreover, "[t]he total of all aid funds available for population matters from all donors, official and private, is less than 2 percent of the total flow of official aid to development." Philander P. Claxton, Jr., "United States Population Policy—Origins and Development," *The Department of State Bulletin* 63, 1630 (September 21, 1970): 320-321. (Presumably Mr. Claxton's last phrase refers to official aid from *all* governments.)

8. This charge is convincingly documented by Heather Dean, "Scarce Resources: The Dynamic of American Imperialism," pp. 139-154 of K.T. Fann and Donald C. Hodges, eds., *Readings in U.S. Imperialism* (Boston: Porter Sargent Publisher, 1971).

9. Ibid., 149.

10. *The Liberal Tradition in America* (New York: Harcourt, Brace & World, Inc., 1955).

11. William Barclay, Joseph Enright, and Reid Reynolds, "Population Control in the Third World," North American Congress on Latin America *Newsletter* 4, 8 (December 1970): 1-18.

12. Elihu Bergman, *The Politics of Population U.S.A.: A Critique of the Policy Process* (Chapel Hill: Carolina Population Center, Population Program and Policy Design Series: no. 5, 1971). See also Chapter 3 in this volume.

13. Michael Parenti, "The Possibilities for Political Change," *Politics and Society* 1, 1 (November 1970): 88.

14. The distribution of the social advantage is a useful concept developed by Neil W. Chamberlain, *Beyond Malthus: Population and Power* (New York and London: Basic Books, Inc., 1970): 16-20.

15. David Chaplin, "The Population Problem in Latin America," pp. 1-22 of David Chaplin, ed., *Population Policies and Growth in Latin America* (Lexington, Mass.: D.C. Heath and Co., 1971): 6.

16. Clinton (n. 1), especially pp. 94-137.

17. This point is made cogently by Richard M. Morse, "The Strange Career of Latin American Studies," *The Annals of the American Academy of Political and Social Science* 356 (November 1964): 106-112.

18. Cf. Theotonio Dos Santos, "The Structure of Dependence," pp. 225-236 of Fann and Hodges (n. 3); Susanne Bodenheimer, "Dependency and Imperialism: The Roots of Latin American Underdevelopment," *Politics and Society* 1, 3 (May 1971): 327-358; Osvaldo Sunkel, "Big Business and 'Dependencia': A Latin American View," *Foreign Affairs* 50, 3 (April 1972): 517-531.

19. Less indicative of this generally low level of discourse is the obviously tactical decision of the opponents of population limitation to equate programs to make family planning services available with programs which oblige people to limit the size of their families. That this transparent maneuver so often goes unchallenged, however, *is* further evidence of the low level of discourse.

20. Two perceptive statements of the nature of nationalism are Kalman H. Silvert, "The Strategy of the Study of Nationalism," pp. 3-38 of Kalman H. Silvert, ed., *Expectant Peoples: Nationalism and Development* (New York: Random House, 1963), and Arthur P. Whitaker and David C. Jordan, *Nationalism in Contemporary Latin America* (New York: The Free Press, 1966).

21. One of the most eloquent and sensitive discussions of the distrustfulness which permeates Latin American society is that of Octavio Paz, *The Labyrinth of Solitude: Life and Thought in Mexico*; translated by Lysander Kemp (New York: Grove Press, Inc., 1961). For a more empirical attempt to deal with this phenomenon, see Joseph A. Kahl, *The Measurement of Modernism: A Study of Values in Brazil and Mexico* (Austin: University of Texas Press, 1968). An interesting effort to tap this dimension of Latin American character by using the theory of games may be found in R. Kenneth Godwin, *Attitudes and Behavior Related to Modernization* (Chapel Hill: Carolina Population Center, Population Program and Policy Design Series: no. 6, 1972).

22. Thomas G. Sanders, "Opposition to Family Planning in Latin America: The Non-Marxist Left," American Universities Field Staff *Reports*, West Coast South America Series 17, 5 (March 1970): 1.

23. Cf. Bergman, (n. 12) and Chapter 3 in this volume, and Barclay et al., (n. 11).

24. Dean (n. 8): 147. These plans are contained in a publication entitled "Resources in America's Future," compiled by an organization called Resources for the Future. See Dean (n. 8): 142-143.

25. For a very well informed discussion of the Latin American Church vis-à-vis this matter, see Thomas G. Sanders, "The Relationship between Population Planning and Belief Systems: The Catholic Church in Latin America," American Universities Field Staff *Reports*, West Coast South America Series 17, 7 (April 1970). Also see the pertinent chapters in J. Mayone Stycos, *Human Fertility in Latin America: Sociological Perspectives* (Ithaca, New York: Cornell University Press, 1968), and the same author's *Ideology, Faith, and Family Planning in Latin America: Studies in Public and Private Opinion on Fertility Control* (New York: McGraw-Hill Book Company, 1971).

26. I am grateful to Professor Arnold S. Nash, Department of Religion,

University of North Carolina at Chapel Hill, for stimulating my thinking on this matter.

27. Herman E. Daly, "A Marxian-Malthusian View of Poverty and Development," *Population Studies* (London) 25, 1 (March 1971): 30.

28. Robert L. Heilbroner, "Counter-Revolutionary America," pp. 241-259 of Irving Howe, ed., *A Dissenter's Guide to Foreign Policy* (Garden City, N.Y.: Doubleday & Co., 1968): 249. Moreover, Heilbroner goes on to say, "there is the necessity of calculating what is likely to happen in the absence of the revolution whose prospective excesses hold us back. Here one must weigh what has been done to remedy underdevelopment—and what has not been done—in the past twenty years; [and] how much time there remains before the population flood enforces its own ultimate solution. . . . " (p. 250). For further thoughts along these lines see my "Portents for Politics in Latin American Population Expansion," *Inter-American Economic Affairs* 25, 2 (Autumn 1971): 31-46.

29. This perception may be accounted for in part by the exponential increase in funds earmarked exclusively for population matters, particularly since the funds available for other developmental activities have not only not been increasing but have in many cases declined. The appearance of the disproportion between these different types of aid is therefore heightened.

30. Barclay et al. (n. 11): 15.

31. The wider anti-social implications of this culturally conditioned egotism are discussed by Stanislav Andreski, *Parasitism and Subversion: The Case of Latin America* (New York: Schocken Books, 1966): 47-54.

32. A survey carried out in Lima toward the end of 1966, with a sample of 1,000 residences selected randomly from a sampling frame of 4,948 urban blocks (including marginal neighborhoods), found that the proportion of persons who considered numerous children to be a guarantee for one's old age was one in four for the middle class as compared to fewer than one in ten for the upper class (and one in two for the lower class). Carlos A. Uriarte, "Encuesta de actitud sobre el tamaño de la familia," *Estudios de Población y Desarrollo* (Lima) 2, 2 (1968): 12.

33. This phenomenon was described by Banfield, in his study of an impoverished southern Italian town, as "amoral familism." Cf. Edward C. Banfield, *The Moral Basis of a Backward Society* (New York: The Free Press, 1958). See also Kahl (n. 21).

34. An analogous situation exists in the more developed countries, for, as Judith Blake and Kingsley Davis have pointed out, alternative sources of psychic satisfaction, self-fulfillment, and social approbation must be created, particularly for women, if people are to be asked to limit the size of their families to one or two children. See Judith Blake, "Demographic Science and the Redirection of Population Policy," *Journal of Chronic Diseases* 18, 11 (November 1965): 1181-1200; and Kingsley Davis, "Population Policy: Will Current Programs Succeed?" *Science* 158, 3802 (10 November 1967): 730-739.

35. Cf. Josué de Castro, *The Geography of Hunger* (Boston: Little, Brown, Inc., 1952). Admittedly, of course, the alternative suggested here is an intuitively derived one; whether there is a high frequency of intercourse among peasants in isolated villages is an empirical question better investigated by anthropologists than by political scientists.

36. Clarence H. Haring, *The Spanish Empire in America* (New York and Burlingame: Harcourt, Brace & World, Inc., 1963): 198.

37. See Miguel Jorrín and John D. Martz, *Latin American Political Thought and Ideology* (Chapel Hill: University of North Carolina Press, 1971) 216.

38. Cf. Rachel de Queiroz, "O Côntrole de Natalidade," *O Cruzeiro* (Rio de Janeiro) maio 27, 1967, and Darcy Ribeiro, "Genocidio con píldoras," *Vispera* (Montevideo) 2, 7 (octubre de 1968): 66-70, cited in Herman E. Daly, "The Population Question in Northeast Brazil: Its Economic and Ideological Dimensions," *Economic Development and Cultural Change* 18, 4, part 1 (July 1970): 536-574. See also Darcy Ribeiro, *The Americas and Civilization*; translated by Linton Lomas Barrett and Marie McDavid Barrett (New York: E.P. Dutton, 1971).

39. Quoted in Sanders (n. 22): 3.

40. See, for instance, Ronald Freedman and John Y. Takeshita, *Family Planning in Taiwan: An Experiment in Social Change* (Princeton, N.J.: Princeton University Press, 1969), and James T. Fawcett, "Population Policy as a Response to Internal Social Pressures: The Case of Thailand," *Concerned Demography* 2, 4 (March 1971): 26-29.

41. "To the contrary, the population problem makes the necessity of economic aid even greater, because the possibility of keeping up with the rapid population growth of the next generation is a real one only if the economic possibilities are realized, and because a decline of fertility is much more probable in a context of spreading education and social and economic change." Ansley J. Coale, "The Economic Effects of Fertility Control in Underdeveloped Areas," pp. 142-162 of Roy O. Greep, ed., *Human Fertility and Population Problems* (Cambridge, Mass.: Schenkman Publishing Company, Inc., 1963): 149.

42. Msgr. Hélder Câmara, archbishop of Recife, reacted to President Johnson's statement on the occasion of the twentieth anniversary of the United Nations as follows: "I will never forget the words of President Lyndon Johnson—five dollars applied to birth control is a better investment than a hundred dollars used in development. I still retain that impertinence in my hearing, and I thank the Pope for taking a position although it creates problems for the underdeveloped countries. . . . " Quoted from *Jornal do Brasil* (Rio de Janeiro) septembro 28, 1968, by Sanders (n. 15): 3. See also Y.N. Guzevaty, "Population and World Politics," *International Affairs* (Moscow) October, 1967, reprinted in its entirety on pp. 3-6 of *Studies in Family Planning* no. 49 (January 1970): 5.

43. A sampling of the uniformly denunciatory editorial reaction in one Latin American country, Peru, to Robert McNamara's statement of September 29,

1969, would include: Ignacio Basombrío Zender, "Población y préstamos," *Correo* (Lima) 6 de octubre, 1969; Federico Prieto Celi, "No a la tesis de McNamara," *La Prensa* (Lima) 4 de octubre, 1969; Guillermo Bolaños, "La planificación familiar de McNamara," *La Crónica* (Lima) 1 de octubre, 1969; and the unsigned lead editorials which appeared in *Expreso* (Lima) 1 de octubre, 1969; *Extra* (Lima) 2 de octubre, 1969; and *La Crónica* (Lima) 3 de octubre, 1969.

44. Paul Ehrlich's ill-advised remark elicited a hue and cry in Peru from *El Comercio* (Lima) 6 de diciembre, 1969, and *Expreso* (Lima) 5 de diciembre, 1969.

6

The Structure of Mass Attitudes in the United States and Latin America: Implications for Policy

R. Kenneth Godwin

There are vast numbers of knowledge, attitudes, and practice (KAP) studies which have shown that important differences exist between the number of children a woman says she wants and the number of children she actually bears. Moreover, the number wanted is almost always substantially lower than the number born. In addition to these KAP surveys there are numerous studies which have attempted to relate social and psychological factors to desired and actual fertility.[1] To a large extent these two types of surveys provide the basis for alternative population policy recommendations. A major difficulty in evaluating these alternative proposals has been the lack of information concerning the relationships between the attitudes and values described in these surveys and future fertility behavior. The aim of this chapter is to discuss possible ways of overcoming this difficulty by concentrating on the structure of attitudes rather than simply accepting or rejecting the verbally expressed opinions gathered in attitude surveys as indicators of future behavior. The principal proposition of this study is that the knowledge of the structure of attitudes, values, and beliefs can aid us in the evaluation of different policy recommendations. The assumptions upon which this proposition is based are:

1. values, beliefs, and attitudes which persons perceive to be important to them are related in some consistent manner; and,
2. persons rationally choose among competing values in decisions which affect their fertility behavior.

It is definitely not my assumption that these attitudes and values are consistent in a logical manner or even in what interviewers or questionnaire designers consider a "rational" sense; rather I am assuming only that the individual chooses to behave in a given way because he, for some set of reasons, believes his choice will maximize his benefits.

Policy As Coercion

In any discussion of population policies individuals should first make clear their normative assumptions concerning the legitimate uses of coercion. If we accept the definition of policy as "a general statement by a governmental authority defining an intention to influence the behavior of citizens by the use of positive and negative sanctions,"[2] then we must conclude that every policy is coercive. The coercion may vary as to whether it directly or indirectly affects the individual and in its strength or weakness; but the policy is, nevertheless, coercive. Thus whether a policy attempts to create new family planning centers, develop new contraceptives, use antinatal propaganda in the schools, or sterilize people, it is using compulsion.

Once we realize that to implement a policy means to coerce someone, the question becomes, "In what situations can we justify policies?" As Steven Garland and Robert Trudeau discuss in Chapter 2 of this volume, writers in the population policy literature generally attempt to justify coercion on the basis that the needs of the society must take precedence over the rights of the individual. As this use of the word "society" signifies the totality of individuals, present and future, who live in a given area; a more correct justification of coercion would be to show that the expansion of individuals' choices in one area is sufficiently important to contract individuals' choices in another area. For example, a policy which paid for research for the development of new contraceptives would reduce our number of choices to the extent that we are taxed to pay for this research. The taxation is justified on the basis that at some future date we will have more valuable choices in our sexual and reproductive behavior and in our living conditions.

The obvious difficulty of exchanging one set of choices for another is that different individuals value different sets of choices. Because of the variation of preferences, there are no universally accepted criteria for justifying the use of coercion in one area to expand a set of choices in another. To this writer the most appropriate criteria are: (1) to place the burden of proof upon those who argue for a new policy; (2) to use the lowest level of coercion possible; (3) to insure that whenever possible the coercion is placed upon those individuals who presently have the widest range of choices; and, (4) to use the coercion whenever possible to expand the choices of those who presently have the least number of alternatives.[3] These criteria stem from my beliefs that the government should not expand its coercive powers unless the harm from inaction is "clear and present"; that by keeping governmental coercion to a minimum we usually maximize individual choice; and, that those persons who are presently least free (in the sense that they have the fewest number of alternatives available to them) should be the last to be coerced and the first to have their arena of choices expanded.

Existing Population Policy Proposals

To a large degree the existing population policy alternatives, both in the United States and abroad, have developed from the combination of two sets of variables: the perceived severity and immediacy of the population problem, and the interpretation of information gathered in KAP and social-psychological studies of fertility. Depending on his interpretation of the "population crisis" and the studies of fertility determinants, a researcher will advocate certain types of policies with different amounts of governmental coercion and intrusion into the fertility behavior of individuals. To simplify discussion of the different policy proposals I will place them in three classes: low, medium, and high coercion.

In the first category, low coercion, are those policies which suggest that the first (and possibly the only) steps in the development of a successful population policy are to make available cheap and efficient contraceptives which are not related to coitus and to insure that the population is aware of the availability of the contraceptives and knows how to use them. At the other extreme are those highly coercive policies which would control fertility by direct intervention into the life of individuals through sterilization or economic penalties directed against families which exceed the "allowable" number of children. In between these two groups are the advocates of policies which are designed to change current norms regarding the acceptable number of children.[4]

The advocates of low coercion policies, those which concentrate solely on voluntary contraceptive practices, usually base their recommendations on the assumption that the effects of rapid population growth have not yet reached crisis proportions and on the evidence of KAP studies which show that throughout most of the world women say they desire only two to four children. The advocates of these policies assume that the differences between actual fertility behavior and the verbally expressed preferences result from the lack of knowledge about and availability of contraceptives. It is argued that if this knowledge gap is bridged people will voluntarily lower their fertility rates to acceptable levels. Another assumption which may accompany this position is that if a country's health facilities develop to the extent that children born alive have a high probability of living to maturity, then the desired family size will also drop. Figure 6-1 shows the basic assumptions about fertility determinants which are made by the advocates of low coercion policies. On the basis of these assumptions typical policy proposals of this group include the establishment or extension of family planning services, liberalization of abortion laws, and the development of maternal-child health facilities.[5]

Persons advocating highly coercive policies assume that the verbally expressed, private opinions about desired family size which are recorded in the KAP studies are not predictive of fertility behavior and that the availability of contraceptives will not greatly alter such behavior. Rather, in their view, fertility behavior is more closely related to social norms which are often pronatal and not easily changed. (See Figure 6-2 for a diagrammatic representation of these assumptions.) Therefore, even if contraceptives were readily available and potential users knew about them, the rate of population growth would remain

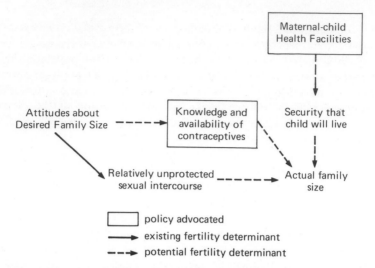

Figure 6-1. Assumptions Concerning Fertility Determinants — Low Coercion Advocates.

unacceptably high, as people would continue to want "too many" children. To support their case, advocates of highly coercive policies point to two facts: that in those countries where fertility rates are low the drop in this rate preceded modern contraceptives, and that the successes of family planning programs in countries with high fertility norms have not been overwhelming.

If the assumptions of the advocates of high coercion policies are correct and fertility behavior is related to social norms which are highly pronatal, stable, and difficult to change, then rather strong incentives or sanctions are required to insure "acceptable" fertility behavior. Typical policies emanating from this school of thought include strong economic incentives or disincentives, licenses for marriages and children, and compulsory sterilization.[6]

Between the high and low coercion policy advocates is a group which also

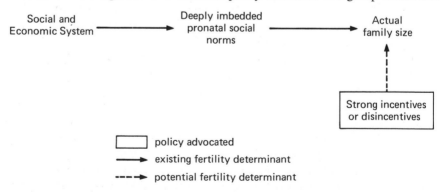

Figure 6-2. Assumptions Concerning Fertility Determinants — High Coercion Advocates.

believes that family planning programs alone are not sufficient, but at the same time rejects those policies which would directly intervene in the choice of couples to have as many children as they desire. As can be seen in Figure 6-3, this group assumes that although attitudes concerning ideal and desired family size are not now predictive of behavior, this situation can change by making such attitudes more salient. In addition, persons advocating medium level coercion assume that social norms concerning fertility can be changed relatively quickly if the underlying causes of these norms can be identified and modified. On the basis of these assumptions, the advocates of medium level coercion argue that intensified educational and propaganda campaigns would be the most appropriate policies for the reduction of fertility rates.[7]

From this simplified view of the three types of population policies and their respective assumptions, the reader can see the relationship of each policy to the findings of KAP studies and social-psychological surveys. The advocates of policies of low coercion assume that verbally expressed attitudes would be related to behavior if contraceptives and knowledge of their use were readily available. The advocates of highly coercive policies assume that fertility behavior is more closely related to social norms than the attitudes measured in KAP studies. These norms are often pronatal and are not readily changed. And the assumptions of the middle group are similar to those of the advocates of high coercion except that the advocates of medium coercion assume that social norms are subject to rapid change and attitudes concerning desired family size can be made relevant. Thus, to evaluate the different policies the first priority is to examine the interrelationships among norms, attitudes, and behavior.

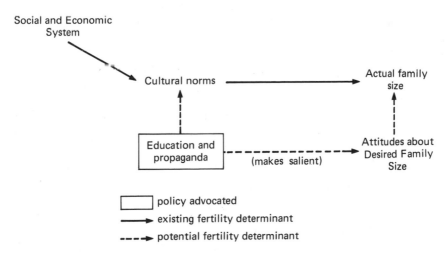

Figure 6-3. Assumptions Concerning Fertility Determinants — Medium Coercion Advocates.

Fertility-Related Attitudes and Their Structure

In the material presented below I will attempt to examine the structure of those attitudes, values, and beliefs which might be expected to be related to fertility behavior. The data for this study were gathered through interviews with a stratified random sample of males fifteen years of age from Durham, North Carolina, and Cuernavaca, Mexico.[8] These interviews consisted of questions chosen from previous KAP and social-psychological studies.[9] Rather than examining the data by the more usual techniques, however, I will attempt to look for a structural pattern which might indicate how these attitudes, beliefs, and values were formed. Following an examination of these data I will examine the implications of any structures which emerge for existing policy alternatives.

The data base on which this survey is built has one important limitation—the individuals involved have had relatively little sexual experience. To partially overcome this limitation I will include information from previous research including that of Joseph Kahl who asked some of the same questions in a nationwide sample of adults in Mexico.[10] In this way the reader will have a chance to check the reliability of the sample used in the present analysis.

To broaden the rather narrow focus of many previous studies concerning fertility attitudes, the present study included not only scales for those attitudes usually found in KAP studies, but also scales for Modernism, Activism, Individualism, Family Modernism, and Integration with Relatives.[11] These scales were included because such attitudes and values have often been postulated as being important in the development of fertility norms.[12]

Upon first examination of the data it would appear that the advocates of highly coercive policies are correct in their assumption that there exists a constellation of attitudes and values highly favorable to large families in countries with high fertility rates. A comparison of the mean responses of the samples in the United States and Mexico shows that there are substantial differences between the two countries in both the number of children desired by the individual for himself and in the perceived ideal family size for rich, poor, and middle class families. (See Table 6-1).

In addition to preferences for larger families, Mexican youths were more likely than their American contemporaries to express the opinion that larger families are good for the country, that the number of children is something for the parents to decide without outside interference, that it is necessary to have many children to protect oneself in old age, and that marriages without children are incomplete. In contrast to the more pronatal attitudes of the Mexicans, youths in the United States were more likely to favor the government distribution of birth control information to whoever wants it and to favor the government's encouraging couples to have fewer children. There were no differences between the two samples in their opinions that the father of many children is more of a man than the father of few children or in the opinion that couples should have only the number of children they desire.

Table 6-1
Mean Scores of Americans and Mexicans on Fertility-Related Questions*

Item	U.S. Mean	Mexican Mean	Difference
1. Desired family size for self	2.25	3.81	1.56**
2. Ideal number of children for a rich family	3.29	5.80	2.51**
3. Ideal number of children for a middle class family	2.54	4.38	1.84**
4. Ideal number of children for a poor family	1.60	2.87	1.27**
5. Number of children in own family	3.39	5.84	2.45**
6. Large families are good for the country	2.87	2.31	.56**
7. The number of children should be decided by the mother and father without outside interference	1.74	1.59	.15
8. It is necessary to have many children to protect oneself in old age	3.15	2.50	.65**
9. The government should give birth control information to whoever wants it	1.45	1.75	.30
10. A marriage without children is incomplete	2.35	2.08	.27
11. The father of many children is more of a man than the father of few	3.08	3.08	.00
12. Couples should have only the number of children they desire	1.54	1.58	.04
13. The government should actively attempt to convince couples to limit the size of their families	2.57	2.71	.14
14. Couples should follow the teachings of the Church with respect to contraceptive practices	–	2.38	–

*Items 6 through 14 were scored 1 = agree very much, 2 = agree a little, 3 = disagree a little, 4 = disagree very much.
**Significant at the p. $<$ .01 level.

Although the data presented in Table 6-1 would give strength to the arguments for highly coercive policies, such strength is dependent upon whether or not such a pattern actually causes behavioral differences. To assert such causality is untenable, however, for two reasons. First, even in these aggregated statistics the differences between the means of the responses to statements 6 through 13 are small, usually below statistical significance, and in only one case (Statement 6) are the mean scores of the two samples on different sides of the agree-disagree continuum (2.5 would be exactly halfway on this continuum). And second, if any of the attitudes shown in Table 6-1 are to affect fertility behavior, they must do so on an individual level. To derive any conclusions about individual behavior from the aggregate data would be to commit the ecological fallacy.[13] Thus it is necessary to use techniques which study the relationships among the variables on the level of the individual.

Although it is not possible to measure the connection between fertility behavior and the attitudes of the youths studied here, it is possible to make some estimates concerning the probable effects of these attitudes on their future fertility behavior. These estimates are based on the proposition that if an attitude is predictive of behavior there exists a consistent structure among the related attitudes.[14] This proposition has been tested and verified in previous research on fertility attitudes and behavior by Insko, Blake, Cialdini, and Mulaik.[15] Thus if the attitudes examined in this study (and in other KAP and social-psychological studies of fertility) are important in the determination of fertility behavior, we would expect to find reliable and consistent patterns among these attitudes.

Attitudes and Values Related to Desired and Ideal Family Size

Because the object of this paper is to look not only for correlations among different fertility-related attitudes but also to examine how such attitudes might be formed, the data analysis is divided into two distinct parts: (1) the analysis of social and social-psychological factors which might be expected to influence the formation of fertility attitudes; and, (2) the analysis of the fertility attitudes themselves. Because a full description of the first of these analyses is available elsewhere,[16] I will simply review these findings and move to the second analysis which is the more important one for the evaluation of policy alternatives.

Social and Social-Psychological Factors

In this analysis ten independent value scales and one interdependent scale were used as the independent variables in two separate step-wise multiple regression analyses. In the first analysis desired family size for self (Question 1 in Table 6-1) was the dependent variable; and, in the second analysis, ideal family size for others, (a scale composed of questions 2, 3, and 4, Table 6-1) was the dependent variable. The eleven independent variables were adaptations of scales used by Kahl[17]—measures of Activism, Individualism, Family Modernism, Integration with Relatives, Stratification of Life Chances, Stratification of Community, Manual Labor, Trust, Occupational Primacy, Risk Taking and Overall Modernism. The regression analyses were carried out separately for each country.

Neither in the United States nor in Mexico did this analysis explain much of the variance in scores on Desired Family Size for Self. In the United States all eleven independent variables could explain only 19 percent of the variance, and in Mexico these variables explained only 16 percent of the variance. Similarly in the analysis of Ideal Family Size for Others the value scales could explain less than 20 percent of the variance in each country. In these regression equations the more important predictors (each of which could explain between 2 and 8 percent of the variance) were Overall Modernism, Family Modernism, Activism, and Attitude Toward Manual Labor. When it is remembered that the correlation between expressed attitudes and overt behavior is often quite weak (this will be discussed more fully later in the chapter), it would seem that the relationships discovered and the information obtained in the above analyses are not likely to aid us in the prediction of fertility behavior.

At this juncture the reader may ask if the above findings can be generalized to adults, as it would seem likely that fifteen year old males have not given sufficient thought to their fertility attitudes to have developed a consistent belief structure. The answer to this question is a conditional yes. As was stated earlier, Kahl asked quite similar questions to a nationwide survey of adult men in Mexico. The mean number of children considered ideal in Kahl's sample was 3.9,[18] while in my own sample the mean was 3.8. In addition, the relationships between the scores on the value scales and Ideal Family Size were also quite similar. Table 6-2 shows the similarity in the strength of the relationships found in Kahl's study and in the present study. The only relationship which appeared in Kahl's study but did not appear in the present study is the relationship between Ideal Family Size and Family Modernism.[19]

The results of this study also appear to be representative of the U.S. adult population. In the United States Clifford studied the relationship between Modernism and Desired and Ideal Family Size.[20] Clifford found the correlations between Modernism and these two variables to be −.10 and −.22, respectively. The correlations between the scores on the Modernism scale and Desired and

Table 6-2

A Comparison of the Relationships Between Value Scales and Ideal Family Size in Mexican Adults and Youths

Value Scale	(Kahl) Adult	(Present Study) 15 Year Old
Modernism	−.22	−.27
Integration with Relatives	−.27	−.23
Family Modernism	−.25	−.02*
Activism	−.15	−.13
Class	−.24	−.27

*Differences between the two correlations statistically significant at the .05 level.

Ideal Family Size in the present study are −.12 and −.15. These differences are not statistically significant.

What are the implications of the above findings for population policy recommendations? First, if an advocate of a certain policy is relying on more "modern" values to lower the desire for a large number of children, he is likely to be quite disappointed. And second, those who argue that fertility norms are closely linked to values such as individualism, activism, and integration of family are incorrect. If fertility norms are related to some set of values, we must look to sets of cultural norms and values other than those usually studied in KAP and social-psychological studies of fertility. For reasons which I will discuss below, such a search would likely be unrewarding.

Attitudes and Values Directly Concerned with Fertility

If the above conclusions concerning the weakness of the relationships between "modern" attitudes and fertility attitudes are correct, what can we say about the strength of attitudes and values which are much more proximate to attitudes concerning family size? Is there a consistent pattern among attitudes and values which might be expected to be closely intertwined with family size ideals? To study this question I analyzed the responses of both the U.S. and Mexican samples to the fourteen questions and statements listed in Table 6-1. The results of this analysis show that there is little structure among these attitudes.

As a first step in the analysis of these attitudes I examined their intercorrelations. As Tables 6-3 and 6-4 show, almost all the correlations in both the United States and Mexico are of a low order. This is true in spite of the fact that several of the items (see questions 1 to 4 in Table 6-1) are quite similar. It is possible that the low correlations found among these items are not due to inconsistencies or an absence of connections among an individual's fertility attitudes and values, but are caused by the fact that other sets of constraints, constraints which I did not anticipate, are operating. It is also possible that the anticipated constraints do exist and are reasonably strong, but the statements employed in the questionnaire were not easily interpreted by the respondents. If this were the case, large amounts of unique variance would have obscured the existing structure.

To test these possibilities I factor analyzed the responses to the fourteen items and used the squared multiple correlation coefficient as the communality estimate. If the low correlations among the items were caused by unique variance, such a communality estimate should reduce this problem.[21] The factor analysis would reveal whether the structure which I had anticipated was, in fact, the one which existed.

The results of this analysis are shown in Table 6-5. I had originally anticipated that three factors would be present: (1) number of children desired and

Table 6-3
Intercorrelations Among Fertility Questions—U.S.A.

	1	2	3	4	5	6	7	8	9	10	11	12	13	14
1		.10	.24	.08	.02	.01	.36	.07	−.07	−.02	−.05	.01		−.07
2			.04	−.16	−.06	.17	−.01	.16	−.20	−.28	−.16	.01		.03
3				.09	−.28	.08	.06	.01	−.24	.07	.05	.00		.09
4					.12	−.29	.14	.05	.10	.43	.34	.19		.11
5						−.01	−.05	−.04	.13	.19	.07	−.04		.12
6							.02	.07	−.07	.11	−.14	−.17		.18
7								−.15	−.02	−.05	−.11	−.03		.02
8									.07	.09	.04	−.04		−.02
9										.04	−.06	.01		−.25
10											.38	.22		.28
11												−.09		.11
12														−.05

13 question not included in U.S.

Table 6-4
Intercorrelations Among Fertility Questions—Mexico

	1	2	3	4	5	6	7	8	9	10	11	12	13	14
1		.35	.52	.07	.04	.08	.21	.11	.18	−.30	−.22	.03	.09	−.14
2			.14	−.04	.21	.01	−.04	.14	.05	−.08	−.21	.16	.12	−.04
3				.18	−.07	.13	.13	−.04	.03	−.50	−.34	−.18	.07	−.24
4					.09	.10	.04	.10	.06	.39	.45	.19	−.03	.18
5						.13	−.08	−.30	.25	−.03	.17	.03	.04	.18
6							−.07	−.05	.12	−.06	.07	−.13	−.10	.02
7								.22	.03	−.03	−.17	−.04	.19	−.04
8									.12	.16	−.04	.07	.34	.14
9										.01	.20	.04	.20	−.14
10											.53	.50	.04	.35
11												.17	.03	.07
12													.01	.16
13														−.19

considered desirable; (2) social pressures to increase or limit family size; and (3) the public or private nature of the decision. These three factors were, in fact, the only ones on which two or more items loaded with even moderate strength in the United States and were the three dominant factors in Mexico. Thus it would appear that the constraints which do exist among these items have a structure which might normally be expected. However, even with the use of a reduced communality estimate, the factor loadings of the different items were

Table 6-5
Factor Loadings of the Fertility Questions

Question	Mexico		United States
		Factor 1 Number of Children	
1	.36		.31
2	.79		.72
3	.64		.68
4	.63		.67
		Factor 2 Social Pressures	
6	−.38		−.53
8	−.56		−.49
11	−.17		−.37
14	−.38		
		Factor 3 Private Matter	
7	−.47		−.47
9	−.41		−.52
13	−.49		−.56

generally low and tended to show that the constraints which do exist are quite small.

In addition to the low level of constraints within each of the three factors, the factor analysis also showed that the factor underlying the number of children desired and considered desirable was almost completely unrelated to either of the other factors. What this means to the policymaker is that knowing that an individual is in favor of family planning adds nothing to the ability to guess whether or not he wants fewer children!

The Salience of Fertility Attitudes to
Fertility Behavior

Unfortunately the history of KAP studies has been characterized by the failure of researchers to realize that the attitudes and values they perceive to be salient to fertility behavior are not necessarily (and perhaps not even usually) the attitudes and values which are salient to the populations being studied. This lack of awareness on the part of KAP researchers has led to some unfortunate misconceptions concerning the actual determination of fertility behavior.

Previous studies which have attempted to relate attitudes and behavior have run into rather severe difficulties. As early as 1934, Richard LaPiere, in his classic study of attitudes and behavior, showed that knowledge of attitudes expressed verbally may not be of any value whatever when we want to predict overt behavior. His comments demonstrate how difficult it is to predict behavior on the basis of an attitude questionnaire:

The questionnaire is cheap, easy, and mechanical. The study of human behavior is time consuming, intellectually fatiguing, and depends for its success upon the ability of the investigator. The former method gives quantitative results, the latter mainly qualitative. Quantitative measurements are quantitatively accurate; qualitative evaluations are always subject to errors of human judgment. Yet it would seem far more worthwhile to make a shrewd guess regarding that which is essential than to accurately measure that which is likely to prove quite irrelevant.[22]

And, in a similar way, Fishbein sums up the results of the last seventy-five years of attitude research:

After more than seventy-five years of attitude research, there is still little, if any, consistent evidence supporting the hypothesis that knowledge of an individual's attitude toward some object will allow one to predict the way he will behave with respect to that object. Indeed, what little evidence there is to support any relationship between attitude and behavior comes from studies showing that a person tends to bring his attitudes into line with his behavior rather than studies demonstrating that behavior is a function of attitude.[23]

The difficulties involved in predicting behavior from verbally expressed attitudes stem from three major sources of error: (1) situational determinants; (2) competing attitudes and values; and, (3) the lack of saliency of an attitude.

The private attitudes which the respondent relates to the interviewer constitute only one variable in the determination of behavior; situational determinants also play an important role. As Melvin DeFleur and Frank Westie have written:

The lack of a straight-line relationship between verbal attitudes and overt action behavior . . . may be explained in terms of some sort of social involvement of the subject in a system of social constraints, preventing him from action (overtly) in the direction of his convictions.[24]

The conventional measures of attitudes do not examine these norms or constraints, and for this reason cannot correctly predict an individual's behavior when the value (norm) of the group in which the individual is socially involved is different from the individual's own desires.[25]

Hence it may well be that, as J. Mayone Stycos has explained, poll type surveys are often a most unreliable predictor of fertility behavior:

It is usually assumed that the "private, anonymous, and confidential" interview provides us with the most "valid" data, or at least the data which best predict behavior. However, . . . the articulations of an Indian woman in the presence of her in-laws might be a better predictor of her fertility than her more "honest" private thoughts articulated to a stranger with a notebook.[26]

Thus existing KAP studies and other surveys which attempt to predict behavior from attitudes are incomplete to the extent that they neglect to study the individual's perceptions of the social norms and standards of conduct which are involved in the situation as well as the importance he attaches to these norms and standards.

The second major obstacle to the prediction of behavior from attitudes develops from the fact that there exist competing attitudes and values in the determination of any behavioral act. For example, an individual may want five children, but for reasons of economy, concern for overpopulation, or worries about the mother's health he may limit his family size to only two children. To use another example, an individual may want only two children, but because he has unfavorable attitudes toward contraceptives he could end up with five children. It is important to remember that these competing values and attitudes are not static but are likely to change as an individual's situation changes.

A third barrier to the prediction of behavior from attitude questionnaires results from the structure—or lack of it—of an individual's attitudes, beliefs, and values. If an attitude is to be useful in the prediction of behavior the individual must make a connection between the attitude under study and the behavior which is being predicted (i.e., the attitude must be salient). Unfortunately for KAP researchers, however, the attitudes which they attempt to study are often not at all connected to the behavior they are endeavoring to predict.

The untrustworthiness of even the most basic assumptions concerning how an individual relates his attitudes to his behavior is illustrated by the assumption that the number of children a woman says she wants is important in the determination of how many children she will have. Although it may appear to the reader that an individual's response concerning the number of children she desires is salient to fertility behavior, this is not necessarily the case. This lack of saliency may be especially prevalent in the less developed countries. Among women in Lima, Peru, Stycos found that a majority of lower class women had *never* thought about how many children they wanted, and even among the upper classes one-third of the women had never given the subject any thought.[27]

If the above results are at all representative for much of the rest of Latin America and the Third World, it is difficult to imagine anyone attempting to predict behavior or make policy on the basis of an answer to a question about which individuals rarely think. Of course, even more remote to most individuals would be such questions as:

All things considered, do you think having a larger population would be a good thing or a bad thing for the country?

All things considered, how would you feel about a birth control program to encourage people in (survey country) to have fewer children—would you approve or disapprove of such a program?

Yet the United States Information Agency sponsored studies in twenty-two countries and collected data on 17,000 individuals asking precisely these questions.[28]

Frederick Stephen as early as 1962 discussed the above problems and warned future researchers of several common pitfalls in the measurement of fertility attitudes:

1. The attitudes which are the object of measurement probably do not exist in individuals in crystallized form.
2. The complexity of the relationship between attitudes and behavior may be ignored and therefore mistakes will be made when behavior is predicted from the few attitudes and motives which are usually measured.
3. Research may focus only on the individual's private attitudes rather than including the influence of the larger social group.
4. Simple ordering and ranking of preferences are not sufficient; better measurement techniques are needed and less reliance should be placed on survey interviews.[29]

In spite of Stephen's article and other similar critiques of attitude studies, researchers have continued to pursue KAP studies and fertility surveys with little regard to the degree of salience of the questions they ask or the complexity of the behavior they try to predict. Yet, until we begin to examine more closely the structure of the situations, values, goals, norms, and attitudes which are related to fertility, we have little basis for evaluating proposed policy alternatives. Because a successful program to reduce fertility requires the cooperation of many millions of decision-makers who are making their decisions beyond the view of governmental authorities, appropriate policies must be based on an understanding of how attitudes are learned and reinforced, which personality functions are served by fertility attitudes and behavior, under what situations given attitudes are likely to become salient, and by what means attitudes, values, and norms are most likely to be changed.[30]

Given the shortage of knowledge on most of the above questions, how can we begin to evaluate existing population policies? I think we can make several important conclusions which can aid us in determining the worth of the different types of policies. First, the advocates of policies of low coercion are probably incorrect in their belief that persons would have the number of children they say they want if only ideal contraceptives were available. The belief structure relating to fertility is far too complex and the salience of desired family size (as measured by the questionnaire) is far too low for family planning programs alone to be successful. Although it is easy to ask persons how many children they want, and easy for them to answer two or three or some other number, KAP studies do not give us any indication of what "want" means in this context.[31] In a twenty-year study of fertility, Westoff, Mishler, and Kelly found that the expressed desire of couples prior to child-bearing explained only 9 percent of the variance in the number of children actually born to these couples.[32]

The findings of the Westoff study and my own conclusions from the data gathered from the Mexican and American youths give support to the advocates of the medium and high coercion policies. In the Westoff study, while previously expressed desires could only explain 9 percent of the individual variance, the overall expressed mean of the young couples (2.64 for the males and 2.79 for the females) differed very little from the actual fertility of the group (2.62).[33] In my own study, the single variable which could predict desired family size better than *all* other variables combined was country. Thus it would appear that the particular social norms of a country are a major determining factor in fertility behavior. This process appears to work much as Ronald Freedman has suggested: social norms about reproduction are likely to specify a range of permissible behavior which if violated are likely to lead to sanctions by the society.[34]

If Freedman is correct in his estimation of the importance of social norms, the relevant question in the evaluation of high and medium coercion policies would be: How susceptible to rapid change are these social norms? If these norms are closely tied to relatively fixed social structures, patterns of behavior, and highly salient desires of individuals, then the fertility norms will be difficult to change and highly coercive policies may be necessary. If the norms are not securely fastened to such structures, patterns, and desires, then policies of a medium level of coercion are likely to be successful.

An example of a country in which these norms seem quite susceptible to change is the United States, which is currently in the midst of rapid change. In just five years (1965-1970) the expected family size among women in their twenties dropped by one-half child.[35] Although this change in expectations is the result of a combination of quite complex factors such as the current economic picture, the increase in the percentage of single women in their early twenties, concern about overpopulation, and new ideas concerning the role of women in society; this precipitous drop in fertility expectations shows that the society has moved a long way from the norm of the early sixties that "you should have as many children as you can afford because to do otherwise would be selfish."[36]

Although it would be foolhardy to generalize from only the experiences of the United States since 1965, the drop in both expected and actual fertility in the United States indicates that fertility attitudes and behavior can change rather rapidly in response to new situations or sets of choices. This evidence from a so-called "developed" country fits nicely with the findings of researchers in the "less developed" countries who have found that the completed family size will drop when alternatives to child-rearing are available for women,[37] when the quality and availability of land is restricted,[38] when the opportunities for and cost of education for children rise,[39] and when there are means other than a large number of children for guaranteeing security for old age.[40] All of the above findings would indicate that the fertility behavior of individuals is the result of rational responses to the material conditions of their lives and that if the alternatives to high fertility are expanded then the social norms will respond readily.

Appropriate Policies and Levels of Coercion

The level of knowledge concerning the determinants of fertility behavior is not high, and the findings of the data analysis in this chapter and of the other research cited are quite tentative and incomplete. Nevertheless, several countries have already adopted explicit population policies, and the United States Agency for International Development is presently attempting to influence other nations to adopt programs which will attempt to reduce fertility rates. What recommendations can be made concerning appropriate policies and levels of coercion?

I think that there can be little doubt that family planning policies alone will not accomplish a rapid reduction in birth rates. The structure and salience of fertility attitudes and beliefs are too low to create the type of demand for contraceptives which would be required for effective population control. The development of this demand requires that either the social norms about appropriate family size be changed or that sufficiently high sanctions or incentives be present. Thus the choice appears to be between policies employing medium or high coercion.

Although we do not have adequate information on most societies to determine whether a medium or a high amount of coercion is required, I would recommend that highly coercive policies should not be used at the present time. I argue this for three reasons, one normative and two practical. First, given the normative assumptions made at the beginning of this chapter, I believe the dangers of governmental intervention are sufficiently strong reasons to advocate that the government should not force individual decisions in this area until other, less coercive, means can be proven ineffective.

A second rationale for medium rather than high coercion is that most governments have neither the desire nor the capability to develop and implement effective birth control policies of a highly coercive nature. This lack of capability is particularly true in the less developed countries where most governments cannot collect taxes much less enforce a birth control policy upon an unwilling population. The third reason for attempting policies in the medium range of coercion stems from the findings in this article that most attitudes related to fertility are neither well structured nor highly salient. Because of the low saliency and structure of these attitudes, beliefs, and values they might be susceptible to rapid change through information or propaganda programs which can aid individuals in relating low fertility to highly desirable social norms and important individual desires. Once desired family size becomes salient to the individual then a family planning program could be effective. In fact, it would seem likely that existing family planning programs can be useful in making appropriate fertility-related attitudes salient to the community.

Before any medium range policy can be implemented it is necessary to make a careful analysis of the choices available to the population. This type of study cannot be done by an interviewer simply conducting an "improved" KAP survey. Rather, both *behavior* and the *environment* within which it occurs must be studied to determine the major pressures which are producing high fertility behavior. Such a study would aid the policymaker in his efforts to design a program applicable to the situation in his country. For example, if an analysis of the determinants of fertility showed that fertility norms and behavior were closely tied to economic considerations such as having children as a form of old age insurance, then the policymaker would know that his program to reduce fertility rates would need to include economic incentives such as increased welfare for the aged as well as the educational or propaganda efforts which would be needed to make this alternative salient to the potential consumers of the program.

In addition to an understanding of the structure of fertility-related beliefs and attitudes and an analysis of the strength of the different competing factors in the decision to engage in unprotected sexual intercourse, an understanding of each government's capacity to implement alternative policies is essential to a successful birth control program. It is often forgotten that a bad policy can be worse than no policy if the incorrectly conceived attempt at lowering the birth rates results in either a strong reaction by the citizenry or the development of an interest group dedicated to the maintenance of the bad policy.[41] The capacity of different governments to effect different types of birth control programs must be a priority subject for political scientists interested in population policy research.

Conclusions

In the examination of the interrelations among the different attitudes and values usually believed to be associated with fertility behavior we have found that the logical and constrained structure often attributed to these attitudes and values is quite weak. In fact, the salience of most of the attitudes usually studied in KAP studies is quite low. These findings lead us to reject those policies which rely solely on the family planning approach, since it is unlikely that such policies, by themselves, will significantly lower fertility. The reason for this expectation of failure is that "desired family size for self" is rarely thought about among significant sectors of the population, is unrelated to other fertility attitudes and values, and is, therefore, not likely to be related to behavior.

The more important factor in the determination of the number of children born is the social norm concerning the "appropriate" family size. This norm is itself a combination of many other factors such as economic and family structures. The importance of social norms means that birth control policies must either change these norms or provide sufficient sanctions to overcome them. Because most governments have neither the desire nor the capacity to enforce strong sanctions, because it is not desirable from the individual point of view that they do so, and because the weak structure of fertility-related attitudes and values suggests that the norms are capable of rapid change, it would seem that policies of medium level coercion are at present most appropriate. The exact nature of these policies must be determined by a careful analysis of the relationship of fertility norms to the choices available to the individuals within each society.

Notes

1. For an extensive bibliography of studies which attempt to relate social and psychological factors to fertility see James T. Fawcett, *Psychology and Population: Behavioral Research Issues in Fertility and Family Planning* (New York: The Population Council, 1970).

2. Theodore Lowi, "Population Policies and the Political System" Chapter 3 of Richard L. Clinton, William S. Flash, and R. Kenneth Godwin, eds., *Political Science in Population Studies* (Lexington, Mass.: D.C. Heath & Co., 1972): 45-91.

3. The last two criteria are adapted from Christian Bay, *The Structure of Freedom* (Palo Alto: Stanford University Press, 1958).

4. Obviously the above trichotomy is not representative of any particular set of writers, and it is doubtful that any one writer would fit exactly either the low or high coercion types. Most writers will, however, fit fairly closely one of the three categories. For examples of the differing views see Daniel Callahan, ed., *The American Population Debate* (Garden City: Doubleday, 1971).

5. A list and explanation of most of the recent population policy proposals can be found in Bernard Berelson, "Beyond Family Planning," *Studies in Family Planning*, no. 38 (February 1969): 1-16.

6. A full list of these proposals can be found in Berelson (n. 5): 2-3, sections B, D, E, and F.

7. Examples of this group of policy advocates are Sloan Wayland, "Family Planning and the School Curriculum," in Bernard Berelson et al., eds., *Family Planning and Population Programs* (Chicago: University of Chicago Press, 1966), pp. 353-362; and Pravin Visaria, "Population Assumptions and Policy," *Economic Weekly* 8 (August 1964): 1343.

8. These particular samples were chosen on the basis of criteria which were important to the study of attitudes and behavior believed to be related to modernization. I am well aware of the difficulties involved in using this age group to study fertility attitudes and values. Nevertheless, evidence which will be presented later in this chapter indicates that the attitude structures of these persons are quite representative of the adult populations of the United States and Mexico.

9. *Selected Questionnaires on Knowledge, Attitudes, and Practice of Family Planning*, Volumes I and II (New York: The Population Council, Demographic Division, 1967).

10. Joseph Kahl, *The Measurement of Modernism: A Study of Values in Mexico and Brazil* (Austin: University of Texas Press, 1966).

11. These scales were adapted from those developed by Kahl and were changed only slightly to correct for the response set bias of Kahl's questionnaire. For the entire questionnaires used in both studies see Kahl (n. 10): 30-34, and R. Kenneth Godwin, *Attitudes and Behavior Related to Modernization* (Chapel Hill: The Carolina Population Center, Program Design and Policy Analysis Series, no. 6, 1972): 170-210.

12. At the heart of the theory of the demographic transition is the postulate that modernization and more "modern" attitudes create more antinatal attitudes and values. A more complete discussion of this hypothesis can be found in Godwin (n. 11), Chapter 7, and William Clifford, "Modern and Traditional Value Orientations and Fertility Behavior: A Social Demographic Study," *Demography* 8, 1 (February 1971): 37-48.

13. A discussion of the ecological fallacy can be found in W. Phillips Shively, " 'Ecological' Inference: The Use of Aggregate Data to Study Individuals," *American Political Science Review* 63, 4 (December 1969): 1183-1196.

14. For discussions of the importance of the structure to behavior see Phillip Converse, "The Nature of Belief Systems in Mass Publics," pp. 205-260 of David Apter, ed., *Ideology and Discontent* (Glencoe, Illinois: The Free Press, 1964); C.R. Tittle and R.J. Hill, "Attitude Measurement and the Prediction of Behavior: An Evaluation of Condition and Measurement Techniques," *Sociometry* 30, 3 (September 1967): 199-213; and Chester Insko, Robert Blake, Robert Cialdini, and Stanly Mulaik, "Attitudes Toward Birth Control and Cognitive Consistency: Theoretical and Practical Implications of Survey Data," *Journal of Personality and Social Psychology* 16, 2 (1970): 228-237.

15. Insko, Blake, Cialdini, and Mulaik (n. 14).

16. Godwin (n. 11).

17. Kahl (n. 10).

18. Ibid., 74.

19. Actually this overall similarity in results is even more surprising when it is realized that Kahl's measure of ideal family size consisted of only one question while the measure used in the present study was a summed scale of three questions. Also all value scales used in the present study were slightly different from those used by Kahl because I attempted to correct the response set bias found in Kahl's questionnaire.

20. Clifford (n. 12): 37-48.

21. A discussion of this problem and the correction by means of a lowering of the communality estimate can be found in the factor analysis chapter of Norman Nie, D.H. Bent, and C.H. Hull, *Statistical Package for the Social Sciences* (New York: McGraw Hill, 1970): 208-244.

22. Richard LaPiere, "Attitudes versus Actions," pp. 26-31 of Martin Fishbein, ed., *Readings in Attitude Theory and Measurement* (New York: John Wiley and Sons, Inc., 1967): 31.

23. Martin Fishbein, "Attitudes and the Prediction of Behavior," in Fishbein, ibid., 477.

24. Melvin L. DeFleur and Frank R. Westie, "Verbal Attitudes and Overt Acts: An Experiment on the Salience of Attitudes," *American Sociological Review* 23, 6 (December 1958): 667.

25. Ibid., 668.

26. J. Mayone Stycos, "Opinion, Ideology, and Population Problems: Some Sources of Domestic and Foreign Opposition to Birth Control," pp. 533-566 of National Academy of Sciences, *Rapid Population Growth: Consequences and Implications* (Baltimore and London: The Johns Hopkins Press, 1971): 533.

27. J. Mayone Stycos, *Human Fertility in Latin America* (Ithaca, New York: Cornell University Press, 1968): 155-158.

28. These were two of four questions which the United States Information Agency gathered from over 17,000 interviews in twenty-two countries, quoted in Stycos (n. 26): 534-536.

29. Frederick F. Stephen, "Possibilities and Pitfalls in the Measurement of Attitudes and Opinions on Family Planning," in C.V. Kiser, ed., *Research in Family Planning* (Princeton, N.J.: Princeton University Press, 1962): 423-431.

30. Fawcett (n. 1): 112.

31. Stephen (n. 29): 426.

32. Charles Westoff, Elliot Mishler, and Lowell Kelly, "Preferences in Size of Family and Eventual Fertility Twenty Years After," *American Journal of Sociology* 62, 5 (March 1957): 491-497.

33. Ibid., 494.

34. Ronald Freedman, "Expectations About Family Size." Paper prepared for a luncheon roundtable discussion at the annual meeting of the American Sociological Association, San Francisco, California, August 1967. Quoted in S.O.

Gustavus and Charles B. Nam, "The Formation and Stability of Ideal Family Size Among Young People," *Demography* 7 (February 1970): 43.

35. Charles Westoff and Norman Ryder, 1970 *National Fertility Study*. Reported in *The New York Times* (November 5, 1965): 281.

36. Lee Rainwater, *Family Design: Marital Sexualtiy, Family Size, and Contraception* (Chicago: Aldine Publishing Co., 1965), p. 281.

37. Marc Nerlove and Paul Schultz, *Love and Life Between the Censuses: A Model of Family Decision Making in Puerto Rico, 1950-1960*, The Rand Corporation, RM-6322-AID, September 1970, and Julie DeVanzo, *The Determinants of Family Formation in Chile, 1960: An Econometric Study of Female Labor Force Participation, Marriage, and Fertility Decisions*, The Rand Corporation, R-830-AID, February 1972.

38. David S. Kleinman, "Fertility Variation and Resources in Rural India, 1961," *Economic Development and Cultural Change* (forthcoming).

39. Paul Schultz, "An Economic Perspective on Population Growth," pp. 148-174 of National Academy of Sciences (n. 26): 154, and Oliver Finnigan, III, and T.H. Sun, "Planning, Starting, and Operating an Educational Incentives Project," *Studies in Family Planning* 3, 1 (January 1972): 1-7.

40. Finnigan and Sun, ibid.

41. For a discussion of problems created when a policy change is attempted see Lowi (n. 2), and Peter Bachrach and Elihu Bergman, "Participation and Conflict in Making American Population Policy" paper prepared for the Commission on Population Growth and the American Future, 1971.

Gerald C. Wright, Jr.

The increase in concern for population problems within the United States can be seen as a product of its place on two fronts of current political activism: the role of family planning in combating poverty, often cited as central to "breaking the poverty cycle" and, second, the "population problem" as a central factor contributing to the deterioration of the physical and cultural environment.

Anticipating vastly increased expenditures in the area of fertility control, the questions must be addressed of where and in what manner this money is to be used. The purpose of this paper is to examine the need for family planning services among the poor in North Carolina and suggest in a preliminary manner possible strategies for the effective implementation of family planning programs in the south.

The data analyzed here were collected as part of a larger survey conducted by the Research Triangle Institute in 1965 under the auspices of the North Carolina Fund.[1] The total sample for the whole survey contained over 13,000 respondents; this paper focuses on a subsample of 2,788 respondents. These are the females of reproductive age who responded to the series of questions concerning attitudes toward family planning and the usage of different contraceptive methods.

I. Focus and Concepts

The purpose of this study is to ascertain the extent of need for public family planning services and to identify areas where these activities need to be increased. Past research indicates that the poor have larger families yet, in general, desire families of the same size desired by the middle class. The outstanding exception to the general pattern that the poor desire families of sizes equal to those of the middle class are the Southern blacks of rural background.[2] Summarizing a number of studies conducted nationally and in Northern cities, Hill and Jaffe write:

These analyses strongly suggest that continuing high fertility is more a consequence of the Negro's disproportionately low socio-economic status than any other factor. This conclusion is reinforced when one unique variable—Southern farm background—is independently traced. Current higher fertility levels among nonwhites are the result partly of the unusually high fertility of the minority of nonwhite couples who presently live in the rural South and partly of the *moderately* high fertility of the many nonwhite couples who were born on Southern farms and have since emigrated.[3]

It is this exception that necessitates separate study of the poor of the South in formulating local family planning policies appropriate to that region. The article quoted above suggests that mobile blacks assimilate the family size norms of the middle class and that the major objective and needs of population policy will then be the same for all races. In North Carolina, as in much of the South, we are dealing with a rural population which is relatively stable, and whose norms and practices concerning family size cannot be assumed to be subject to significant change by assimilation. Thus one purpose of this paper is to examine this question with the goal in mind of discovering the degree to which effective population policy ought to consider racial characteristics and, if so, what these considerations ought to be. In short, population policies formulated and successful in other parts of the country cannot be assumed to be the optimal policies for the South.

Need

The central concept of this paper is "need" for family planning services. The various operational definitions current in the literature of family planning can be divided into two categories. First, need may be defined by the observer. A rather sophisticated definition of "excessive births" is used by C. Horace Hamilton which is based on the age of the mother and order of the newborn child. For example, a child born to a woman age twenty-eight who already has two children is not considered an excessive birth. If the same woman had already given birth to three children, the offspring would be considered "excessive." The justification for this type of observer-defined need is threefold: (1) the desire for "some sort of reasonable and convenient statistical criterion," (2) "such limits are in the interest of both the individual family and society," and (3) to maintain the population.[4]

A number of objections can be raised concerning an observer-defined criterion of what constitutes an excessive family size. At a minimum, such criteria could tend to shift the emphasis of population programs from policies designed to assist the individual control his family size and spacing to policies designed to regulate family fertility. Moreover, observer-defined criteria, if widely accepted over a long enough period of time, could help lay the foundation for coercive policies which would constitute serious infringements on what many, including this writer, feel are basic human rights.

The vision of coercive, highly regulatory population policies in the United

States is not a completely imagined danger. Bills for the compulsory sterilization of unwed mothers have been introduced in at least nine state legislatures.[5] In his article "Beyond Family Planning" Bernard Berelson surveys a number of potential "involuntary fertility control" politics which have been advocated by various groups and individuals. These range from marketable licenses to have children to compulsory induced abortion for all illegitimate pregnancies.[6]

Coercive policies such as these are certainly undesirable, and the data presented here indicate, unnecessary. A prerequisite for coercive policies is that the policymaker rather than the individual defines one's need for fertility control services. To the extent that need for contraceptive services is defined by the policymaker there may be a tendency for family planning to be something that is done *to* a person. A preferred alternative is to view family planning as something done *by* a person, with governmental assistance as it proves necessary.

If birth control is something done by a person, it follows that the individual also decides when it is necessary—"need" is, therefore, defined by the individual. By saying a woman is "in need' of contraceptives, it is meant that she is of reproductive age and has expressed a desire not to have any more children. It does not mean that she consciously desires artificial contraceptives, but only that through her responses during the interview she has indicated the desire to limit her family to at least its present size. One of the goals of this paper is to find the relationship between expressed desires not to have more children and usage and attitudes toward contraceptives.

It should be pointed out that consideration of the spacing or interval function of contraceptives is omitted in this study. The data simply do not allow this question to be addressed. If we were able to measure this important aspect of need, the estimates of the proportion of women in need of family planning services would be considerably greater.

Operationally a woman is defined as being in need if she indicated that (1) she wished to have no additional children or (2) her present number of children either equals or exceeds the number she gave for the "best number of children to have." This second factor was included because of the large number of cases coded "not answered" and "don't know" for the additional children measure. The comparison of the actual and ideal number of children serves as a reliability check on the first measure. For the cases in which there were valid responses on the additional children measure, the vast majority of classifications agreed with the comparison measure.

Attitudes

To determine a person's disposition toward contraception each respondent was asked: "Many people do things to keep from getting pregnant. Do you think that this is a good idea?" The answers were coded: yes, depends, no. All other responses (did not know, refused to answer) are excluded from analysis. The respondents were then asked why they felt as they did. The four response categories with more than 5 percent of the respondents are financial reasons, endangers health, large families are a burden, and religious or moral reasons.

Usage

Women were classified as (current) contraceptive users if they stated they were using at least one of the following means of contraception: pills, diaphragm, condoms, tube jellies, foam, the IUD, or if they had had an operation which prevented conception.

Unmet Need

The most relevant group for the policy formulator consists of those mothers who (1) are in need of contraceptives, but (2) are not currently utilizing an accepted means of reliable birth control. These persons are termed as having an "unmet need" for family planning services. They are the focal group of this paper; we seek to find out their racial, economic, educational, and residential characteristics. Then the task is to ascertain their attitudes toward the use of contraceptives and, finally, by inference, to suggest some possible reasons why they are less successful in limiting their families at their desired level.

Location of Residence

Characteristics of the place of residence—"city" or "rural"—are taken from assessments of the interviewers. Homes said to be in a city or town are classified as city; if the place of residence was a farm or rural non-farm it is classified here as rural. These do not refer to the Bureau of the Census' distinction based on Standard Metropolitan Statistical Areas.

The remaining variables of our analysis—race, educational level, and income—are self-defining.

II. Data and Analysis

An overview of the relationship of the actual and desired number of children for the different demographic groups can be seen in Table 7-1. By subtracting the mean desired number from the mean actual number of children we get a rough index of how successful each of these groups is in attaining their ideal family size. The whole sample has .17 children less than what they would like. One can readily see, however, that it is among the very poor (under $3,000 per year family income), the poorly educated, and the blacks that the present family size exceeds what is desired. (A positive value for the index indicates that there are more children than desired.) This is true in spite of the fact that these groups consistently desire larger families than the more advantaged. The largest differentiation is on the variable of education. We would conclude that this is a function of having a larger number of categories were it not for the very strong support received in related research.[7] Because of the importance placed on the Southern rural black by Whelpton et al., as an exceptional case, the data will be analyzed in terms of four groups defined by the intersection of place of residence and race.

With no more knowledge than that contained in Table 7-1, one would be inclined to conclude that the greatest need is among blacks, families making less than $3,000/year, and mothers with less than a high school education. But there is also likely to be the suspicion that the relationship between race and fertility is spurious, since we can be quite sure that race is strongly associated with income and education. The relationship, however, is not that simple.

Table 7-1
Mean Number of Children and Desired Number of Children Among the Poor on Selected Variables*

Poverty Indicator	$\bar{X}$ Actual No. of Children	$\bar{X}$ Desired No. of Children	Difference Actual–Desired
All respondents	2.90 (2164)	3.07 (2286)	−.17
Income			
Under $3,000	3.27 (907)	3.11 (773)	.16
$3,000-$5,000	2.77 (581)	3.07 (496)	−.30
Over $5,000	2.51 (676)	3.00 (564)	−.49
Education			
0-6th grade	3.51 (347)	3.31 (282)	.20
7-9th grade	3.32 (741)	3.16 (637)	.16
10-12th grade	2.59 (1362)	2.97 (1145)	−.38
Some college	2.09 (271)	2.92 (220)	−.83
Race			
Black	3.33 (1146)	3.11 (955)	.22
White	2.48 (1516)	3.01 (1286)	−.53
Residence			
Rural	3.07 (959)	3.20 (787)	−.13
City	2.74 (1745)	2.99 (1481)	−.25

*The figures in parentheses in this and succeeding tables are the N's on which calculations are based.

When the differences between black and white are compared, with education and location of residence controlled (Table 7-2), we see that each of these factors is independently related to fertility (actual number of children). Blacks with the least education living in rural areas have the most children. Those with the smallest families are blacks who have attended college and live in more urbanized areas. They are followed closely by college educated rural blacks and city dwelling whites of equal education. An interesting pattern emerges if one takes smaller families as evidence of an assimilation into middle-class norms and life style, for then education appears to serve as a vehicle for the adoption of middle-class norms of family size. The effect of increased education on the desire for smaller families appears to be greater for blacks than for whites.

From Table 7-2, one also can conclude that there is a much greater consensus on the best size for a family than is attained in practice. The difference between the actual and the desired number of children can serve as an index of how successful the respondents were in limiting their families to their desired size. With the exception of those who have attended college, the average black family at each educational level already had larger families than they wanted. In contrast, only whites with less than a seventh grade education had families which were, on the average, larger than they would like.

The severity of the discrepancy between the actual and the ideal is perhaps an even more important dimension than the relative number of groups which have larger families. In these terms the serious problems of the woman's inability to contain her fertility at desired levels are centered in the low educated rural black segment of the population. It is this group which is having *more* children than they would like. These women may be referred to as "hyperfecund" so as to succinctly distinguish them from those who have exactly the number of children they desire and desire no more, "parity," and those who wish to enlarge their families, "subfecund."

The addition of those who are hyperfecund and at parity yields the number of women who are seen as in need of some means of contraception. The incidence of this need is shown in Table 7-3 for the race/residential groups controlling for our poverty indicators.

The percentages in the table refer to the proportion of the women in each category (e.g., rural blacks with less than a seventh grade education) who desire not to have any more children. Though there is some relationship of race and poverty to the desire not to have more children it is in the opposite direction from what many would expect. The less educated, the low income, and generally blacks have a higher proportion of their number wishing to stop the growth of their families. In terms of interest to the policy formulator, the desire to halt family growth is found more among the poorer groups than the middle class. Of course, this is merely a restatement of the earlier findings that it is the poor who are least successful at attaining parity.

Table 7-2

Comparison of Desired and Actual Number of Children for Race/Residential Groups by Education

	Blacks				Whites			
	X̄ Actual No. of Children	X̄ Desired No. of Children	Difference Actual-Desired	N	X̄ Actual No. of Children	X̄ Desired No. of Children	Difference Actual-Desired	N
Rural								
0-6th grade	4.48	3.78	.70	(50)	3.73	3.46	.27	(44)
7-9th grade	4.66	3.52	1.14	(93)	3.05	3.24	-.19	(156)
10-12th grade	3.15	3.07	.08	(85)	2.17	2.99	-.82	(286)
Some college	2.20	2.80	-.60	(5)	2.35	2.69	-.34	(42)
City								
0-6th grade	3.23	3.17	.06	(115)	3.16	3.06	.10	(63)
7-9th grade	3.29	3.05	.24	(198)	2.61	3.01	-.40	(177)
10-12th grade	3.01	2.96	.05	(335)	2.25	2.95	-.70	(407)
Some college	1.87	3.02	-1.15	(63)	2.20	2.97	-.77	(103)

Table 7-3

Percentage in Need of Contraception for Race/Residential Groups by Education and Income

Poverty Indicator	Percentage in Need of Contraception									
	Rural Blacks %		City Blacks %		Rural Whites %		City Whites %		Total %	
Education										
0-6th grade	78	(50)	66	(111)	66	(44)	76	(62)	70	(267)
7-9th grade	76	(93)	65	(190)	65	(155)	59	(175)	65	(613)
10-12th grade	65	(85)	63	(328)	57	(270)	55	(396)	59	(1079)
Some College	60	(5)	46	(61)	67	(42)	53	(100)	54	(208)
Income										
Under $3,000	75	(146)	67	(331)	59	(123)	58	(131)	65	(731)
$3,000-$5,000	54	(37)	59	(143)	58	(123)	57	(166)	58	(469)
Over $5,000	80	(10)	56	(78)	68	(145)	61	(306)	62	(539)

Usage of Contraceptives and Unmet Need

The most successful means of fertility control is through the use of artificial contraceptives; hence the immediate goal of family planning programs is the greater use of more reliable contraceptives. Of interest, therefore, is the present incidence of the use of modern means of birth control. Table 7-4 shows the percentage of respondents using contraceptives. It is immediately apparent that the use of artificial contraceptive methods is strongly related to the indicators of socioeconomic poverty.

Table 7-4

Percentage of Contraceptive Users by Racial/Residential Groups by Education and Income

Poverty Indicator	Percentage Using Some Type of Contraceptive									
	Rural Blacks %		City Blacks %		Rural Whites %		City Whites %		Total %	
Education										
0-6th grade	10	(68)	11	(140)	22	(51)	21	(78)	15	(337)
7-9th grade	23	(115)	17	(236)	32	(180)	29	(203)	25	(734)
10-12th grade	20	(110)	26	(405)	42	(348)	40	(498)	35	(1361)
Some College	43	(7)	29	(77)	33	(55)	45	(130)	38	(269)
Income										
Under $3,000	21	(180)	18	(401)	20	(149)	25	(153)	20	(883)
$3,000-$5,000	21	(44)	27	(172)	46	(152)	37	(209)	35	(577)
Over $5,000	20	(15)	31	(99)	47	(190)	41	(380)	41	(684)

The city-rural differences are smaller and less consistent than the differences based either on race or education and income. It is rather surprising that city dwellers do not use contraceptives at a consistently higher rate than those in rural areas. It was expected that the greater flow of information and more intensified heterogeneous social interaction associated with more urbanized living would facilitate the individual's exposure to and eventual adoption of modern contraceptive methods. Clearly, however, at least these data do not support this thinking.

A program designed to bring contraceptives to those who need them would optimally not be based on just those who do not want more children, nor on those who are not using contraceptives, but on both these groups. That is, the primary focal group of a family planning program would initially be those who wish to limit the size of their families *and* who are not presently utilizing the methods by which to accomplish this. This focal group is here referred to as those respondents with an "unmet need" for contraceptives. Knowing that the desire to have no more children is greater among the rural poor (Tables 7-2 and 7-3), and that the use of contraceptives is associated with being white and having more education and income, one could predict that the highest unmet need is among the poor. Table 7-5 shows this to be the case. For the entire sample the differences between the highest and lowest categories of education and income are 33 percent and 20 percent, respectively. The percentages of each race/residential group with unmet need for family planning services are as follows: rural blacks, 54%; city blacks, 45%; rural whites, 32%; and city whites, 32%.

Combining this with the data presented in Table 7-5 one can see that each of the factors of race, place of residence, income, and education is independently related to the extent of unmet need. The only exception is that place of residence does not appear to be consistently related to unmet need among whites.

Table 7-5
Percentage with Unmet Need Among Race/Residential Groups by Education and Income

Poverty Indicator	Rural Blacks %		City Blacks %		Rural Whites %		City Whites %		Total %	
					Percentage with Unmet Need					
Education										
0-6th grade	66	(50)	58	(113)	52	(46)	57	(63)	58	(272)
7-9th grade	54	(97)	50	(199)	38	(163)	39	(184)	45	(643)
10-12th grade	50	(91)	43	(343)	27	(294)	29	(426)	34	(1154)
Some College	17	(6)	27	(64)	33	(46)	23	(113)	26	(229)
Income										
Under $3,000	54	(152)	54	(344)	45	(127)	45	(136)	51	(759)
$3,000-$5,000	49	(39)	39	(150)	26	(134)	33	(176)	34	(499)
Over $5,000	55	(11)	29	(83)	30	(164)	31	(334)	31	(592)

What can one infer from these results? Our interpretation is that the inability to limit one's family to the size one would like stems from the same causes which account for the other "inabilities" of the poor: the inability to achieve a higher economic status, the inability to attain a higher education, the inability to find better employment, and the inability to fully utilize what governmental help has been made available; in short, the inability to achieve a better life for one's self and one's family. Further, the failure to utilize contraceptive methods must be seen in a larger picture of poverty than just the economic aspect. Some readily available contraceptives are not prohibitively expensive, though some families are no doubt so economically deprived that the purchase of a pack of condoms must be balanced against the cost of feeding one's children. More often it is probably a function of what is commonly referred to as the "culture of poverty." That is, the use of contraceptives is not a part of the relevant subculture for many of the poor. The information which is most often received concerning contraceptives probably comes through peer groups rather than from competent medical personnel. If this is true (we have no way of testing this with our data) it is quite likely that the existing beliefs about fertility control methods are less than conducive to their use.

Surprisingly, no research was found that addresses the question of the extent to which attitudes toward contraceptives are products of peer group and/or subcultural norms. Though we will examine some attitudes toward the use of contraceptives below, it is unfortunate that we will not be able to state the extent to which these are determined by the adoption of norms and mores of "relevant others." Given the extent to which many political and social attitudes/behaviors may be attributed to familial and social interactions, this is probably a useful perspective from which to view the attitude transmissions concerning the use of contraceptives.

Attitudes toward Contraception

In the design of a strategy or strategies of a family planning program, it would be useful to know the extent to which the poor's failure to utilize contraceptives is a function of negative attitudes and the extent to which the failure is a matter of simply not engaging in approved forms of behavior. Further, in the attempt to emphasize the attractiveness of contraceptives to those in need of them, one would want to know what the poor see as both positive and negative reasons for their use, for the success of an educational campaign is largely contingent upon the degree of the congruence of the values of the potential recipient and the values emphasized in the campaign.

First, we will examine the general predispositions of the poor toward birth control. Table 7-6 shows the distribution of positive responses to the question of whether or not the respondent thinks it is a good idea to do things to keep from

Table 7-6

Percentages of Approval of Birth Control for Race/Residential Groups by Education and Income

Poverty Indicator	Rural Blacks %		City Blacks %		Rural Whites %		City Whites %		Total %	
			Percentage Approving of Birth Control							
Education										
0-6th grade	32	(63)	39	(135)	51	(47)	44	(72)	41	(317)
7-9th grade	42	(106)	52	(223)	52	(176)	65	(196)	54	(701)
10-12th grade	48	(103)	58	(386)	71	(332)	71	(488)	65	(1309)
Some college	57	(7)	61	(70)	82	(55)	80	(128)	75	(260)
Income										
Under $3,000	40	(169)	54	(383)	49	(142)	60	(151)	52	(845)
$3,000-$5,000	46	(41)	57	(162)	68	(148)	61	(200)	60	(551)
Over $5,000	71	(14)	57	(94)	75	(185)	76	(373)	73	(666)

getting pregnant. As with the usage of contraceptives and the other dimensions we have looked at, approval of the use of contraceptives is positively related to education, income, living in a city, and being white. It should be noted however, that the proportions approving are considerably higher than the proportions using contraceptives. The effect of one's place of residence discriminates more consistently among blacks than among whites on this variable. Also of interest is the finding that the respondents are more widely distributed on the education dimension than on that of income. This provides partial support for the thinking that, while poverty is commonly thought of in economic terms, many of the norms and behavioral patterns are better attributed to informational variables of which education is a rough indicator.

Whatever the causal factor(s), it is important to realize that those most in need of contraceptives are also those least predisposed to utilize them. The low percentages of the blacks and of the poorly educated who are favorable to birth control suggest strongly that the solutions to the population problem among the poor may have to go deeper than merely making contraceptives available.

If we look at the primary policy focal group, that is those with an unmet need for some type of birth control, the patterns are quite similar (Table 7-7). We have not controlled for education and income in this table because the small cell frequencies would be very unstable. Fifty-seven percent of those in need of contraceptives but who are not using them are in favor of their use. These people, it would seem, would be the most susceptible to family planning services if they were readily available. Expansions of the present family planning programs in North Carolina, which are primarily making contraceptives available (and to a much lesser extent making it known that they are available), would probably get most of their new clients from this group.

Table 7-7

Attitudes Toward Contraception Among Those With An Unmet Need for Birth Control by Race/Residential Groups

Favor Contraception?	Rural Blacks %	City Blacks %	Rural Whites %	City Whites %	Total %
Yes	41	56	55	67	57
Depends	10	12	21	16	15
No	49	32	24	17	28
	100	100	100	100	100
N =	(123)	(311)	(175)	(245)	(854)

The "depends" group are probably ambivalent; not being strongly opposed they could probably be reached through an intensified educational campaign. Such campaigns should emphasize those positive values which the group is already inclined to see and correct what erroneous ideas they may now have.

The explicitly opposed group presents a challenge of a different order. In some cases, the woman may be morally opposed to the use of contraceptives as a matter of religious doctrine. In such cases the advocates of family planning can probably do no more than emphasize the values of a small family economically and encourage the use of less reliable techniques such as the rhythm method. A portion of these women, however, may be opposed to the use of artificial contraceptives on the basis of ideas they have which may be quite in error. Changing such incorrect notions as to what the consequences of the use of contraceptives may be is largely a matter of education. Strongly held beliefs on this subject are not likely to be dispelled on the basis of a few mass mailings or on the word of a welfare worker. Rather the proper information will be most effective if channeled through existing sources considered legitimate and reliable by the potential user. More innovative policies along these lines will have to be developed and implemented if the approximately 40 percent of blacks and 20 percent of whites who are in need of contraception are to be able to limit the size of their families at the level they desire.

What are the explanations offered for positive and negative attitudes toward family planning? What values do people see as involved with the idea of contraception? Table 7-8 shows the types of values cited by the respondents with an unmet need for contraceptives as explanations for their attitudes.

Only those categories which contained at least 5 percent of the total sample are represented. A small number of respondents gave reasons such as family planning was a means of population control, it is up to the individual, and that it was "not wrong." Because "population control" is often associated with charges of family planning programs as subtle forms of genocide or with excessive governmental interference in the individual's private affairs it might be thought

Table 7-8

Reasons Explaining Attitudes Toward Contraception for Race/Residential Groups for Those with Unmet Need

Favor Use of Contraceptives?	Rural Blacks %	City Blacks %	Rural Whites %	City Whites %	Total %
Yes N = 459					
Financial	57	61	66	64	63
Large Families a Burden	22	16	7	8	12
Endanger Health	7	1	3	2	2
Religious	2	2	–	1	1
Other	13	20	24	1	22
Depends N = 117					
Financial	58	35	52	46	45
Large Families a Burden	–	3	–	–	1
Endanger Health	8	16	16	5	12
Religious	–	5	–	5	3
Moral	–	–	–	–	–
Other	33	41	32	43	39
Opposed N = 222					
Financial	–	–	3	3	1
Large Families a Burden	–	2	–	–	1
Endanger Health	59	36	27	30	39
Religious	34	41	53	51	43
Other	7	21	18	16	16

to evoke strongly negative feelings. Somewhat surprisingly, however, the majority of those who cited population control were in favor of contraception. In any case these responses were very rare.

Among those with a favorable disposition toward birth control its predominant virtue is seen in financial terms. It appears that a large proportion of the respondents perceive the role family planning can play in combating poverty. Though they may not speak of it in such terms, clearly they are aware that children cost money—money that they are able to visualize as being spent in other ways.

One of the major findings of previous research is the wide-spread concern of parents for the life opportunities of their offspring. There seems to be a common wish to be able to "give my kids the breaks I never had as a kid."[8] Whatever the nature of the psychological mechanism which connects fertility and one's finances, it is clear that the majority of those favorable to birth control do make this connection.

The only other factor that was given any large frequency was that large families impose a burden. Unfortunately we are unable to say what the nature of the burden is. Presumably it is in economic or social terms: overcrowding of the home, too much work for the mother, etc. There is little difference on this question between race/residential groups, though rural blacks appear to see the advantages slightly more in terms of alleviating the burdens of a large family.

The undecided group can be broken into two sections: those assigning a positive value to contraception and those citing primarily negative aspects. As with those in favor of contraception, the majority of these women focused primarily on the financial dimension. A large portion of this group apparently base their attitude on idiosyncratic factors that were difficult to code—hence over a third of the reasons given were classified as "other." The rural-city distinction appears to differentiate the respondents in this category according to the frequency of financial reasons cited. People in more urbanized areas apparently are undecided more often about the non-economic aspects of contraception than those in the rural areas, who are more prone to see the financial benefits of birth control. But having recorded a positive reason for their attitude toward contraception, we are at a loss to account for their indecision. A minority of the undecided showed concern for the possible dangers to one's health, with an even smaller proportion giving religious or moral reasons for their hesitance.

Opposition to contraception among those who do not want more children lies in moral-religious objections and concerns of dangers to one's health. Rural blacks were most concerned about the health hazards, while the modal responses for the other groups were religious and moral in nature.

The religious and moral objections to contraception are a bit confounding. Only about 5 percent of the sample were Roman Catholic, which is usually seen as the major group giving moral objections to the use of artificial contraceptives. One student has suggested that these objections are intimately related to the fundamentalist ethos which is prevalent in the South.[9] According to this thesis the fatalism associated with the fundamentalist view of the world works to inhibit the adoption of contraceptives, which are seen as interference with the will of God. This is in line with one of the major interpretations of the role religion has played for the Southern black. For the totally oppressed, the hope of a better life to come, if one bears this life's burdens, makes one's existence more tolerable. With the forces of oppression decreased, however, this view of the world becomes dysfunctional for making the best of this life. In short, some contend that the fundamentalist perspective has outlived its usefulness for the Southern black and now works as an inhibiting force to his economic and social advancement.

There is a good deal of plausibility to this theory, and the data can be interpreted in these terms. To the extent that one does rely on this view, however, he is forced to conclude that whites are more affected by it than blacks. Of those who opposed the use of contraceptives, a majority of the whites gave religious-moral reasons, whereas this reason was given by only some 35 percent of the blacks.

It is unfortunate that more questions were not asked on this matter. As it is, we are restricted in our ability to say a great deal about why the poor feel the way that they do about contraception. Nevertheless, these data can serve as a basis for some preliminary suggestions for possible strategies in future family planning programs.

Conclusions and Recommendations

The major conclusion, and one of which we can be quite certain, is that there is a tremendous need for greatly expanded publicly subsidized family planning services. Approximately 40 percent of the poor and near poor in the state of North Carolina are in need of these services. This need is most severe among poorly educated blacks living in rural areas. On a per capita basis, the greatest need for subsidized services exists among blacks generally and among whites with little formal education.

Further, we have found that effective programs will have to go considerably beyond the present activities of simply setting up clinics which are open to the poor. Some actions in this direction are already underway in the form of the Office of Economic Opportunity's "outreach" program which consists of sending people hired locally out into the community to acquaint others with the services that are available.

Increased efforts at bringing the benefits of family planning to the poor must take a two-pronged approach. First, over 50 percent of those in need of these services appear ready to accept them if they are made aware of their availability and their utilization does not demand too great an effort. Existing clinics, however, are generally open but a few hours a week and in some cases only a few hours monthly. Distances no doubt play a factor also. An increase in the number and accessibility of relatively cost-free family planning clinics can be expected to reach most of this group. On the whole this group is aware of the economic benefits of limiting one's family size. This awareness should be reinforced in the clinic's approach to the client.

An intensive and sustained educational campaign will be necessary to reach those who are not so sure about contraceptives or are explicitly opposed to them. A large number of the undecided did see positive economic benefits in contraception, and this factor should be emphasized to them. The idea that contraceptives are a danger to one's health presents an especially difficult problem. One of the greatest benefits of a reduced number of pregnancies is the *advantages* to the mother's health. Quite clearly, this is not perceived by the poor. Blake and his associates found that of the nine reasons offered for using birth control to his sample of public housing residents, respondents rated this the lowest.[10] They therefore recommended that the role of birth control in helping "the wife to be healthy and have a good figure" not be emphasized in educational programs. Our findings suggest that not only is the health of the mother not perceived as improving with the use of birth control, but in fact a large minority believe deleterious effects will result. Thus we strongly suggest that the correction of misperceptions concerning the health aspects of contraceptives must be emphasized if birth control is to gain acceptance among this segment of the community.

Blake and his colleagues also found that the husbands play a crucial role in deciding whether or not the couple will engage in family planning. They did not, however, ascertain the extent to which the husband actually vetoes the wife's desire to use contraceptives. A check on our data showed that overwhelmingly the wife stated that her husband was in agreement with her in her attitudes toward the use of contraceptives. This suggests the possibility of increasing the success of educational programs by considering the husband as well as the wife as part of the target population. This could entail such minor changes as alterations in the "outreach" contacts to the evening hours to increase the husband's direct exposure to the campaign to use of male outreach workers operating through the husband's work environment.

Objections stemming from religious or moral beliefs probably will not be greatly affected by information about the economic and health aspects of contraception. A wholly different strategy is called for in this instance. Since there is not an explicit doctrinal objection to family planning found in religious beliefs of most of the poor of the South, a direct strategy might be the most effective one. Consideration ought to be given to the possibilities of working through the local ministers and church social organizations; if the minister can be convinced of the advantages of family planning and is willing to take some action to let his parishioners know of his feelings on this matter a good deal of the battle has been won. The minister is probably the most legitimate and believed spokesman, not only on matters of the hereafter, but on a wide variety of subjects. Further, for many of the poor the church is the only organization of which they are a member. Educational campaigns channeled through the local church would not only carry the sanction of the most respected institution of the poor, they would be able to reach a greater number of those in need than would any other single organization.

A greater use of the mass media would also be of great value. While mass mailings could play a role, the relevance of such an approach to the target group must be careful. One possible avenue that has yet to be adequately explored is that of television. Planned Parenthood-World Population has broken the ice, though to date the messages have been very low key. A more vigorous utilization of this medium holds forth considerable promise. If it is permissible to use television and the methods of Madison Avenue to sell everything from breakfast cereal to politicians, surely it can be used in an attempt to sell the advantages of family planning and moderately sized families.

In conclusion, the data examined here show that a large percentage of those who desire to limit the size of their families are favorably disposed to contraceptive techniques. A more vigorous utilization of the traditional strategy of making contraceptives available can be expected to effectively reach most of this group. For the remainder of those with an unmet need for contraceptives more innovative strategies are needed. At a minimum these expanded programs should make use of communications channels familiar to the particular target groups and should systematically reinforce the positive attitudes and correct erroneous ideas which are dominant in the target population. The success of such efforts is likely to be maximized by designing programs, not on some national model which may work in theory, but by investing in programs which are designed with the culture and attitudes of the potential clientele in mind. This paper has been an exploration of these attitudes among a population felt to be typical of the southern poor.

Notes

1. I am indebted to George Esser, Director of the North Carolina Fund, for making these data available.

2. Pascal K. Whelpton, Arthur A. Campbell, and John E. Patterson, *Fertility and Family Planning in the United States* (Princeton, N.J.: University of Princeton Press, 1966): 334-370.

3. Adelaide C. Hill and Fredrick S. Jaffe, "Negro Fertility and Family Size Preferences: Implications for Programming of Health and Social Services," in T. Parsons and K.B. Clark, eds., *The Negro American* (Boston: Houghton Mifflin, 1965): 208-209.

4. C. Horace Hamilton, "The Need for Family Planning in North Carolina," *The University of North Carolina Newsletter* 53, 3 (November 1968).

5. Fredrick S. Jaffe, "Family Planning, Public Policy and Intervention Strategy," *The Journal of Social Issues* 24, 4 (October 1967): 153-154.

6. Bernard Berelson, "Beyond Family Planning," *Studies in Family Planning* no. 38 (February 1969): 1-16.

7. Whelpton, Campbell, and Patterson (n. 2): 94.

8. Charles F. Westoff, Robert G. Potter, Jr., Philip C. Sagi, and Elliot G. Mishler, *Family Growth in Metropolitan America* (Princeton, N.J.: Princeton University Press, 1961): 248.

9. John R. Hofley, *Lower Class Religion: The Moral Basis of a Backward Society*, Ph.D. dissertation, Chapel Hill, N.C., 1968.

10. Robert R. Blake, Chester A. Insko, Robert Cialdini, and Alan Chaikin, *Beliefs and Attitudes About Contraceptives Among the Poor* (Chapel Hill, N.C.: Carolina Population Center, Monograph no. 5, 1969): 32.

The Prospects of Demographic Transition in a Mobilization System: China

Pi-chao Chen

Elsewhere I have described the ways in which the Chinese government has organized its birth control program and the strategy it has adopted to promote birth control.[1] In pushing for birth control the government has displayed great ingenuity, resorting to various measures to overcome limitations posed by resources and personnel shortage, and employed various incentive and sanctions to surmount inertia and resistance and to encourage compliance. To the extent that many of the measures adopted are harsh by "non-Chinese" standards, they reflect the determination and seriousness with which the government presses for population control. How effective has the Chinese action program been? What has been its impact, if any, on the fertility level? Unfortunately, we do not have the program specifics, the demographic data, and results to make even a rough appraisal. When it comes to making predictions demography does not fare better than other social science disciplines. Projecting population trends is often a hazardous task, inasmuch as the necessary assumptions about the vital trends may either be faulty or not hold beyond a short length of time. In the case of China, projections are rendered more difficult by the lack of comprehensive and reliable statistical data. In spite of this, a few demographers have taken on the thankless task of projecting population trends of China for the decades ahead.[2] In this chapter I do not intend to duplicate the work the demographers have done elsewhere. Rather, I shall attempt a "speculative" discussion of the likely impacts of recent political and social changes wrought by the Communist government on fertility trend in the years to come.

I. The U.N. Threshold Hypothesis and the Prospects of Fertility Decline

Until recently, historic demographic transitions have been accounted for in terms of the theory of demographic transition, in one version or another.[3] According to this theory, the shift of both mortality and fertility from near-balance at a high level to near-balance at a low level is regarded as a function of socioeconomic modernization. The theory postulates a three stage process of transition: a near equilibrium between fertility and mortality at a high level in the pre-transition stage; a precipitous mortality decline and a slowly declining fertility during the transitional stage; restoration of near equilibrium at a low level at the end of the transition. In the process, a "population explosion" occurs. Underlying this conceptualization is a causal model, with the social, economic, and some demographic factors viewed as independent variables, and vital trends as dependent variables. The latest attempt at a rigorous formulation of this model is the U.N. threshold hypothesis. It attempts to quantify the degree of socioeconomic modernization required for fertility to decline by cross-sectional examination of present day statistical data.[4] In spite of its theoretical deficiency, the U.N. threshold hypothesis does have some heuristic merit. If nothing else, it demonstrates that obtainment of a certain degree of modernization is either conducive to or a necessary (but not a sufficient) condition for a secular fertility decline to begin. To the extent that this causal chain is valid, we shall juxtapose the value of the twelve indicators of development in China with that of the U.N. threshold zone. Table 8-1 presents this juxtaposition. The tentative and crude nature of the comparison must be emphasized. Much of the quantitative data for China are not available. For those that are available, some data are educated guesswork at best and patent speculation at worst.

As Table 8-1 shows, of the twelve indicators for China in the 1950s, urbanization comes closest to the U.N. threshold zone. Income per head, non-agricultural activities, newspaper circulation, and radio receivers lag far behind, and only two indicators, cinema attendance and early marriage, surpassed the threshold zone. While in some instances (i.e., cinema attendance and early marriage) the reliability of the data is highly doubtful, in others (i.e., urbanization) differences in definition of the term may account for the favorable status accorded it in China. Still, in other instances (i.e., newspaper circulation and radio receivers per 1,000 population) the indicators used simply cannot reflect the extent of social communication obtained because they do not take into account the ingenious devices (such as the ubiquitous small groups, massive wired radio networks, and roving propaganda and cultural teams) with which the regime reaches and communicates to the vast majority of rural population of China. All told, however, the inescapable conclusion derived from the juxtaposition of data is that the prospects for immediate spontaneous fertility decline in China are not sanguine at all, if the U.N. hypothesis holds for China.

It is, however, necessary to point out that the U.N. hypothesis is neither flawless nor well verified. To begin with, the U.N. study is a cross-sectional examination of present day statistical data rather than a careful analysis of time series relating to countries that have undergone demographic transition. Recent studies that have done precisely the latter reveal that while fertility decline has been in general associated with the development of a secular-rational attitude, religious changes and differences, the improvement in women's status, decline in mortality, urbanization, industrialization, and so forth, and while examples can

Table 8-1

A Comparison of U.N. Reduced Threshold Zone for A Shift from High to Low
Fertility with the Values of Various Social and Economic Indicators for China in
the 1950s-1960s

Indicators	U.N. Reduced Threshold Zone (1)	China in 1950-60s	
Income per head of household (U.S. dollar equivalent annually)	230-339	95.3-108.1	(2)
Energy Consumption (equivalent kg. of coal annually per head)	360-1012	190-280	(3)
Urbanization (percentage of total population in localities of 20,000 or more inhabitants)	16.0-33.0	13.48	(4)
Non-agricultural activities (percentage of economically active males)	44.7-61.0	21-33	(5)
Hospital beds (per 1,000 inhabitants)	5-6	9.65	(6)
Life expectancy (expectation of life at birth, both sexes, in years)	58.5-64.4	30-44	(7)
Infant mortality (annual number of infant deaths per 1,000 live births)	77.5-44.3	N.A.	(8)
Early marriage (percentage of women aged 15-19 years, married)	15.3-11.4	15-10	(9)
Female literacy (percentage of literates in female population 15 years of age and over)	61.7-74.9	50-60	(10)
Newspaper circulation (per 1,000 inhabitants)	80-99	2.9	(11)
Radio receivers (per 1,000 inhabitants)	87-88	14.3-26.6	(12)
Cinema attendance (average annual attendance per individual)	6.3-9.7	10.2	(13)

Notes:

(1) U.N., *Population Bulletin*, no. 7 (1963): 149.

(2) The lower figure (95.3) refers to 1955 and the higher figure (108.1) 1965. Figures are
from Ta-chung Liu, "The Tempo of Economic Development of the Chinese Mainland,
1949-65," *An Economic Profile of Mainland China* (Washington, D.C.: U.S. Government
Printing Office, 1967): 50. Also T.C. Liu and K.C.Yeh, *The Economy of the Chinese
Mainland* (Princeton: Princeton University Press, 1965): 224.

(3) The lower figure (190) refers to 1957 while the higher figure (280) refers to 1960. The
figures for energy consumption are from Y.L. Wu, *Economic Development and the Use of
Energy Resources in Communist China* (New York: Praeger, 1963): 192.

(4) The figure refers to 1956 and is derived from "Data on the Population of Our Country,
1949-56," *T'ung-chi Kung-tso*, no. 11 (June 14, 1957): 25. This figure should be regarded as
a rough indication of the degree of urbanization for the following reasons. First, in quoting
the urban total, the State Statistical Bureau did not provide a definition of the term "urban
population." The proportion of urban population used here by no means refers to
"percentage of total population in localities of 20,000 or more inhabitants" as the U.N.
study used. Second, the urban total is more likely to represent undercount rather than

Table 8-1 (cont.)

overcount. Third, official rural-urban dichotomy is probably based on administration rather than on the demographic characteristics of the population. If this is the case, the expansion of administrative jurisdiction of municipalities by incorporating the surrounding rural areas, as was the case in recent past, may result in increase in the absolute number and relative proportion of the "urban population," even if the demographic characteristics of the residents thus brought the municipal jurisdiction may not have undergone change. The figure used here may be regarded as a quantitative trend of the degree of urbanization in the 1960s, inasmuch as the urban population has shrunk drastically following the Great Leap campaign, which witnessed great rural-urban migration.

(5) The figures refer to 1955. The higher figure is calculated on the basis of Liu and Yeh's estimate, while the lower figure on Emerson's estimate. Liu and Yeh's estimate of total non-agricultural employment for 1955 was 58.95 million in 1955. Their estimate of total non-agricultural female employment was 11.67 million in 1955. Subtracting 58.95 million by 11.67 million gives the figure of 47.28 million, which should be the total non-agricultural male labor force for 1955. Dividing 47.28 million by 143 million (the total male labor force) gives 9.33, which should be the proportion of non-agricultural male labor force for 1955. Emerson's estimate of total non-agricultural employment in 1955 was 38.864 million. He did not give figures of distribution of non-agricultural employment by sex. Liu and Yeh give the ratio of male to female non-agricultural labor force in 1955 as 80.2:19.8. Multiplying 38.864 by a factor of 0.802 yields 31,092 million, which should be the total figure of non-agricultural male labor force in 1955. Dividing this figure by 143 million yields 0.21, which should be the proportion of male labor force employed in non-agricultural sector. The figure of 143 million—the total active labor force for China in 1955—is derived from Chu Yuan-chi'en, "The Problem of Agricultural Surplus Labor in China at Present," *Chiao-hsueh yu Yen-chiu*(Teach and Research), no. 2 (February 4, 1957): 17-20 and Wang Kuang-wei, "Opinion on Allocating Agricultural Labor Force," *Chi-hua Ching-chi* (Planned Economy), no. 8 (August 9, 1957): 6-9. For Liu and Yeh's estimate, see T.C. Liu and K.C. Yeh (n. 2): 207-209. For Emerson's estimate, see J.P. Emerson, *Non-Agricultural Employment in Mainland China: 1949-58* (Washington, D.C.: U.S. Department of Commerce Bureau of the Census, 1965): 128.

(6)The figure is derived from The State Statistical Burea, *The Great Ten Years* (Peking: Foreign Language Press, 1960): 220.

(7) The figures quoted assume mortality levels ranging from 20 to 25 per 1,000 population for China in 1953. See J.S. Aird, "Population Growth," in A. Eckstein, W. Galenson, and T.C. Liu, *Economic Trends in Communist China* (Chicago: Aldine Publishing Co., 1968): 285.

(8) The figure for infant mortality is not available and cannot be estimated in the absence of relevant information.

(9) The low figure is based on the assumption (1) that the majority of females do not get married before 18, the legal minimum age of marriage and (2) that the government promotion of late marriage since 1962 has raised the average age of marriage to higher than 18.

(10) For the justification for giving such high figures see A. Doak Barnett, *Cadres, Bureaucracy, and Political Power in Communist China* (New York: Columbia University Press, 1967): 386-388.

(11) The figure is from Alan P.L. Liu's unpublished doctoral dissertation "Communications and Political Integration in Communist China," (M.I.T., 1967): 62.

(12) From Alan P.L. Liu, ibid. The lower figure refers to radio receiver distribution per 1,000 population while the higher one refers to loudspeakers per 1,000 population in 1964.

(13) From Alan P.L. Liu, ibid., 382.

be cited to illustrate the presumed influences of each of the variables, counter-examples or exceptions are nearly as abundant and prevalent.[5] Although the U.N. study has demonstrated that the countries studied are bimodally divided into two distinct groups, with one group characterized by low fertility and high modernization and the other by high fertility and low modernization, it remains an insufficient proof of the validity of the threshold hypothesis which the study is meant to prove. The fact that there are no significant correlations within each of the two groups remains to be explained. As Simon Kuznets aptly points out, the U.N. threshold hypothesis is merely a reformulation of the insensitivity of certain supposedly dependent variables (fertility) to a set of supposedly independent variables (the twelve indicators) within a given range, rather than a successful identification of the independent variables and a formulation of their interrelationship that contribute to the levels and range of the insensitive dependent variables.[6] For these reasons, our comparison should not be taken too seriously.

II. Taiwan vs. China

In recent years, three Chinese cultural areas outside the People's Republic of China, namely Taiwan, Hong Kong, and Singapore, have experienced a secular fertility decline as shown by Table 8-2.

Since organized birth control programs were not introduced into those areas

Table 8-2
Birth Rates in Taiwan, Hong Kong and Singapore, 1955-1966

	Taiwan	Hong Kong	Singapore
1955	45.3	36.3	44.3
1956	44.8	37.0	44.4
1957	41.4	35.8	43.4
1958	41.7	37.4	42.0
1959	41.2	35.2	40.3
1960	39.5	36.0	38.7
1961	38.3	34.2	36.5
1962	37.4	32.8	35.1
1963	36.3	32.1	34.7
1964	34.5	30.1	33.2
1965	32.7	27.7	31.1
1966	32.5	24.9	29.9

Source: United Nations, *Demographic Yearbook, 1965*, New York, 1966 and United Nations, *Population and Vital Statistics Report*, 1 July 1967, Statistical Papers. Series A, Vol. XIX, No. 3.

until early 1960, the decline may be attributed to the fact that these areas have reached the minimum level of socioeconomic modernization required. The populations of Hong Kong and Singapore are highly urbanized in that a very significant proportion live in highly congested areas and are employed in the non-agricultural sector. In Hong Kong, the recent fertility decline has been due to the anomalies in the age-sex structure arising from migration and other factors.[7] On the other hand, the demographic dynamics of the population of Taiwan are less affected by such anomalies. All this argues against the usefulness of comparing China with Hong Kong and Singapore; it seems more sensible to compare Taiwan with China, in terms of degree of modernization, as an approach to roughly assessing the degree in which the population of China has approximated the U.N. threshold.

The same U.N. study referred to above includes Taiwan in its analysis. In order to minimize the influence of minor variations which may arise from errors of measurement or estimates, the U.N. study divides the value of each of the twelve indicators into six levels.[8] The level of the indicators for Taiwan quoted by the U.N. study refers to the 1950s. Table 8-3 presents the comparative levels of social and economic development obtained by Taiwan and China. At these levels of modernization, the population of Taiwan reached the threshold of secular fertility decline, which began in 1959.

As the table shows, China has approximated Taiwan in income per head, urbanization, hospital beds, and early marriages, surpassed Taiwan in cinema

Table 8-3

A Comparison of Levels of Social and Economic Development Obtained by China and Taiwan in 1950s

Indicators	Taiwan[1]	China[2]
Income per head	VI	VI
Energy Consumption	IV	V
Urbanization	V	V
Non-agricultural Activities	IV	V-VI
Hospital Beds	VI	VI
Life Expectancy	III	VI
Infant Mortality	III	N.A.
Early Marriage	IV	IV
Female Literacy	IV	IV
Newspaper Circulation	IV	VI
Radio Receiver	IV	V
Cinema Attendance	IV	III

Sources:
1. U.N. *Population Bulletin*, no. 7 (1963): 139.
2. Computed from Table 8-1.

attendance, and lagged behind Taiwan in radio receivers and newspaper circulation, infant mortality, life expectancy, non-agricultural activities, energy consumption, and female literacy. The fact that China was behind Taiwan in eight indicators requires no explanation, but the fact that China was ahead of Taiwan in one indicator and approximated in three others does require one. What are being compared here are not the exact values of the indicators, but rather the levels, or the range of values divided into six levels, as indicated above. That China surpassed Taiwan in cinema attendance is questionable if the measurement used is conventional, but may not be so if one takes into account the roving movie teams that roam the countryside to bring movie entertainment to the peasants. All this shows that mainland China has a long way to travel before it reaches the threshold zone, if Taiwan's experience has relevance for China. Even so, one is cautioned against taking the comparison too seriously because it tends to show China in a more favorable light than it deserves.

III. The Institutional and Social Changes and Their Likely Impacts on Fertility Trends

From the above discussion, the conclusion is obvious that China is and will remain an economically backward country for a long time, and that in leaving it to the forces of economic changes a significant spontaneous fertility decline is most unlikely to occur in the near future. This statement stands in spite of the fact that the demographic hypothesis against which we measure the degree of China's modernization is full of theoretical deficiency and conceptual ambiguity. For while we do not have a verified theory capable of accounting for all demographic transitions, past and present, we do know something about the prevailing social, economic, and demographic correlates of fertility decline. Secular fertility decline occurs either as a concomitant to or as a consequence of the kind of changes in literacy, female roles, mass media, urbanization, industrialization, rise in child survival ratio, and so forth, which we usually refer to as modernization. By itself each of the measures of modernization tells us very little about the degree of development, but together they reflect the extent of development. Societal development is essentially an interactive and cumulative process in which all the components tend to develop concomitantly, and the efficient functioning of any one of the components tends to require the efficient functioning of all the others. Significant variation in the activity of one component tends to relate to significant variation in the activities of all the others. To say this is to say that in the absence of other developmental concomitants, significant fertility change is most unlikely.

Although the economic modernization effected by the Communist regime may prove as yet too weak to exert pressure on fertility, the institutional and cultural changes under the Communists' auspices have been nothing short of revolutionary. Some of these changes are either highly conducive to the spread of birth control or tend to facilitate the government's efforts to make information, supply, and service accessible to the population. In this section we are to engage in a "speculative discussion" of the likely impacts of these recent great changes on the fertility trends in the years ahead. Specifically, we shall focus on the following aspects of the changes: (1) improvements in public health; (2) mortality decline; (3) acceleration of the family revolution; (4) improvements in women's status; (5) "socialist transformation" of the economy; (6) expansion of the mass communication; and (7) expansion of the education system.

Expansion of the Public Health Network

When the Communists came to power, China had only a few trained medical personnel, no adequate hospital facilities and no nationwide public health network. Within a decade, they established a nationwide public health network (albeit primitive by Western standards), suppressed major epidemic diseases, and effected some decline in the mortality rate. Faced with crushing health problems and yet with very limited material resources, the government quite early opted for a labor-intensive approach. This approach places minimal emphasis on capital-intensive medical services, and instead relies on fundamental changes in communication, organization, and environmental sanitation.[9] For example, travelers to China have often commented on the fly-free cities, a result of the "patriotic anti-four-pest" campaign—a mass campaign that mobilized millions of people to eliminate flies, mosquitoes, rats, and sparrows. Such mass mobilization campaigns have been largely responsible for bringing epidemic diseases under control and lowering mortality.

Prior to 1949 modern medicine had hardly made an inroad into China; the few modern doctors and hospitals were concentrated mainly in a few urban centers and treaty ports. The vast majority of the Chinese population, the peasants, did not have access to modern doctors and hospitals, and had to look to the traditional herbalist doctors. Take maternal and child care. Before the liberation there were only 81 maternal and infant hospitals, with a total of 1,736 beds, and only two children's hospitals, with 173 beds. The vast majority of deliveries were handled by old-style midwives who had no knowledge of modern hygiene. Under such circumstances, infant and maternal mortality was bound to be high.

Determined to improve maternal and child care rapidly and yet having limited capital and trained manpower, the government opted for "walking on two legs"—i.e., using both the traditional and the modern medical facilities and personnel to their maximum limit. One of the first steps taken in this direction was the retraining of old-style midwives in modern delivery methods. By 1953, more than 242,000 had been retrained. At the same time, the government began to train modern women and child health workers; by 1953 there were about 10,000 trained. By the end of 1956, more than 79,500 delivery stations had been established and were staffed with retrained old-style midwives or newly trained modern midwives and women and child health workers. By then the number of maternal and infant health personnel trained had reached the following numbers: obstetricians, 3,769; pediatricians, 3,769; modern midwives, 34,000; woman and child health workers, 44,000; retrained old-style midwives, 578,000; and nurses, 356,000.[10] Although we do not have statistics from 1956 on, there seems to be little doubt that the number of personnel trained has continued to grow.

As part of the communization drive of the Great Leap, each commune set up its own health center, and many production brigades their own small health stations. A vast (though unknown) number of medical workers of all kinds were sent from cities to staff the new rural health centers and stations.[11] Every commune is reported to now have one or more trained resident nurses, though only a small proportion of them have resident modern doctors. Since 1958 the government had made it a rule to send newly graduated medical doctors to rural health centers as a part of their training. They are required to stay there up to five years, one year for each year of the training provided by the state. The proportion of modern doctors, as opposed to herbalist doctors, in rural health centers is therefore likely to increase over time. The medical doctors and nurses are assisted by a few auxiliary (part-time) nurses recruited mostly from woman pioneers and "activists." Together they constitute the public health service in the rural areas.

Since the outbreak of the Proletarian Cultural Revolution, one-third or more of all medical and health workers have reportedly been transferred to rural areas to set up "rural health bases" and to "reinforce the rural medical set-up," at Mao's insistence. Plans have been drafted to train a large number of urban and rural health personnel and midwives who are not to be divorced from production, and a large number of rural doctors who are to be part-time doctors and part-time farmers (the so-called "bare-foot doctors"). Middle schools have been ordered to provide short courses for health workers and midwives. The provisional plan requires that within three to five years the health center in each commune be staffed with four or five doctors, every production brigade with one or two bare-foot doctors and one or two midwives, and each production team with one or two health workers not divorced from production. Minor diseases and injuries are to be treated in villages, ordinary ones in every commune, and grave ones at the *hsien* level medical hospital.[12] Needless to say, all these are but further extensions and intensifications of the mass-line and walking-on-two-legs approaches to public health. This newly expanded and strengthened rural public health network will be an asset to the government in its attempt to bring birth control information and services to the vast majority of the Chinese population.

At the present stage of development, China is certainly in a position to train and deploy an army of birth control field workers. The level of training required should not be exaggerated.[13] After a short period of training, the field workers should be competent to teach the peasant women elementary reproductive physiology and to instruct them in various conventional birth control methods. When conventional methods fail to prevent pregnancy, the field workers may refer the case to nearby hospitals where facilities and trained personnel are available for performing vacuum-type induced abortion, which takes several minutes and requires no hospitalization and hence is very inexpensive.

Mortality Decline

With some notable exceptions secular fertility decline has been historically preceded by decline in mortality, especially infant mortality.[14] With more children surviving fewer births are needed to achieve a desired family size, a condition highly conducive to birth control.

In Taiwan, quite independent of the island-wide birth control program introduced in 1963-1964, fertility began a secular decline in 1958. At that time, Taiwan's crude mortality rate had already dropped to 8.5 per 1,000 population, a considerable gain over the 33.4 per 1,000 population recorded for 1906. If the Taiwan experience has any relevance for China, it is that spontaneous fertility decline tends to follow a major mortality decline.

The available official data on mortality in China in 1952-1957 are given in Table 8-4. Pressat and Chandrasekhar obtained these figures in 1958 from the State Statistical Bureau. The fact that the figures were much lower than the vital rates derived from pre-war sample surveys or those found in Manchuria and Taiwan at comparable stages of development and other known facts has made

Table 8-4
Mortality Rates in China, 1952-57

Year	Death Rate	
	Chandrasekhar	Pressat
1952	18	17
1953	17	
1954	13	13
1955	12.4	
1956	11.4	
1957	11	11

Source: Roland Pressat, "La Population de la Chine et son Economie," *Population* 13, 4 (October-December 1958): 570; S. Chandrasekhar, *China's Population: Census and Vital Statistics* (Hong Kong: Hong Kong University Press, 1959): 50.

some demographers skeptical of their accuracy. John Aird, for instance, has questioned the reliability of the figures.

The vital rates obtained by Chandrasekhar give evidence of the progressive deterioration of registration . . . The death rates show a suspiciously abrupt decline from 1953 to 1954, when food and cloth rationing began, and thereafter decline continuously. The change may have been due partly to changes in the population covered. Pressat's 1952 figures and Chandrasekhar's 1953 figures were probably based on the vital rates surveys of 1951-1954 . . . In any case, increasing underregistration is probably a contributing factor in the downward trend of both birth and death.[15]

Skeptical of the Chinese official statistics, Aird subsequently constructed four models of demographic trends for China for the period 1953-1965. His estimated rates for 1965 range from a high of 21 to a low of 16 per 1,000 population.[16] Assuming that the lowest figure most closely approximates the actual level of mortality, China's crude death rate in 1965 was still much higher than that of Taiwan, 8.5 per 1,000 population, when secular fertility decline began.

Admitting that Aird's skepticism is well taken, we have, however, reasons not to believe that the decreasing official rates reflect "progressive deterioration of registration." It is difficult to reconcile the deterioration of registration with the known fact that during the same period the Chinese government increased its administrative penetration of the society. Furthermore, this period also witnessed progressive expansion and intensification of the low-cost, labor-intensive mass campaign approach to public health—i.e., implementation of the "walking-on-two-legs" approach and the "patriotic hygienic" mass campaigns.

Thanks to major medical inventions (i.e., antibiotics and DDT, etc.), development of low-cost effective public health techniques and expansion of public health networks, a significant mortality decline has taken place without profound economic development in many presently low-income underdeveloped countries. This is in sharp contrast to what happened to the presently developed countries at earlier times, with respect to mortality decline. In our times profound economic transformation may be a sufficient but certainly not a necessary condition for a major mortality reduction to occur. It is not particularly helpful to reject the Chinese official figures obtained in pre-war Taiwan or in Manchuria in the 1930s (for which relatively reliable statistics are available) much less with the figures obtained from the pre-war sample surveys. The conditions (including political condition) are so drastically different as to make this kind of comparison not very relevant and helpful.

Whatever the actual level of mortality in recent years, there seems to be little doubt that the level at present is much lower than it was prior to the Communist era. Whether the government will be able to register significant gains in mortality reduction in the years ahead without substantially raising the living standards remains to be seen. However, barring unforeseeable natural calamities, large-scale famine, and collapse of the unified central authority, mortality is likely to continue to decline at an undeterminable pace. Since much of the reduction in mortality typically occurs in childhood, child survival ratio is likely to increase as mortality rates further decline. This trend, together with other forces arising from development, is likely to exert increasing pressure on the family with an adequate number of surviving children to adopt family planning.

Acceleration of the "Family Revolution"

Marriage in traditional China was not so much an affair between a mature man and woman as an affair between two families. Its primary purpose is not the romantic happiness of the marrying couple but the fulfillment of the sacred obligation of perpetuating the family line, the acquisition of a daughter-in-law for the service and comfort of the parents, and the begetting of sons for the security of the parents' old age. It was a sacred obligation for a mature man to have at least one surviving son; this obligation in turn fell upon his wife.[17] Under conditions where about half of all infants died before reaching maturity, the anxiety about having sons, even about the assured survival of at least one son, naturally provided a positive incentive for bearing many children.

Mainly as a result of the intrusion of the West and western ideas and the resultant collapse of the traditional order, a "family revolution" has been set in motion since the early twentieth century.[18] As a revolutionary regime bent on breaking up the networks of human relations and uprooting many of the age-old cultural values, the Communists have realized from the very beginning that if they are to succeed in their socialist construction they must storm the very bulwark of the old institutions and culture—the traditional family. Since family begins with marriage, the assault must begin with the reform of marriage law. Thus one of the first significant laws promulgated by the Communist regime upon its rise to power was the New Marriage Law, issued in May 1950. By its own choice, the government has thus embarked upon a campaign aimed at accelerating the family revolution and at the eventual destruction of the traditional family system.

Although the regime has attacked the traditional family system for its own political and economic reasons, the campaign may turn out to have unintended demographic consequences. The traditional system, with its inequality of sexes, and with its emphasis on perpetuating the family lineage, on the parental authority, on strong kinship ties, and on the family as a predominant unit of production, education, and consumption was conducive to the big family idea and hence high fertility.[19] The family revolution ushered in during the Republican period and accelerated from the beginning of the Communist era has had the effect of eroding the traditional familial idea and practice and fostering modern familial idea and practice.

The new Marriage Law forbids the "arbitrary and compulsory" form of marriage, that is, parental interference in their children's marriage. To get married, the couple has only to register in person with the local government, and the marriage is then legal as long as it complies with the provisions of the marriage law. Marriage has now become an affair of the couples concerned, intended for their own common life rather than for the perpetuation of the ancestral lineage. A wife now has the right to custody of her children in divorce. A woman's status in the family is no longer dependent upon bearing children, especially sons. As a result there has occurred a reversal of the authority relationship between married couples and their parents. Although many parents still live with their married sons, the controlling position in the family has passed to the young couples, with parents as adjuncts and not masters. Such families may retain the traditional three-generation membership, but their internal structure departs radically from the traditional pattern.[20] The abolition of begetting male offspring as the principal purpose of marriage and the weakening of kinship ties should have the effect of reducing the pressure for bearing many children, especially sons. The new Marriage Law may thus have the unintended consequence of removing one of the major factors that in the past tended to sustain high fertility norms.

Another part of the new Marriage Law which has implications for fertility trends is the rise in the age of marriage. The traditional emphasis on producing large numbers of male offspring tended to encourage marrying the children as young as possible. We have no quantitative data about the extent to which this ideal was actually realized. There is, however, scattered evidence to show that during the Republican era the practice of early marriage was widespread, with the mean age of marriage at 19-20 years of age for men and 17-18 or probably younger for women.[21] The Marriage Law now sets 20 as the minimum legal age of marriage for men and 18 for women, instead of the minimum of 18 for men and 16 for women as was provided in the Nationalist Law.

Since 1962 the government has "recommended" late marriage—28 to 32 for men and 25 to 28 for women. Presumably it would be easier for the government to force this recommendation upon certain segments of the unmarried population—i.e., urban, educated, employees of public enterprises and agencies, upwardly mobile aspirants, and so forth. To what extent it can enforce the recommendation among the rest remains a moot question. To the extent that the government is able to enforce this "optimal age of marriage" among certain segments of the population, it will effect some fertility decline. Raising the mean age of marriage can substantially reduce the birth rate even when the ultimate mean size of the family remains constant. This point is illustrated by projections made by Pressat. Assuming that the nuptiality rate remains constant, he examines the effect on the fertility of a fictitious cohort of a progressive increase in the mean age at marriage from 19.7 years to 24.3 years in the space of ten generations. Although the proportion of women ever married remains constant in all the generations (i.e., 993 women out of 1,000 will eventually marry), the fact that marriages will increasingly be delayed will result in a considerable reduction in the current nuptiality rate. His projection shows that the effect will be spread over forty years. During this period, it will be as if 4.5 female generations contracted no marriage at all.[22]

The possible demographic effects of the Communist Marriage Law discussed so far all tend to favor fertility reduction. There is, however, one aspect of the Law that tends to raise the fertility level, the right of a widow to remarry. Under the traditional order, if his wife died, a widower was allowed to take another wife or a concubine, whichever he preferred. The death of a wife therefore had no consequence for the overall fertility level. If anything, it tended to raise the fertility level (provided that the proportion of wives dying was high and that the proportion of the widowers remarrying was as high), since the second wife or concubine was likely to be younger than the deceased wife. However, the traditional order imposed severe restrictions on the remarriage of widows, as a way of enforcing the solidarity of the family group. More likely than not, if a widow desired to remarry, the family would prevent her from doing so. If the attempt to prevent remarriage failed, she would likely be denied custody of her children, legally or otherwise; this denial would in most instances prevent her from remarrying. Under such circumstances, a widow seldom remarried as long as the husband's family could support her. During the Republican period, although there was general agitation against the traditional restrictions, the problem did not catch major attention and received little emphasis in the marriage laws. Under the Communists the issue of a widow's freedom to remarry received major emphasis for the first time. In accordance with the general principle of non-interference in the freedom of marriage by any third party, the law specifically forbids interference with a widow's remarriage. In pursuance with the general principle against "exacting money or gifts in connection with marriage," demanding a price for a widow's remarriage is also explicitly prohibited.[23]

What has been the effect of abolishing the traditional restrictions against a widow's remarrying? Without comprehensive statistics about the proportions of widows remarrying before and after 1949, we cannot answer this question. We do have, however, some fragmentary statistical evidence from pre-Communist era: sample census figures of nine *hsien* in the Szechuwan province in 1947 showed a ratio of one widow to every 3.15 married women, and sample studies of nine localities in northern, eastern, and southwestern regions showed a range of one widow for every 3.02 to 4.15 married women fifteen years of age and over. Compared with one widow for every 5.55 married women of fifteen and over in the U.S.A., these ratios are much higher. Probably the only counterpart would be India, where there is one widow to every 3.14 married women.[24] With the removal of restrictions, the proportion of widows remarrying undoubtedly has risen. Since widows age 44 or over are unlikely to remarry, the abolition of the restrictions are likely to raise overall fertility levels to some degree, if significant proportions of widows remarry.

Improvements in Women's Status

In pursuance of the principle of equality of the sexes, the government has put into statute women's right to work: "Both husband and wife shall have the right to free choice of occupation and free participation in work and in social activities."[25] To translate this legal stipulation, the government quite clearly institutionalized the principle of equal pay for equal work in the urban-industrial sector. The same principle has also been introduced into the farming sector with less success. All these measures, of course, tend to improve the economic and social status of women in the family and in society. Furthermore, status improvement and widening employment opportunities have combined to bring into the nation's labor force increasing numbers of women. Women's participation in white-collar and industrial occupations jumped from 420,000 in 1949 to 1,900,000 in 1954, an increase of 450 percent.[26] Comprehensive statistics for the subsequent period are, however, unavailable.

In the agricultural sector, the growth of women's participation has also been impressive. As pointed out previously, as early as 1955 Mao perceived agricultural cooperativization as an effective device for mobilizing women's participation in agricultural production. In 1954 and 1955, women supplied one-third of all the work-days in the agricultural producer's cooperatives. (This figure compares favorably with John L. Buck's land utilization survey in 1937 which found that women supplied 16.4 percent of farm labor, mostly in the form of helping with the harvest during busy seasons, weeding, and other secondary chores.[27]) The communization drive of 1958-1959 further inflated the ratio of women's participation. We do not know for sure whether the collapse of the Great Leap led to the reduction of the proportion of women in agricultural activities. Whatever the magnitude of the reduction, if it has occurred, it is highly unlikely that the proportion now is lower than it was before 1954. To facilitate women's participation in the labor force, nurseries and kindergartens of various kinds— seasonal and long-term, day and boarding—have been set up.[28]

In the West, improvements in women's status in the family and society proved to be highly conducive to the spread of birth control. The legal guarantee of the principle of sexual equality, the extension of education and other privileges to women, and the encouragement of women's participation in gainful employment outside the household are objective tests of improved status and widened opportunities for women. Since the burdens of pregnancy and child care are theirs, women presumably respond to these improvements by practicing birth control. In the West, however, improvements in women's status and the spread of birth control took place in a context in which agriculture remained in private hands and most working women were engaged in non-agricultural, especially white-collar, activities. This raises the question: Will women respond to outside gainful employment opportunities by limiting childbirths when most of the opportunities are restricted to collectivized agriculture? On the one hand, there are reasons to believe that the spread of birth control requires not only outside employment but also that the employment be non-agricultural in nature. In the West the increase in female employment was partly related to the change in norms governing women's participation in outside employment and partly related to increasing industrialization (measured by the increasing proportion of the labor force in non-agricultural sectors). Most non-agricultural employment makes it necessary for women to work at a place separated at some distance from the house, entailing a drastic rearrangement of family life and childrearing, whereas farm work does not. On the other hand, there are also reasons to believe that the drastic reorganization of economic and family life impelled by collectivization and the employment of a high percentage of women in agricultural production may have a precipitous and depressing effect on rural fertility as evidenced by the rural Soviet Union, the fertility of which gradually but steadily declined since the 1930s following the collectivization.[29]

The crude birth rate in the rural Soviet Union dropped from 45 per 1,000 population in 1928 to 32.2 per 1,000 population in 1935, and further down to 31.5 in 1940. Needless to say, the almost universal fertility differentials due to such factors as degree of education, the type of residence, and occupational difference, ethnic origins, and religion have persisted. It was of course quite possible that the precipitous decline in fertility in rural Soviet Union might be attributed to: (1) the massive rural-urban migration accompanying the rapid industrialization of 1930s and the siphoning off from the rural areas a disproportionately large percentage of persons or couples of reproductive age; (2) the socioeconomic transformation brought about by the draft industrialization; (3) the psycho-cultural shocks caused by the massive purges and random terror; and (4) the separation of families effected by the forcible resettlement and imprisonment of large number of males in the concentration camps. During this period, not only were living standards in the rural Soviet Union not improved but actually deteriorated, thanks to the ruthless and brutal collectivization. Having said what we did, the fact however remains: given the present stage of our knowledge we simply cannot have a definite answer to the question posed above. Different answers to the question, however, will have drastically divergent implications for the childbearing practice and hence fertility trends in China for the years to come. For the sake of speculation, let us assume for a moment that working outside as a wage laborer with pay scale almost as high as male, regardless of the nature of employment, is a force sufficient to motivate the rural married women to practice family planning. If this assumption holds, then the condition required for birth control to spread in rural China is already in existence in China, thanks to the communization of agriculture. If the assumption does not hold, then the prospects will be less bright. Whatever the case, the institutional changes and "cultural revolution" experienced by the post-1949 China, the magnitude and intensity of which has yet to be surpassed by any of the Third World, are more likely to facilitate, rather than obstruct, the government's attempts to spread family planning in the vast rural China.

Socialist Transformation of the Economy

In traditional China, the family was predominantly a unit of production and of organization of labor, of capital, and land for the acquisition of goods and services to meet the needs of the members of the household. This pattern was as dominant in commerce and industry as in agriculture. Children assisted in the family farm or shop when they were young. When they grew up they brought additional income home, either by contributing their labor to the family farm or business or by earning wages outside. By law and custom, the grown-up sons supported their aged parents. Expenditure on education was not part of the cost of bringing up children. Under such conditions, where the cost of raising children was marginal and the children's contribution to the family welfare increased proportionally as they grew up, there was every incentive to bear many children, especially when the survival ratio was so low. An additional child or children created no unbearable economic burden, for the family could always somehow squeeze out enough to take care of the additional one. Private ownership of the means of production (including land) therefore tended to be conducive to high fertility.

However, the factors that tend to sustain high fertility when the means of production are in private hands become much weakened when the means of production are socialized. After the socialist transformation of industry and commerce in 1955-1956 and cooperativization and communization of agriculture in 1955-1956 and 1958-1959, the average Chinese ceased to be an owner of the means of production. A chief source of family income now comes from the husband's and the wife's (depending upon the cases) salaries or wages, based upon accumulated labor points. The only supplementary income for a farmer is the yields from the private plots, which he may either consume himself or dispose of on the free market for cash. Income from this source is meager, however, because private plots represent on the average only 5 percent of the collectivized areas.[30] An unwanted child (or children) may therefore create an unbearable financial burden for the family. Furthermore, pregnancy, post-natal leave of absence, and child-care all entail the loss of the wife's income, if she works outside of the household. Unlike previously, education now is mandatory. School-age children must attend either a full-time school or a part-time study and part-time work school, depending upon the available facilities. While primary education is compulsory wherever feasible, it is not free; parents are required to share the burden of their children's education.[31] All this means that young children cease to be an economic asset of some marginal value, and the cost of rearing children rises; they cannot be expected to contribute to the family economic welfare by working, except after school. When a child reaches fifteen or sixteen years of age he is considered a full-fledged worker in agriculture, and then he may contribute to the family welfare by earning a full-time wage. But within a few years he is ready for marriage. When he gets married he may set up his own household and thus cease to contribute to the family income. Even if he continues to live with his parents, his contribution is bound to decrease in time, because in addition to bringing back a wife he may soon produce children of his own. From a purely economic point of view, having numerous children ceases to be an unmixed blessing. While the investment in raising numerous children rises sharply, the expected returns from the investment decreases. Under such circumstances, economic calculation may provide a motivation strong enough to lead married couples to plan and limit the number of children.

In traditional China, as in most pre-modernized societies, concern for security at old age constituted a powerful motivational force in favor of high fertility. Nothing was more dreadful than the prospect of facing old age without at least one offspring, preferably a male one. In contemporary China, one of the economic functions of the traditional family, the support of aged parents by grown-up children, has now been taken over in part by the collective. In the urban-industrial sector, social security and pension systems have been established. In the rural sector, a rudimentary social security system has also been introduced. In a commune (or production brigade, depending upon the period and areas), before the total income is distributed among the members, a specific percentage is set aside as the public welfare fund, earmarked for taking care of the widows of revolutionary martyrs, dependents of men in armed services, and childless old people.[32] To be sure, the provision for the aged people thus far introduced is no match for the social security system long institutionalized in the advanced countries. It is, however, to be expected that with the collective increasingly replacing the immediate kins as the provider of security for the aged, a major motivational force that in the past sustained high fertility norms and practices is likely to be weakened in proportion.[33]

To recapitulate, in traditional China the family performed the vital function of providing material care and security to the individual throughout his entire life cycle—raising him from infancy, providing him with the means or channels of livelihood in his adult years, and supporting him in old age. The economic functions it performed and the psychological security and gratification it provided combined to make the traditional Chinese family system one of the most enduring social institutions in history. The economic function of the traditional family was closely intertwined with private ownership of the means of sustenance and production, which in most cases are self-sufficient. With the socialization of the means of production and with the weakening of family solidarity under communism, the family ceased to be a dominant unit of production, and its economic functions were severely undermined. Radical change in economic institutions under communism may foster a radical change in the norms and practices relating to childbearing. Whether the causal chain posited here is sheer fantasy or a plausible hypothesis, only the future can tell. By itself the causal chain between the abolition of private ownership and childbearing practice may be too weak, because it requires an exceptional degree of rational calculation and foresight. But the welfare consequences of decisions to have children do not appear to the parents until years after the decisions are made.[34] Unreinforced by other development forces and pressures (i.e., a rise in children survival ratio, rise in aspirations for selves and the children stimulated by rising income, a growing awareness of the possibilities of meaningful alternatives to raising children for women, an improvement in the cultural level, a replacement of fatalism by rationalism, and so forth), pure economic calculation is most likely to prove to be too weak to break the high fertility norms and to lead to conscientious family planning.

Expansion of Mass Communication

The level of fertility has been found to be highly correlated with the mass media circulation rate. Studies in Taiwan have indicated that frequency of exposure to mass media is significantly correlated with practice of birth control and number of children born.[35]

Like the Bolsheviks in the Soviet Union and unlike the governments of many developing countries, the Chinese Communist government has from the very beginning attached high priority to the development of mass media. As a consequence, post-1949 China has witnessed an enormous expansion of mass media, especially oral media.

Between 1947 and 1959, the total circulation of newspapers increased by a nearly seven-fold.[36] Although the growth has been spectacular in temporal terms, the current newspapers' circulation is small by the standards of advanced countries. In 1960 the circulation of newspapers was 2.9 per 1,000 population, in contrast to 6.6 per 1,000 in Taiwan. Low income and the relatively low level of literacy rates have been primarily responsible for this relatively small circulation rate. "The mass media flourish," Lerner says, "only where the mass has sufficient skill in literacy, sufficient motivation to share 'borrowed experience,' and sufficient cash to consume the mediated products."[37]

Cognizant of the fact that newspaper circulation could not grow rapidly, the government quite early opted for rapid development of radio broadcasting. In the early years, it concentrated on erecting radio monitoring networks. This is an ingenious device, utilizing the limited broadcasting facilities for mass communication by combining radios with propagandists and agitators, who serve as "opinion leaders" and relay the message transmitted via the central broadcasting system. This device represents a Chinese version of "two-step flow" communication. The monitoring system was considered a temporary measure to maximize the utility of a few radio sets, and it was gradually phased out after 1955. In its place a permanent wired radio broadcasting system was created; the system grew spectacularly during the two campaigns of the agricultural cooperativization of

1955-1956, and the communization drive of 1958-1959. Alan P.L. Liu estimates that there was one radio for about every seventy persons in China. With such a ratio, the government obviously could not hope to reach the majority of its people via radio communication. However, by connecting loudspeakers with radio sets the penetrating power can be multiplied in proportion to the number of loudspeakers installed. Loudspeakers were installed in factories, shops, offices, and schools. In rural villages, loudspeakers were also installed in large quantity. Given the multiplying effect of the loudspeaker system, the extent of the Chinese population exposure to radio broadcast should not be measured simply in terms of the number of radio sets or the total broadcasting kilowatt power per 1,000 population.

We do not know precisely what is being transmitted via the wired broadcasting systems, other than production techniques, ideological messages, news, and entertainment. If the government chooses to, it certainly can employ the system to diffuse various birth control methods as well as to inculcate small family ideas. It is quite possible that the government has in fact done this since 1962.

The expansion in mass media summarized above, however, does not adequately reflect the extent of social communication in China. What the society lacks in material resources, the government makes up by mobilizing its abundant human resources in order to reach and communicate with its people. Through the ubiquitous small groups and production teams (which meet frequently and into which virtually every Chinese is organized), the mobile movie, culture and propaganda teams (which roam the countryside and bring the entertainment and the government's message to even the most remote villages otherwise inaccessible by cars or other modern means of transportation), and intensive person-to-person communication so characteristic of the Chinese Communist approach to mass communication, the Chinese government has succeeded in reaching and communicating to its population in a way and degree a government in the Third World can hardly dream of.

Since the early 1960s production of transistor radios has apparently surged tremendously, and distribution of radios in rural villages has spread wide and far. The Myrdals who revisited the same village (Liu Ling in northern Shensi) in 1969 after seven years of absence reported that the villagers now have radio sets of their own. "Transistors are being spread all over China. There is not a village without a radio. In 1962 there was a central radio for the village; in 1969 the families had their own radios."[38]

We do not know to what extent the higher rural fertility, universally in all pre-industrialized societies, is a function of the peasants' ignorance and unawareness of the alternative to pregnancy and childbearing and of the availability of contraceptive methods other than *coitus interruptus*,[39] and to what extent it is a function of fatalism, a lack of high aspiration for life and their offsprings, and concern for security at old age. More likely than not it is a function of both. To the extent that ignorance of birth control methods plays an important part (as it still does even in the United States), increase in mass communication and especially transmitting the birth-control-related message via the mass media can partially overcome the rural inertia with respect to birth control practice. Thanks to its success in creating human networks of communication to compensate for the lack of physical facilities, the Chinese government is in a much stronger position to diffuse the birth control knowledge among the people than any other government at a comparable stage of modernization.

Expansion of the Education System

Educational level is found by many studies to be significantly correlated with the practice of birth control and the number of children born.[40] Under communism, China has made great strides in mass education. As in other fields, however, reliable statistics are hard to come by. We do not know, for instance, exactly what proportions of the population is literate. The reported proportions of school-age children in school vary from one year to another; Leo Orleans quotes the following figures: 50.7 percent in 1953; 61.3 percent in 1956; 85 percent in 1957 and 1958; and 87 percent in 1959 and 1960.[41] While the term school-age children is not defined, it obviously refers to children of primary school age, 6 or 7 to 12 or 13 years of age.

In 1950 the government launched an ambitious drive to wipe out illiteracy. As of the mid-1960s, the program operated mainly at the production brigade level, in the form of the People's School for Elimination of Illiteracy. Evening classes for adults were held in the local primary school.[42] Although it is impossible to make an exact estimate of the campaign's achievement, partly because literacy has never been officially defined and partly because the government has not published comprehensive statistics since late 1950s, continuing progress in wiping out "illiteracy" can be taken for granted.

Literacy is not an isolated social phenomenon; its growth usually parallels general social and economic modernization. In spite of the vigorous attack on illiteracy, therefore, China is unlikely to achieve universal literacy (by the standards of advanced nations) in the near future. The trend toward universal literacy is unmistakable, however, as progressively increasing proportions of young people attain some schooling and as they gradually replace the older, less literate population. It is significant that among the young people who are about to enter or just entering the childbearing age, the literacy rate was already close to 90 percent in mid-1960. This cannot fail to eventually exert some impact on the childbearing practice and hence on fertility.

The effect of the possible widespread use of schools and the literacy campaign as an instrument of the birth control program merits attention. Since 1962 the government has used schools as means of inculcating small family ideas and of diffusing birth control knowledge. The age cohort who were schooled under communism in the 1950s are now entering the childbearing age. If the attempt in this respect succeeds (and there is no reason it cannot), the result could be revolutionary.

IV. Concluding Remarks

In the foregoing sections we have dwelt on the forces obstructive of as well as conducive to secular fertility decline in China. On the one hand, we have shown that the extent of economic development and related changes (e.g., urbanization) are likely to be as yet too weak to precipitate a substantial decline in fertility. On the other hand, we have shown that some aspects of the profound cultural and institutional changes initiated by the Communists since 1949 have the effect, intended or otherwise, of removing or undermining many of the forces that in the past tended to encourage and sustain the traditional "way of life" with its high fertility norms and practices, characteristic of virtually all agrarian pre-modernized societies. We have also dwelt on the government's efforts to bring public health, mass communication, and popular education to the people. Progressive expansion of such infrastructure will increasingly facilitate not only the government's attempt to provide the services as intended but also its attempts to make available to the people birth control information, education, supplies, and technical services.

How is one to draw a conclusion from all this? And how much of the conclusion, if any, is valid, definite, and certain? As mentioned earlier, we do not have a valid theory capable of explaining the demographic transitions in the past, much less demographic transitions in the future. The conclusion one draws will inevitably reflect the relative weight one assigns to each, or a combination of some, of the sociological factors believed to be either correlates of low fertility or causal factors responsible for fertility decline.

A theory that convincingly explains the transitions in the past (assuming that such a theory actually exists) may not accurately predict the transition in China, and the experience of countries that have completed their demographic transition is no reliable guide to what may take place in China or, for that matter, in the presently underdeveloped high-fertility countries in general. In other words, to predict the socioeconomic changes and the time required for China to complete its transition on the basis of the experience of today's low-fertility countries is misleading at best and a futile intellectual exercise at worst, for the conditions have changed profoundly. First, the pace of mortality decline from a high level characteristic of a pre-industrialized society to a low level typical of an economically advanced society has accelerated over the past century. Thanks to breakthroughs in medical science and public health techniques, China, like some other underdeveloped countries, has experienced a substantial decline in mortality without profound economic transformation. Second, many reliable, inexpei. sive, and convenient contraceptives available today did not exist in the earlier period. Third, fertility declined in Europe and elsewhere without the benefit of large-scale organized efforts and publicity to promote birth control. In fact, with the possible exception of post-war Japan, birth control spread and fertility declined in a climate hostile to such practices. Fourth, the government of China has erected a physical-cum-human network of social communication, linking the average peasants in rural villages to the outside world, making them aware of the possibility of alternatives to the traditional way of life, and raising their sense of personal efficacy.[43] Fifth, what disadvantage the Chinese government faces in having to promote birth control in an economically backward society may be compensated to some, albeit undeterminable, extent by its organizational innovativeness. The extent to which the Chinese government has been able to reach the masses of China, to rearrange their daily life, to transform their values, to manipulate reward and punishment in order to induce compliance and deter defiance, and to mobilize and unleash their energy—all this was unheard of in the presently developed countries (with the possible exception of the Soviet Union) at their comparable stage of development, and all this is hardly dreamed of by the governments in other presently underdeveloped countries. Any serious attempt to assess the probability of the Chinese government's ability to realize its stated policy goal (of reducing the birth rate to below one percent by the end of this century) must take these facts into account. Because of the drastically changing conditions, the past is no guide to the present and the future.

The foregoing observation in turn leads to the question: Will the fertility decline be hastened by a nationwide organized effort to promote birth control? Important as this question is, there is no simple answer to it. So far in man's history there has been no instance in which a major fertility transition took place as a result of organized efforts.[44] Fertility in the West and elsewhere declined mainly as a result of the initiative taken by millions of married couples in response to the pressures generated in the process of profound social and economic changes. To say this is not, however, to say that organized efforts are bound to fail because of the absence of precedent, but merely that such efforts have not been made in the past.

Recent experience in Taiwan and Korea has demonstrated that a well-organized and vigorously pursued campaign can indeed accelerate the spread of birth control. In Taiwan it was found that before the promotional campaign started, the practice of birth control was strongly associated with the usual indices of modernity. But once the program was launched, the rate of acceptance of birth control among the traditional and lower strata of the population was proportionately the same as that among the general population. It was also found that the input of program efforts (i.e., deployment of personnel and resources) was a powerful determinant of the acceptance rate. (However, prior to the introduction of the organized program the forces released by modernization in Taiwan had already shown signs of exerting pressure on some segments of the population to adopt family planning.)

To the extent and assuming that the Taiwan experience is relevant, then the immediate prospect of widespread birth control in China is very good, thanks to the organizational innovativeness and penetrative capabilities of its government. To say this is not, however, to say that it will be an easy task to bring birth control to a population the size of China's. For all its organizational triumphs, the task if formidable. Finally, even if China were to achieve the feat of zero population growth in a decade—a next-to-impossible prospect—her population would continue to grow for several decades before finally stabilizing, due to the recent high levels of fertility. Regardless of how the population responds to the government's efforts and of the resulting pace of fertility decline, therefore, China's population will certainly reach the one billion mark before it can complete its demographic transition.[45]

Notes

1. See my "China's Birth Control Action Program, 1956-64," *Population Studies* 24, 2 (July 1970): 141-158. See also H.Y. Tien, "Sterilization, Oral Contraception and Population Control in China," *Population Studies* 22, 3 (March 1965): 215-235; Leo Orleans, "Evidence from Chinese Medical Journals on Current Population Policy," *China Quarterly* no. 40 (October-December 1969): 137-146.

2. Roland Pressat, "The Present and Future Demographic Situation in China," in *The Proceedings of the World Population Conference, 1965* (United Nations, 1967) vol. 2: 29-33; United Nations, *World Population Prospects As Assessed in 1963* (New York: 1966): 51-53; John S. Aird, "Population Growth," in Alexander Eckstein, Walter Galenson, and Ti-chung Liu, eds., *Economic Trends in Communist China* (Chicago: Aldine, 1968),: 183-328.

3. Warren S. Thompson and David J. Lewis, *Population Problems* (New York: McGraw-Hill, 1965), chapters 6 and 16; Kingsley Davis, "The World Demographic Transition," *The Annals of the American Academy of Political and Social Science* 237 (January 1945): 1-11; Irene B. Taeuber, "Japan's Demographic Transition Re-examined," *Population Studies* 14, 1 (July 1960): 28-40; Ronald Freedman, "The Sociology of Human Fertility," *Current Sociology* 10/11, 2 (1961-62): 35-119.

4. United Nations, *Population Bulletin* no. 7 (1963).

5. Ansley J. Coale, "Factors Associated With the Development of Low Fertility: An Historic Survey," in *Proceedings of the World Population Conference, 1965* (n. 2): 205-207; A.J. Coale, "Decline of Fertility in Europe from the French Revolution to World War II," in S.J. Behrman, L. Corsa, and R. Freedman, eds., *Fertility and Family Planning: A World View* (Ann Arbor:

University of Michigan Press, 1969): 3-24; John Knodel and Etienne van de Walle, "Demographic Transition and Fertility Decline: the European Case," reprint (Princeton: Office of Population Research, Princeton University).

6. Simon Kuznets, "Economic Aspects of Fertility Trends in the Less Developed Countries," in Behrman, Corsa, and Freedman (n. 5): 157-179.

7. Ronald Freedman and Arjune L. Adlakha, "Recent Fertility Declines in Hong Kong: The Role of the Changing Age Structure," *Population Studies* 22 (July 1968): 181-198.

8. For definitions of the levels, see United Nations, *Population Bulletin* no. 7 (1963): 137.

9. William Y. Chen, "Medicine and Public Health," *The China Quarterly* no. 6 (April-June 1961); Robert Worth, "Health Trend in China Since the Great Leap Forward," *American Journal of Hygiene* 78 (1968): 349-357.

10. Li Teh-chuan, "The Development of Woman and Child Health Work," in *Jen-min Shou-tse* (Peking: Jen-min Publishing Co., 1958): 636-637.

11. Robert M. Worth, "Strategy of Change in People's Republic of China—the Rural Health Center," in Daniel Lerner and Wilbur Schramm, eds., *Communication and Change in the Developing Countries* (Honolulu: East-West Center Press, 1967): 216-230.

12. "Mao's Revolution in Public Health," *Current Scene* 5, 7 (May 1968). See also Han Suyin, "Family Planning in China," *Japan Quarterly* 17, 4 (October-December 1970): 438-439.

13. For the training program in Taiwan, which seems relevant to the China case see "Taiwan: Training for Family Planning," *Studies in Family Planning* no. 36 (December 1968): 1-6.

14. In some Latin American countries, birth rates remained high or rose in the period 1910-1950, when death and infant mortality rates declined. See A. Andre Collver, *Birth Rates in Latin America* (Berkeley: Institute for International Studies, University of California, 1965). See also Coale, in *The Proceedings of the World Population Conference, 1965* (n. 5): 208.

15. John S. Aird, *The Size, Composition, and Growth of the Population of Mainland China* (Washington, D.C.: Bureau of the Census, 1961), p. 41. See also John Aird, "The Population of Mainland China," in *Population Trends in Eastern Europe, the USSR and Mainland China* (New York: Milbank Memorial Fund, 1960): 121-122.

16. John S. Aird (n. 2), in Eckstein, Galenson, and Liu, (1968): 303.

17. T'ung-tsu Ch'u, *Law and Society in Traditional China* (Paris: Mouton and Co., 1965): Chapter 2.

18. Marion J. Levy, Jr., *The Family in Revolution in Modern China* (Cambridge: Harvard University Press, 1959).

19. The view that the masses in traditional China practiced the big family idea has come under questioning by a number of social scientists. In their view, the big family idea, such as portrayed in the classical novel, *Red Chamber's*

Dream, was achieved by a few big landlords, gentry-officials, and big merchants. The majority of the common folk could not afford such luxury. As Francis Hsu puts it: "The wealth and more scholarly tended to adhere much more than the poor to the socially upheld big-family idea; this apparently explains the large households among the rich as a whole as contrasted with the poor as a whole." See Francis L.K. Hsu, *Under the Ancestor's Shadow* (New York: Doubleday, 1967): 7. See also Francis L.K. Hsu, "The Myth of Chinese Family Size," *American Journal of Sociology* 47 (May 1943): 555-562. While the masses could not afford big families, they aspired to their realization as something highly desirable. "The Chinese family in this sense was like a balloon, ever ready to expand whenever there was wealth to inflate it. As soon as there was enough land or other forms of production to employ the married sons, they would remain in the father's household, with property and income managed in common under the leadership and authority of the parents, and the process of expansion of the small household into a 'big family' began. Should wealth increase, the membership of the family would expand further by adding concubines and their children. The longer life span of the well-to-do also augmented the size of the expanding family. Sufficient economic means being a necessary ingredient, the 'big family' was more common among large landowners and well-to-do merchants than among the average peasants and workers." See C.K. Yang, *The Chinese Family in the Communist Revolution* (Cambridge: MIT Press, 1959): 9. See also Rose H. Lee, "Research on the Chinese Family," *American Journal of Sociology* 54 (May 1949): 497-504. Field surveys conducted during the Republican period shed some light on the actual size of a family. In North China villages, Olga Lang found that 54 percent of the farm laborers' families were simple conjugal families and only 11 percent were group-families. Among the landlords, however, the proportions were just about reversed. Only 12 percent of these families were conjugal, and 53 percent were extended or joint families. The proportions for the in-between classes show intermediate graduations. See Olga Lang, *Chinese Family and Society* (New Haven: Yale University Press, 1946): 138. In a village west of Shanghai Hsiao-tung Fei found that only 37 families among his series included both a senior married couple and one or more married sons. There were family groups that did not include any married couples. The most common single type, with 138 cases, was a married couple with some kin other than their own children but not with another married couple. See Hsiao-tung Fei, *Peasant Life in China* (London: Boutledge & Sons, 1954): 27-29.

20. Yang (n. 19): 39-44.

21. Ta Chen, *Population in Modern China* (Chicago: University of Chicago Press, 1946): 41-42 and 114; Chi-ming Chiao, "A Study of Chinese Population," *Milbank Memorial Fund Quarterly* 11, 4 (October 1933); and 12, 1-3 (January, April, and July 1934). In a rural community in north China the average age at marriage was found to be 17.2 for men and 17.7 for women. See

Sidney D. Gamble, *Ting Hsien: A North China Rural Community* (Stanford: Stanford University Press, 1968) paperback ed.: 40-41. In the same community it was also.found that age at marriage was closely related to the size of land owned by the family. "The average age for the girls marrying into the families with 50 or more *mu* of land was a full year less than for those marrying into families with less than 50 *mu*, 16.8 as compared with 17.8. For the boys the difference was much more marked. Their average age at marriage was 18.4 for the 50 to 99 *mu* group and to the surprisingly low average of 13.2 in the families with 100 *mu* or over." Ibid., pp. 42-43. If this pattern holds throughout the country (and needless to say it is impossible to ascertain this point), then it should not be very difficult for the government to uniformly enforce legal age of marriage. It should also facilitate the government's efforts to promote "optimal age of marriage" to some extent. In the past persons whose families' land holding was small got married later presumably because they could not afford wedding expenses while relatively young. Now the private ownership of land is abolished, they have all the more the economic disincentive not to get married early. However, this deterring factor is now somewhat offset by the government's strenuous efforts to discourage extravagant wedding practices. For evidence see *Chinese Communist Documents Captured by the Anti-Communist Guerrilla Team in a Raid on Lien Kiang, Fukien*, Photo copy, University of Michigan Asia Library.

22. Pressat (n. 2): 31.

23. Articles 2 and 3 of the Marriage Law of the People's Republic of China, reproduced in Yang (n. 19): 221.

24. Ibid., 46.

25. Article 9 of the Marriage Law, Yang (n. 19): 222.

26. *Hsin Chung-kuo Fu-nu* no. 10 (October 1955): 18-19. In 1955 the proportion of women in the labor force in selected industry and service sectors was 13.1 percent, ranging from 3.3 percent in basic construction to 21.5 percent in culture, education, and health. See "The Size, Composition and Distribution of Workers and Clerks in China in 1955," *Hsin-hua Pan-yeh-kan* no. 2 (January 1957): 87-89.

27. John L. Buck, *Land Utilization in China* (Chicago: University of Chicago Press, 1937): 303.

28. In 1958, at the height of the Great Leap campaign, there were three million nurseries in the rural areas looking after 24 million children, and unknown numbers of kindergartens were taking care of another 25 million children. On the average, 85 percent of the pre-school rural children reportedly went to nurseries or kindergartens for at least part of the work days. See Rebecca Kwan, "The Commune, the Family and the Emancipation of Women," *Contemporary China* 3 (1960): 148.

29. Soviet demographers attribute this precipitous fertility decline to collectivization, growth of obligatory education, and food shortages in the early

1930s. Eason, however, argues that "the age cohorts born during World War I and the Civil War, when birth rates were low, entered the reproductive ages beginning about 1930, and that this alone had a depressing effect on birth rate, other things being equal, for at least a decade or so." See Warren W. Eason, "Population Changes," in Allen Kassof, ed., *Prospects for Soviet Society* (New York: Praeger, 1968): 535, footnote 62. Although this thesis may indeed explain the population dynamics of rural Soviet Union in the 1930s, it can hardly explain the fact that rural fertility continued to decline, dropping to 27 per 1,000 population in 1950 and remaining more or less stable at this level for the rest of the decade only to experience further decline in the 1960s. Nor can the steady fertility decline be accounted for in terms of real economic improvements in the rural areas. Throughout 1940s the living standards in rural Soviet Union were very much the same as they were during the 1930s, if not worse, in view of the devastation of World War II and Stalin's decision to continue the pre-war forced industrialization pace in the immediate post-war period. Lorimer explains the steady decline in overall fertility up to 1936 in terms of widespread recourse to induced abortion, which was legalized shortly after the establishment of the U.S.S.R. and spread widely in the early 1930s. As evidence in support of his thesis, Lorimer points to the fact that following the re-illegalization of induced abortion in 1936, fertility again rose to 39.6 and 38.3 per 1,000 population in 1937 and 1938 respectively. See Frank Lorimer, *The Population of the Soviet Union* (Geneva: League of Nations, 1946), pp. 126-133. This thesis, however, cannot account for the fact that within three years the upward trend was reversed; in 1940 fertility again dropped to 31.2 and 31.5 per 1,000 population for the whole country and rural areas respectively. See Kassof (n. 29): 210-219. Admitting that the explanatory variables referred to above are all valid and together largely account for the population dynamics of rural Soviet Union in 1930s and 1940s, we may still suggest another important explanatory variable, namely the unusually high degree of female participation in the labor force at an early stage of modernization. Due primarily to the loss of over seven million adult males during World War I and the Civil War and its effects (e.g., famine and epidemics), large numbers of women were compelled to work outside of the household since the early Soviet era. The 1926 census revealed that women comprised 46.3 percent of the total labor force and that the proportion of women aged 20 to 54 in the labor force amounted to 78 percent, which was almost twice as high as that in the United States in 1960. See H. Kent Geiger, *The Family in Soviet Russia* (Cambridge: Harvard University Press, 1968): 177. In view of the limited extent of industrialization in 1920s and 1930s, it could be readily assumed that the overwhelming proportion of working women were employed in agriculture, mainly on collective farms as field workers and livestock tenders. The uniqueness of the Soviet demographic experience lies in the fact that in no other society (with the conspicuous exception of post-1949 China) at the comparable stage of modernization has the rural population been forced to undergo the kind of radical, sudden rearrangement of their economic and family life that Soviet peasants had in the 1930s. It is possible that employment of peasant women outside of the household in the context of collectivized agriculture alone has depressing effects on rural fertility, regardless of the type of employment. This point will be further elaborated later in the text.

30. Kenneth R. Walker, *Planning in Chinese Agriculture* (Chicago: Aldine, 1965): 59-100.

31. Leo Orleans, "Communist China's Education: Policies, Problems, and Progress," in *Economic Profile of Mainland China* vol. 2, (Washington, D.C.: U.S. Government Printing Office, 1967): 507-508.

32. Audrey Donnithorne, *China's Economic System* (New York: Praeger, 1967): 70-74.

33. Perhaps the best empirical evidence that tends to support our hypothesis about the depressing effect of collectivization on rural fertility is the demographic experience of the East European countries in the post-war period. Berent, in a careful examination of the demographic experience of the East European countries in the 1950s, has shown that the independent farmers consistently had the highest fertility rates, the cooperative farmers the next highest, the manual workers the next, and the non-manual workers the lowest fertility rates. Of all the countries studied only one, Hungary, did not conform to this pattern. For some unexplained reasons cooperative farmers there had higher fertility rates than the independent farmers. See Jerzy Berent, "Causes of Fertility Decline in Eastern Europe and the Soviet Union, Part II," *Population Studies* 24, 1 (March 1970): 258, table 8. In view of this finding, it is tempting to suggest that collectivization be viewed as an independent factor that tends to depress rural fertility, along with other social and economic forces generated in the process of modernization. What we are suggesting is that independent-cooperative farmers' fertility differentials may be as real as the well-nigh urban-rural fertility differentials and regional-ethnic-religious fertility differentials. For a somewhat vaguely stated and more cautious view, see Demitri B. Shimkim, "Demographic Changes and Socio-Economic Forces Within the Soviet Union, 1939-1959," in *Population Trends in Eastern Europe, the USSR and Mainland China* (n. 15): 262. See also Ronald Freedman, "Statement by Moderator," in *Proceedings of World Population Conference, 1965* (n. 2): 39-41.

34. Nathan Keyfitz, "The Impact of Technological Change on Demographic Patterns," in Bert F. Hoselitz and Wilbert F. Moore, eds., *Industrialization and Society* (Unesco-Mouton, 1966): 228.

35. Ronald Freedman, John Takeshita, and T.H. Sun, "Fertility and Family Planning in Taiwan: A Case Study of the Demographic Transition," *American Journal of Sociology* 70 (July 1964): 16-27.

36. All figures quoted in this section are from Alan P.L. Liu, *Communication and National Integration in Communist China*, Ph.D. dissertation, Department of Political Science, MIT, 1967, pp. 123-125 and 225-229.

37. Daniel Lerner, "Toward a Communication Theory of Modernization," in Lucian W. Pye, ed., *Communications and Political Development* (Princeton: Princeton University Press, 1963): 328.

38. Jan Myrdal and Gun Kessle, *China: The Revolution Continued* (New York: Pantheon, 1970): xi.

39. Ehrlich and Ehrlich suggest that in the United States the high incidence of unwanted children among the poor and near-poor as contrasted with the non-poor (estimated to be 40 vs. 14 percent) appears to lie more in the non-availability of the effective contraceptive methods to them rather than in their lack of knowledge (about such availability). From this it may be inferred that there presumably is no lack of motivation on the part of the poor or near-poor to practice family planning. See Paul E. Ehrlich and Ann Ehrlich, *Population Resources Environmeht* (San Francisco: W.H. Freeman and Co., 1970): 246.

40. United Nations, *Population Bulletin* no. 7 (1963): 127-129.

41. Leo Orleans, *Professional Manpower and Education in Communist China* (Washington, D.C.: National Science Foundation, 1960): 32.

42. A. Doak Barnet, *Cadres, Bureaucracy and Political Power in Communist China* (New York: Columbia University Press, 1967): 387-388. The basis for this assertion is, however, very weak, for the information was supplied by a few refugees interviewed by the author.

43. Cf. Dudly Kirk, "Nationality in the Developing Countries: Recent Trends and Prospects," in Behrman, Corsa, and Freedman, eds. (n. 5): 75-78.

44. Taiwan, Hong Kong, Singapore, and possibly South Korea are the exceptions. However, the relative success of the organized programs in Taiwan, Hong Kong, and Singapore, which happen to be the three major "Chinese cultural areas" outside of mainland China, can be to some extent accounted for by sociological factors apart from the programs themselves. Besides, the demographic transitions in these areas have yet to be completed. For an evaluation of the Taiwan program, see Ronald Freedman and John Y. Takeshita, *Family Planning in Taiwan* (Princeton, N.J.: Princeton University Press, 1969).

45. Of the five U.N. projections of the population of China in the year 2000, using different combinations of assumed mortality and fertility, three projections yield figures above one billion. See United Nations, *World Population Prospects As Assessed in 1963* (New York: United Nations, 1966): 57. For another projection (critical of the U.N. assumptions) for the period 1966-1968, see Aird, "Population Growth," in Eckstein, Galenson, and Liu, eds., (n. 2): 300-302, 276-316, and passim.

The Effects of Liberalized Abortion Laws in Eastern Europe

Robert J. McIntyre

Introduction

Alteration of the terms of availability of induced abortion is an obvious and direct means by which governmental policy may influence the fertility patterns of a population. Recent advocacy of liberalization of the availability of legal abortion in many "western" countries, and scholarly speculation on the likely popular response, should not be allowed to block from view the long and varied record of social experimentation in the countries of Eastern Europe. Beginning with the remarkable but short-lived Soviet law of 1920, and then again in the legislation of the mid-1950s in almost all of the Eastern European countries, abrupt shifts in the legal availability of induced abortion may be observed. The latter period is of special interest because of the occurrence of essentially similar abortion reform movements and legislation in a number of different countries at about the same point in time.

In the twenty-five years after the end of World War II most of the countries of Eastern Europe experienced sharply reduced rates of population growth, with falling birth rates more than offsetting falling death rates. Social and economic factors such as rising per capita income, increased participation of married women in the labor force, and endemic housing shortages partially occasioned by the unprecedented pace of urbanization, all played a role in the declining trend of the birth rate over this twenty-five year period. The first two of these factors appear to represent general tendencies operative in all relatively industrialized societies, while the last condition is somewhat specific to the Eastern European countries.

In the period after 1955 the rate of fertility decline in Eastern Europe has been particularly abrupt, and in the process this group of countries has made a rapid transition from the upper to the lower end of the European fertility spectrum, exhibiting some of the lowest crude birth rates in the world by the mid-1960s. The extent and sharpness of this fertility decline suggest that more than the usual secular factors were at work. The coincident legalization and large-scale popular adoption of induced abortion in these societies offer an obvious and appealing explanatory hypothesis in resolving this demographic anomaly.

The possible explanatory role of induced abortion is especially intriguing in light of the widespread anticipation of similar legislative reform in a number of Western European and North American countries. Preliminary movements toward reform in these western countries, however, bear only a limited resemblance to the sweeping Eastern European laws. It should be stressed that despite presumptions as to the "liberality" of Scandinavian laws in such matters, the permissiveness of the Eastern European abortion legislation of the mid-1950s has not been approached anywhere in Western Europe. The specific historical experience under study here is thus noteworthy both as a record of the process of interaction between fertility-influencing legislation and popular response and because of the remarkable extreme to which a particular type of legislation was carried.

Even in the absence of the abortion factor, such a rapid fertility decline would have an intrinsic appeal to economists who have long been interested in the nature of the interrelationship between demographic and economic phenomena. Besides the traditional Malthusian mechanism whereby increasing levels of real income directly support and foster population expansion, the highly important feedback from population change to economic growth and development has long been recognized. Modern consideration of this latter mechanism probably dates from J.M. Keynes' famous 1937 article in the *Eugenics Review*. This analytical concern was continued in the work of Alvin Hansen and Joseph Spengler,[1] and more recently has reappeared in studies by Kuznets, Easterlin, Demeny, and others.[2]

According to this line of argument the particular pattern of population growth will have both aggregate demand and aggregate supply effects. Variations in the rate of population growth have a direct though delayed effect on the demand for educational facilities, housing, and a broad range of consumer and capital goods. Equally important consequences eventually occur in the labor market, where they result in a changing size, age distribution, and rate of growth of the labor force, and in production where they may force alterations in capital-labor ratios, especially in a fully employed society with little remaining excess rural population.

But it is hardly necessary to labor the point that sharp changes in the growth of the working aged population, or in its size relative to the inactive population, will have significant economic effects. The particular interest of the Eastern European experience lies in the rich record of politically directed institutional change, public response, and ensuing administrative countermeasures that surround the issue of abortion liberalization. This chapter will provide an introduction to this highly political series of events, depicting the nature, extent, and underlying motive of historical events, but stopping short of any systematic evaluation of the net economic consequences of these demographic developments. The effects of various long-term structural changes in the population on observed fertility behavior are evaluated and a preliminary appraisal is made of the extent to which abortion reform by itself explains the abruptness of the decline and the ensuing low level of all important fertility indicators for these countries over the last fifteen years. Special analytical interest also centers around the various socio-demographic policies introduced during the 1960s to attempt to offset declining fertility trends. These pronatalist measures range from assorted "positive" incentive programs to administrative restriction or revocation of induced abortion programs and will be considered in some detail below.

Historical Background of the Recent Abortion Reforms

Slightly more than three years after the October Revolution, in a time of great social dislocation and waning civil war, the Soviet government enacted an unprecedented and almost unrestricted system of abortion on demand. While intended to reduce rampant illegal abortion, the new system was conceived of principally as a social welfare program fulfilling an important part of the socialist program for the emancipation of women. V.I. Lenin himself had explicitly advocated both legalization of abortion and encouragement of contraception as being essential to woman's basic right of choosing when and if to bear children.[3] Abortion was viewed as a temporary expedient, pending general improvement of the standard of living and assumption of major child care responsibilities by the state.[4]

Official distress over the large number of abortions performed under this system led to imposition of a small but significant fee in 1923. After twelve years of further controversy, administrative action was finally taken in 1935 forbidding abortion of first pregnancies and requiring a six-month interval between legal abortions. In June of 1936 the balance of the law of 1920 was substantively repealed. At the same time, a system of family allowances was established and child care facilities were expanded with the explicit hope of stimulating population growth. Although the result was that women in large numbers resorted to illegal abortion, it was not until 1955 that the restrictions of 1935 and 1936 were removed.[5] While homage was paid at this time to the Leninist principle of restoring women's full prerogatives, explicit acknowledgment was also made of the need to reduce damage to "the health of women" resulting from extensive illegal abortion.

After the reliberalization of Soviet abortion laws in December of 1955, all of the European socialist countries, except for the German Democratic Republic and Albania, rapidly enacted similar legislation. In each instance the change in the form and substance of the socio-legal posture toward abortion was enormous, and in each country there was an immediate and clearly visible rise in the number of abortions performed and an apparently related change in birth and population growth rates.[6] In light of the present space constraints, Bulgaria, Czechoslovakia, and Hungary have been selected for detailed analysis. These particular countries exhibit markedly different levels of economic development, as measured by per capita national income, as well as distinct cultural and political histories, and hence are representative of the whole of Eastern Europe.[7] In each of these countries the response to the legal change in abortion availability was sudden and very large in magnitude. The recorded number of legal abortions rose at a remarkable rate, and population growth fell off sharply, seeming to belie the possibility that official abortion statistics had simply begun to encompass previously illicit abortions. In Hungary the number of legal abortions per 1,000 population soon surpassed the number of live births. In each country the rate of population increase, as measured directly, and the potential future growth of the population, as measured roughly by the gross rate of reproduction,[8] fell off sharply. As indicated in Table 9-1, the GRR for Hungary fell from 1.35 in 1955 to .87 in 1962—well below the level associated with a pattern of age-specific fertility which, if continued for an extended period of time, would be just sufficient to maintain a constant population size.[9] In Czechoslovakia the GRR fell from 1.38 in 1955 to 1.14 in 1962, while in Bulgaria the index fell from 1.17 to 1.08 over the same period. In Romania, which has been excluded from the systematic analysis of this study, the fertility decline was particularly abrupt and legal abortions quickly came to outnumber live births, perhaps by as much as five to one, while the GRR dropped from 1.49 in 1955 to .98 seven years later.

Data of the type shown in Table 9-1 provide an interesting and more or less adequate picture of the broad fertility trends. But inspection of specific birth rates and gross rates of reproduction indicates that important structural factors are operating behind these aggregate figures. Note for example the apparent inconsistency between the crude birth rates and GRRs for Bulgaria, Czechoslovakia, and Hungary in 1955, reflecting the differing age structures of the respective populations.[11] Systematic determination of the extent of the direct fertility consequences of the modification in the abortion laws of the Eastern European countries requires that the effects of changes in long-run factors, such as the age and sex structure of the population, the proportion of the fertile female population that is married, and the urban-rural distribution of the

Table 9-1

	Crude Birth Rate			Gross Rate of Reproduction		
	1955	1962	1965	1955	1962	1965
Bulgaria	20.1	16.7	15.3	1.170	1.082	1.004
Czechoslovakia	20.3	15.7	16.4	1.379	1.140	1.151
Hungary	21.4	12.9	13.1	1.354	.868	.875
Romania	25.6	16.2	14.6	1.490	.980	.924
Western Europe[10]	18.3	18.6	18.5	1.227	1.297	1.314

Source: United Nations, *Demographic Yearbook 1965*: 294-297 and 611-616. *Demographic Yearbook 1969*: 262-263 and 475-476.

population, be removed from the observed changes in the basic indicators of fertility. The first step in this analytical process involves detailed evaluation of changes in the age and sex structure of the population which might conceal or confuse the true pattern of intrinsic fertility.[12]

Effects of Changes in the Age and Sex Structure of the Population

A satisfactory treatment of the effects of shifts in the age structure of the population can be built around the analytical categories suggested by Volkov and Berent.[13] This analysis is carried out in terms of the crude birth rate which may be expressed as:

$$(1) \quad \frac{B}{P} = \frac{B}{W^*} \cdot \frac{W^*}{W} \cdot \frac{W}{P}, \text{ where}$$

$\dfrac{B}{P}$ = live births per thousand total population

$\underline{W^*}$ = total female population 15-49 years of age

$\dfrac{B}{W^*}$ = live births per thousand women 15-49 years of age

W = total female population

P = total population

The first multiplicative term represents a recalculation of the birth rate on a more meaningful base—the total number of live births per thousand women in the fertile age range, which is generally considered to be 15-49 years of age.[14] The second term represents the number of fertile women as a proportion of total women, while the last term embodies the male-female ratio for the entire population.

Alteration of any one of the three multiplicative terms, holding both of the others constant, will result in a proportional change in the calculated value of the crude birth rate. Since 1955 was the last full year before either adoption or widespread public discussion of the desirability of abortion reform prior to actual adoption, it is suggested as an appropriate point of reference.[15] In the same way, the year 1962 marks something of a watershed between the initial period of concerned discussion and controversy over the unanticipated fertility consequences of the new reforms and the ensuing period characterized by implementation of explicitly pronatalist remedies.

If the values of two of the terms in equation (1) are held at their 1955 levels and multiplied by the realized values for the third, a series of hypothetical crude birth rates is generated reflecting solely the implications of the historical behavior of the factors embodied in the third term. Each term may in turn be treated in this fashion, thereby fully apportioning the observed changes in the crude birth rate to the variations of the constituent terms, and thereby standardizing for changes in the various age-structural characteristics of the population. This analysis may be summarized as dividing the total change in the crude birth rate into "pure" and "structural" effects, the latter reflecting the total structural effects embodied in the three multiplicative terms in equation (1).[16]

Data for the suggested period of 1955 to 1962 are summarized in Table 9-2, which simply distinguishes between the "pure" and total fertility change—the difference between the two being the change attributable to the various age and sex related structural factors discussed earlier. Careful evaluation of the experience of Czechoslovakia as an example, indicates that the tabular analysis must be supplemented with appropriate historical detail to achieve a rich and relatively satisfactory account of the effects of specific policy changes. Over the entire 1955-68 period the crude birth rate for Czechoslovakia fell by 5.4 points, but the pure fertility change amounted to −5.9 points, sufficient to fully account for the observed reduction of the crude birth rate and to more than offset the small change in the age structure of the 15-49 year old female population, which by itself tended to *raise* the observed fertility level. The proportion of women in the total population did not change significantly during this period, while the proportion of fertile to total women fell from 1955 to 1961 and increased thereafter, finally rising above the 1955 level in 1968. On the basis of analysis across the thirteen year period, it seems clear that shifts in the age structure of the population were not an important factor in observed fertility trends, although inspection of the changes for individual years and apposite subperiods is essential before this conclusion can be accepted without qualification.

In particular, explicit attention should be given to circumstances before and after 1962, since a significant restriction of the Czech abortion laws occurred in December of that year, making abortions less readily accessible to women who

Table 9-2
Changes in Crude Birth Rates: 1955 to 1962

	Bulgaria	Czechoslovakia[a]		Hungary
Total Change	−3.4	−4.6	(−4.3)	−8.5
"Pure" Fertility Change	−1.2	−3.6	(−3.3)	−7.6
Age-Sex Structural Shift Effect	−2.2	−1.0	(−1.0)	− .9
Shift Effect/Total Change	.65	.22	(.23)	.11

[a]Figures in parentheses refer to the 1955-59 period.

were very young and/or who had never borne a child. The fairly sharp rise in
both the pure fertility indicator and the crude birth rate during the following
two years may well be a reflection of this circumstance. A renewed pure fertility
decline in 1965-67 more than compensated for the 1963-64 interlude, but direct
evidence as to an administrative cause for this fluctuation is incomplete.
Information is available on the percentage of applications for abortion that were
in fact granted. This approval percentage fell from approximately 90 percent in
1960-62 to 86 percent in 1963, rising to 89 percent in 1964 and 92 percent by
1965.[17]

As might be expected, the well-advertised implementation of stricter requirements resulted in submission of a reduced number of applications by the public
as well as fewer favorable actions on those applications received. Applications
for legal abortion fell by more than 20 percent during the two year period of
relative administrative stringency in 1963 and 1964.[18] The number of legal
abortions fell by a comparable percentage, dropping from 89,800 in 1962 to
70,500 and 70,700 in the two following years, and then rising steeply for the
next four years, reaching 99,700 in 1968.[19] As might be expected, recourse to
illegal methods also seems to have increased as a result of the reduced availability
of legal abortion during 1963 and 1964. Direct estimates of the number of
"other" abortions suggests a rise from 26,093 in 1962 to 29,387 and 28,513 in

Table 9-3
Number of Maternal Deaths from Abortions: Czechoslovakia 1953-65

Year	Legal Abortion	Spontaneous	Criminal	Total
1953	—		44	44*
1954	—		37	37*
1955	—		37	37*
1956	—		44	44*
1957	8	20	21	49
1958	4	13	19	36
1959	2	4	10	16
1960	2	6	10	18
1961	1	1	12	14
1962	2	6	9	17
1963	0	0	14	14
1964	1	n.a.	14	n.a.
1965	1	n.a.	3	n.a.

Source: Adopted from figures presented by A. Černoch, "Les authorisations d'interrup-
tions de grossesse en Tchécoslovaquie," *Gynaecologia* vol. 160 (1965): 293; and J. Lukás,
"Abortion in Czechoslovakia," in *Sex and Human Relations* (Proceedings of the 1964 IPPF
Conference, London) (New York: Excerpta Medica Foundation, 1965): 98.

*Some additional maternal deaths are likely to have resulted from the relatively small but
still significant number of legal abortions performed prior to 1957.

the following two years.[20] Indirect evidence is provided by the changing pattern of maternal mortality resulting from abortion.[21] (See Table 9-3.) A sharp rise in deaths resulting from criminal abortion can be seen in 1963 and 1964, followed by a sharp decline in 1965 when the regulations were again eased.

Thus, specific abortion and mortality data seem to be consistent with the yearly behavior of the "pure fertility" as revealed in the standardization analysis summarized in Table 9-2. It seems clear that the sharp reversal of the downward trend in the birth rate in 1963 and 1964 is to a significant degree the result of the abortion restrictions of those years. It is interesting to note that the reliberalization in 1965 came after substantial controversy, and perhaps even quasi-political scandal, over the rising number of injuries and deaths resulting from criminal abortion and the apparent rise in the number of suicides among pregnant women.[22] Just how much of the large pure fertility declines in 1965, 1966, and 1967 should be attributed to administrative relaxation of abortion requirements is less clear, although the pattern of the fertility decline closely matches the abortion resurgence, both in the aggregate and in terms of age-specific rates.

For Hungary the influence of shifts in the age and sex structure of the population accounted for only 11 percent of the enormous 8.5 point fertility decline of the 1955 to 1962 period (see Table 9-2). This age-structural influence is almost entirely the result of a rise in the proportion of women in the fertile age groups. The Bulgarian case is quite different, age-structural factors accounting for 65 percent of the relatively small 3.4 point decline in the crude birth rate. The changing distribution of women within the fertile age groups was slightly more important than the declining overall proportion of this group in the total female population in explaining this 2.2 point structurally induced decline in the crude birth rate.

Effects of Changes in the Urban-Rural Population Distribution

Like most modern societies the Eastern European countries have been experiencing a secular shift of population out of the countryside and into the cities. Since birth rates tend to be considerably higher in rural areas, this tendency toward urbanization during the time of the abortion reforms would build in a downward bias to the national crude birth rates that is largely spurious from the analytical perspective of this chapter. As in the case of age-sex structure, it is necessary to develop a distinction between the "pure" behavioral component of the fertility decline and the "spurious" element deriving from a secular trend—in this case the movement of large numbers of persons from the high fertility milieu of the rural way of life to the lower fertility urban environment. It is useful to reflect the urban-rural fertility dichotomy directly in the calculation of the crude birth rate, which can be expressed as:

$$(2) \quad \frac{B}{P} \quad = \text{UBR} \cdot \frac{\text{UP}}{P} + \text{RBR} \cdot \frac{\text{RP}}{P}, \text{where}$$

$$\frac{B}{P} \quad = \text{ live births per thousand total population}$$

$$\text{UBR} \quad = \text{ live births in urban areas per thousand urban residents}$$

$$\text{RBR} \quad = \text{ live births in rural areas per thousand rural residents}$$

$$P \quad = \text{ total population} = \text{UP} + \text{RP}$$

Utilizing a differential form of equation (2) a standardization analysis can be developed which distinguishes between the effects of changes in birth rates within the urban and rural sectors and shifts in the importance of those sectors and thus of their weight in the calculation of the crude birth rate.[23]

Historical data calculated for equation (2) are summarized in Table 9-4 which contains data for the 1955-1962 period for Bulgaria, Czechoslovakia, and Hungary. In Czechoslovakia the urban-rural shift was of negligible importance whether viewed over the five or the eight year period. For Bulgaria and Hungary, increased urbanization had a small depressing effect on the birth rate over the 1955 to 1962 period. In both cases, however, this effect was wiped out by a strong rise in urban birth rates in the ensuing six years. In Hungary the net effect over the entire fourteen year period was nil, while in Bulgaria the remarkable net effect of urbanization was to *raise* the birth rate by half a point.

The analysis of the yearly data on the effects of urbanization in Bulgaria which underlies the summary results in Table 9-4 illuminates both the specific case under study and the analytical method. Of particular note was the sharp rise in Bulgarian fertility in 1968, which was especially evident in urban areas, where the birth rate rose 2.1 points in that single year. This is at least partially a reflection of the restriction in the availability of legal abortion which was put into effect on December 22, 1967,[24] and perhaps anticipated and partially implemented months earlier. Since the urban population is known to be much more likely to seek abortion, reduced access to induced abortion might be expected to have a greater impact on the urban birth rate. It should also be

Table 9-4
Changes in Crude Birth Rates: 1955 to 1962

	Bulgaria	Czechoslovakia[a]		Hungary
Total Change	−3.4	−4.6	(−4.3)	−8.5
"Pure" Fertility Change	−3.2	−4.5	(−4.2)	−7.9
Urban-Rural Structural Shift Effects	− .2	.1	(− .1)	− .6
Shift Effect/Total Change	.06	.02	(.02)	.07

[a]Figures in parentheses refer to the 1955-59 period.

noted that after 1966 the Bulgarian urban birth rate is actually *higher* than the rate for rural areas. This circumstance is certainly unique in the twentieth-century European experience and has yet to be satisfactorily explained. While the urban birth rate reached a low of 15.3 in 1962 and, except for one year, rose thereafter, the rural rate continued to fall until 1968. The broad program of pronatalist incentives introduced in the early 1960s may well play a role here, in that the types of inducements used—greatly extended paid maternity leave, improved child care facilities, access to new and larger apartments, tax advantages, and steeply progressive "children's allowances"—may have had a more conclusive effect in the urban environment, where a greater proportion of mothers are in the labor force away from the home and where the child care advantages of the extended family are less common.

Table 9-5
Bulgaria: Urban and Rural Birth Rates

	1955	56	57	58	59	60	61	62	63	64	65	66	67	68
Total	20.1	19.5	18.4	17.9	17.6	17.8	17.4	16.7	16.4	16.1	15.3	14.9	15.0	16.9
Urban	18.7	17.5	17.1	16.4	16.0	16.1	15.8	15.3	15.5	15.6	14.7	15.5	15.9	18.0
Rural	20.8	20.5	19.2	18.7	18.4	18.8	18.3	17.7	17.0	16.4	15.9	14.4	14.2	15.9

Source: United Nations, *Demographic Yearbook* (various years)

Effects of Changes in Nuptiality

Both intuition and available data suggest that the fertility rate of married women is generally much higher than that of unmarried women. Movements in the aggregate crude birth rate necessarily embody changes in the fertility rates of both married and unmarried women as well as any changes which might occur in the proportion of fertile women who are married and thus presumably subject to greater risk of pregnancy. Again this concealed element in the observed fertility patterns can be directly reflected in the calculation of the crude birth rate, which in this case is expressed as:

$$(3) \quad \frac{B}{P} = \frac{B}{MW^*} \cdot \frac{MW^*}{P} + \frac{B}{UMW^*} \cdot \frac{UMW^*}{P}, \text{ where}$$

$\dfrac{B}{P}$ = live births per thousand total population

$\dfrac{B}{MW^*}$ = legitimate live births per thousand married women*

$$\frac{B}{UMW^*} = \text{illegitimate live births per thousand unmarried women*}$$

$$\frac{MW^*}{P} = \text{married women* as a proportion of total population}$$

$$\frac{UMW^*}{P} = \text{unmarried women* as a proportion of total population}$$

$$P = MW^* + UMW^* + \text{all women 0-14 and over 49 + all men,}$$

and all figures bearing an asterisk refer to women 15-49 years of age. A differential form of equation (3) can be used to separate the effects of changes in married fertility and unmarried fertility from the result of shifts in the proportion of fertile women who are married. The consequences of changes in the proportion of women who are married and thus presumably subject to greater risk of pregnancy is called the shift effect. Historical data for equation (3) are summarized in Table 9-6, which indicates that shifts in nuptiality patterns account for about a fifth of the observed change in the crude birth rate in both Bulgaria and Czechoslovakia over the entire period. The relative importance of changing marriage patterns is reduced somewhat over the 1955-1959 sub-period for Czechoslovakia. For Hungary only five percent of the large 8.5 point decline in the crude birth rate can properly be attributed to shifts in nuptiality. If the impact of changing nuptiality patterns is in general not great, this is another way of saying that a large "pure" fertility decline must have occurred to yield the large aggregate fertility declines. Clearly marital fertility fell in each country and non-marital fertility fell in Czechoslovakia and Hungary, with particularly large reductions in the latter country. Review of the yearly data on the proportion of married and unmarried women 15-49 years of age supports the conclusion of the earlier discussion of the age and sex structure that changes in the proportion of women in the fertile ages had little to do with observed fertility trends in that country.

Table 9-6
Changes in Crude Birth Rates: 1955 to 1962

	Bulgaria	Czechoslovakia[a]		Hungary
Total Change	−4.8	−4.6	(−4.3)	−8.5
"Pure" Fertility Change	−4.0	−3.6	(−3.7)	−8.1
Nuptiality Shift Effects	.8	−1.0	(− .6)	− .4
Shift Effect/Total Change	.17	.22	(.14)	.05

[a]Figures in parentheses refer to the 1955-59 period.

Extent of Pure Fertility Decline

In the preceding sections the effects of changes in the age and sex structure, urban-rural residence, and nuptiality patterns of the three populations have each been separately evaluated. In each section a distinction was made between the direct effects of the particular secular factor under study and the remaining "pure" fertility effect. This latter behavioral effect is different in magnitude in each case since it is defined as including everything that remains after elimination of the full influence of one specific long-run factor. The magnitude of the given structural change is established in a unique manner. It is now possible to bring all three sequentially evaluated structural effects together and determine how much of the observed fertility reductions remain after their cumulative impact is eliminated.[25] Table 9-7 brings together the results of the three separate procedures and indicates the extent to which apparent fertility reductions are the result of underlying "purely demographic" long-term trends.

After adjustment for the three enumerated structural factors it can be seen that the relative significance of the residual "pure" fertility reduction varies greatly between countries. It is relatively unimportant for Bulgaria, but predominant in the case of Hungary, with Czechoslovakia occupying an intermediate position. In explaining this variation it would be desirable to have a full accounting of the significant social and economic elements of the environment in which family planning decisions are made and through which institutional changes such as abortion reform must work before actual fertility patterns are effected. While such an approach would be helpful in explaining the differential response to the abortion reforms, it would necessarily bring in difficult-to-

Table 9-7
Changes in Crude Birth Rates: 1955 to 1962 and 1955 to 1965

	Total Change in the Crude Birth Rate	Less: Effects of Shifts In:			Equals: Pure Fertility Change	
		Age & Sex	Urbanization	Nuptiality	Number	% of Total
Bulgaria						
1955-62	−3.4	−2.3	−.1	− .7	− .3	8.8
1955-65	−4.8	−2.6	−.1	− .6	−1.5	31.2
Czechoslovakia						
1955-59	−4.3	−1.0	−.1	− .6	−2.6	60.5
1955-62	−3.9	−1.0	−.1	−1.0	−2.5	54.3
Hungary						
1955-62	−8.5	− .9	−.6	− .4	−6.6	77.6
1955-65	−8.4	− .9	−	− .5	−7.0	83.3

Source: United Nations, *Demographic Yearbook* (various years) and calculations by the author.

quantify variables such as governmental educational and propaganda efforts, direct fertility-influencing welfare programs, public attitudes toward the future and toward the diffuse concept of desired family size, as well as more readily accessible factors such as the extent and trend of labor force participation by women in the fertile age groups, the level and rate of growth of real per capita income, and the degree of availability of various contraceptive materials and knowledge.

Fortunately, a good number of these factors can be shown either to have worked in a pronatalist direction in the time period under consideration or to vary only slightly between these countries. In this particular temporally compressed historical situation the problem is further simplified by the ability to properly exclude all factors that do not change sharply and differentially at or about the time of the reforms. For example, it has been suggested that the absence of significant pronatalist policy changes in the 1955 to 1962 period permits us the great analytical liberty of ignoring the structure of the social welfare systems and their effects on fertility. But obviously an account principally concerned with the differential nature of the response would want to consider the level and nature of these very systems. Rates of labor force participation presumably also have vital implications for women's attitudes toward motherhood, and serve, at some given level of abstract family size preference, to indirectly reflect the opportunity income of "foregoing" a child care career—an implicit indication of the degree of access of women to relatively rewarding careers. But again we conveniently find that these levels of economic participation were already very high by the time of the reforms and did not evolve systematically in the period under consideration.

Governmental educational and persuasive efforts can be shown to have been consistently directed toward stimulating population growth and discouraging recourse to legal abortion, even while freely offering and subsidizing it. This posture reflects the essentially contradictory nature of the social and economic goals being pursued: the simultaneous effort to eliminate illegal abortion via provision of a legal substitute, while also viewing with alarm and attempting to counteract any decline in aggregate population growth resulting from massive public acceptance of induced abortion as a family planning technique.

This is not the place to go into the implicit economic-demographic theories lying behind this somewhat surprising pronatalist inclination. Suffice it to say that there is evidence of a rational and coherent pattern of governmental concern with the undesirable economic implications of a *sudden* slowing of population growth, relating to the ensuing abrupt termination of labor force growth and the possible development of high dependency ratios, as longevity continues to increase and fertility declines. This concern was evident in Czechoslovakia as early as 1957, the year of the long-anticipated legalization of abortion. At that time, an advisory State Population Committee was established to study ways in which "(1) to prevent the fall of the birth rate and thus to counteract the unfavorable age composition of the population; and (2) to prepare such conditions as would enable families to have a large number of children without affecting their standard of living and to help equalize the standard of living between families with children and childless families."[26] The large numbers of legal abortions performed in 1956 and 1957, as interpretation of existing laws became less strict in anticipation of the reforms of late 1957, and the sharp declines in the number of births in those years presumably played an important role in motivating this early expression of official concern. Similar expressions of concern can be found from the initial period of liberalization in Hungary and Bulgaria, not to mention the Soviet Union. As Berent suggests, these recent fertility developments "have generally been received with surprise, often with incredulity, and always with disapproval."[27] The specific manifestations of this concern in Hungary and Czechoslovakia will be considered below in the context of the discussion of the implementation of active pronatalist policies in the early 1960s. In all of these countries the parallel with the earlier Soviet liberalization of the 1920-1936 period is remarkable, both with regard to the quickly emerging governmental view of the dire consequences that would flow from reduced population growth and in terms of the program of social and financial incentives to large families offered at the same time that state-supported abortion remained available.[28]

In the absence of a completely specified model of fertility determination, some further support for the causal role of abortion reform in reducing fertility can be gained by inspection of the pattern of yearly changes in abortions performed and changes in live births for the three countries. Even if there were no other complicating factors, complete explanation of changes in the number of births in terms of the changes in the number of abortions is not possible because of the methodological conundrums created by the problem of measuring the number of illegal abortions. As we have indicated, substantial reduction of the extent of illegal abortion was a central policy concern of the abortion legalization and reform movement in Eastern Europe. Whatever the unintended nature of the apparent aggregate fertility consequences of these laws, the desired major reduction if not complete elimination of illegal abortion was clearly achieved. Although Eastern European statistics on abortion are unusually good,[29] they are necessarily incomplete, making it impossible to directly deduce the net effect on births by subtracting the reduction in illegal abortion from the increase in legal abortion.[30]

We may hypothesize that the partly invisible reduction in the practice of illegal abortion would probably be greatest in the early years of the new regime, as old individual habits change in the face of progressive community acceptance of legal abortion and conclusive proof of its remarkable degree of safety. While some women will retain allegiance to illegal practitioners either through inertia, geographical isolation, or a particularly strong interest in secrecy,[31] the evidence seems to suggest that the great bulk of those favorably disposed toward abortion will prefer to seek a legal interruption.

Without reference to more elaborate statistical techniques, it is possible to note the extent to which negative (positive) yearly changes in the number of births are associated with positive (negative) changes in the number of abortions for each of the three countries.[32] After an initial period in which the effect on current fertility would seem to have been greatly attenuated by the decreasing practice of illegal abortion, a remarkably coherent pattern emerges. In Czechoslovakia, for example, in the first years of the reform from 1957 to 1961, legal abortions rose by 87,000 while the number of births fell by only 34,300. But in the 1962 to 1964 period of reduced abortion availability, legal abortions fell by 23,600 while births rose by 22,900, and in each of the next four years of more readily available abortion the figures are remarkably consistent and similar in their absolute values. This is all the more impressive in light of the basic inadequacy of the time dimension of the data involved, since some of the abortions performed in the last six to eight months of any given year may be expected to influence births which otherwise would have eventuated in the next calendar year.

Since, except for rare cases involving rape, incest, or serious medical-eugenic considerations, interruption of pregnancy in these countries is legally restricted to the first twelve weeks of pregnancy, the shortest biologically possible lapse between the interruption of a pregnancy and the otherwise anticipated time of the averted birth is six months and the maximum in the vicinity of eight months. Accordingly, the large administratively induced decline in the number of abortions performed in Czechoslovakia during 1962 and 1963 will have an effect on fertility that is limited in 1962, strong in 1963, and that necessarily carries over into 1964 as well. It should be noted that M. Kucera, a leading Czech demographer, writing in 1965, ascribed the 1963 and 1964 fertility rise to the increase in maternity leave to twenty-two weeks and incorrect rumors of its impending extension to 54 weeks.[33] J. Lukás, writing in 1964, offers an amusing alternative explanation which suggests that the decline in abortions and the rise in the number of births was the result of "health education and of education for parenthood."[34]

These views seem improbable, or at least unimportant, in light of the analysis of the application and approval rates for legal abortion presented above. Explanations of this type would have great difficulty in explaining the propitious correspondence of the recession in natality and the suspension of these particular abortion restrictions in 1965. The figures in Table 9-8 seem to support this view, but in the absence of monthly data for both births and abortions, the analysis must be left in this largely speculative state.

For Hungary the pattern is initially similar with yearly increases in the number of abortions from 1955 through 1961 and reductions in the number of births for one additional year. Beyond 1962 the data offer less satisfaction, a weak and irregular rise in the number of abortions appearing with a steadily climbing number of births.[35] Further supportive evidence relevant to the abortion-birth relationship can be drawn from the events of 1952 and 1953

Table 9-8
Yearly Changes In Legal Abortions (A) and Live Births (B) (thousands)

	1955	1956	1957	1958	1959	1960	1961	1962	1963	1964	1965	1966	1967	1968
Bulgaria														
A	—	17.3	13.3	6.4	7.5	9.2	14.0	7.9	6.6	8.2	5.0	5.9	-3.2	-13.0
B	—	-3.1	-6.9	-2.7	-1.4	3.2	-2.2	-3.7	-2.0	-1.2	-5.2	-2.8	1.5	16.9
Czechoslovakia														
A	-.7	1.0	4.2	54.1	17.7	9.2	6.0	-4.5	-19.3	.2	8.9	10.7	6.1	3.3
B	-1.5	-3.2	-9.2	-17.7	-18.1	.3	1.1	-.9	18.5	5.3	-9.6	-9.1	-6.6	-2.2
Hungary														
A	19.1	47.1	40.9	22.2	6.8	9.8	7.8	-6.3	10.1	10.6	-4.1	6.5	.7	13.6
B	-12.9	-17.6	-25.6	- 8.8	-7.2	-4.7	-6.1	-10.3	2.3	- .2	1.0	5.4	10.4	5.5

Sources: Henry P. David, Family Planning and Abortion in the Socialist Countries of Central and Eastern Europe (New York: The Population Council, 1970): A. Klinger, "Demographic Aspects of Abortion," IUSSP International Population Conference vol. 2, (London: IUSSP, 1969): 1153-1165; and United Nations, Demographic Yearbook (various years).

when a concerted offensive against illegal abortion was undertaken. This campaign involved vigorous enforcement and prosecution under existing legislation proscribing induced abortion. Despite a previously declining trend, the number of births rose markedly during this two-year period.

The generally appreciated undesirability of the approach of this anti-abortion program, either in terms of lack of success or unpopularity, led in late 1953 to the establishment of local medical boards with authority to approve applications for abortion on certainly narrowly specified *medical* grounds or indications. The spontaneous liberalization of the standards applied by these commissions can be seen in the distinct upward trend in the number of legal abortions performed, rising from less than 3,000 per year in 1950-1953 to 16,300 in 1954 and 35,400 in 1955, prior to the general legalization of abortion on social grounds, which did not eventuate until June of 1956.

In Bulgaria the generally increasing number of abortions in the ten years following the reform occurred with parallel declines in births in all but one year. When the number of abortions suddenly fell in 1967 and 1968 as the result of administrative restrictions on eligibility for abortion, large increases in the number of live births, of a similar absolute magnitude, appeared for the first time since the very beginning of the 1950s. Again in the case of Bulgaria, significant pronatalist policy changes were implemented in the mid-1960s which generally tended to stimulate fertility and perhaps played a role in subtly augmenting the more powerful and abrupt effect of the anti-abortion policy shift of 1967. Although no abortion data are available for these most recent years, the sharp fall in the number of live births in 1970 after three years of increases, in concert with solid evidence of abandonment of the three-year-old restrictive abortion policy in that same year,[36] suggest that this may be another demonstration of the close abortion-birth nexus.

Concluding Remarks on the Early Period
of Abortion Liberalization

There has been a dramatic decline in the crude birth rates in most of the countries of Eastern Europe over the last fifteen years. In a very brief period the observed fertility pattern of these countries has been transformed, and they have moved from the upper to the very lower end of the fertility spectrum of developed countries. Detailed consideration of events in Bulgaria, Czechoslovakia, and Hungary has made it clear that this fertility decline was not just a statistical illusion resulting from war-induced irregularities in the age structure of the population. Likewise, the rapid urbanization of the period or changes in nuptiality patterns are not adequate to explain the sharpness of the decline. The issue of causation is quite complicated, and it can always be said that the observed fertility declines are simply a reflection of changing conceptions of desired family size. From that perspective, "the possibility of terminating pregnancies can only be a means and not a reason for reduction of family size."[37] One obvious objection to that view consists in pointing out the oddity of the coincidence of the alleged decline in "desired family size" with the sudden availability of legal abortion.

A more conclusive argument can be made by careful consideration of the way in which the information content of the desired family size measure is constrained by certain of its methodological characteristics. On an a priori basis, legalization of abortion would be expected to have at least two distinct effects on the fertility decision-making process. A model of family size determination, along the lines suggested by Schultz[38] is useful as a point of reference. In this model, the birth rate

$$(4) \quad \frac{B}{P} = f(X_1, X_2, X_3)$$

$$\text{where} \quad X_1 = \text{"desired family size"}$$

$$X_2 = \text{a measure of the expected incidence of death among offspring, and}$$

$$X_3 = \text{a measure of the variance of } X_2$$

The variable X_1 is in turn a function of environmental conditions which affect the subjective and/or pecuniary net costs of having children. Prominent among these factors[39] must be some measure of the *full* costs of avoidance of birth, which are drastically altered by introduction of extremely safe, inexpensive, and socially sanctioned abortion. (Obviously this effect will be especially strong in countries and times where other contraceptive practices are not extensively developed, as was the case in much of Eastern Europe in the 1955 to 1965 period.) In terms of simple demand theory, abortion provides a substitute[40] for previous contraceptive practices offering almost absolute certainty of success at a mortality risk lower than that of actually bearing a child, and without the various psycho-sensual drawbacks associated with prior methods. So, at given levels of the other determinants of "desired family size," promulgation of abortion reform completely transforms the cost side of the conception control problem. It should be clear in this sense that any attempt to measure "desired family size" by survey techniques must necessarily assume and presuppose a *given cost structure*. Modifications of this cost structure, whether in the form of real alterations in conventionally defined prices or perceived changes in psychic costs,[41] should naturally be expected to alter the measured "desired family size." Survey results showing declining "desired family size" in Hungary from 1955 to 1966,[42] for example, are hardly surprising when viewed from this perspective. Table 9-9 presents data collected through national samples for Hungary in 1958-1960 and 1965-1966.

Table 9-9
Number of Planned Children in Hungary

Age of Mother	1958-60	1965-66
15-24	2.1	2.0
25-29	2.2	2.0
30-39	2.4	2.1
40-49	2.6	2.3
Total	2.4	2.1

Source: J. Berent, "Causes of Fertility Decline in Eastern Europe and the Soviet Union," *Population Studies* 24, 2 (July 1970): 284.

In addition to this direct cost mechanism, abortion availability may also have a demonstration effect which results in a further modification of parental tastes. According to this line of reasoning, the simple fact of the appearance of many one- and two-child families may in and of itself alter average ideas of what is the "normal" number of children and just what are the desirable ways of drawing pleasure from life. There is also some evidence from longitudinal studies in other countries that successful de facto control of fertility seems to result in the smaller families than were initially deemed desirable.[43]

Availability of legal abortion can be expected to influence observed fertility through these specific cost and "taste" factors operating on the desired number of births and also through at least partial elimination of the inability to adjust the "realized" to the "desired" number of children. It is also possible, however, that the availability of abortion may alter only the timing and spacing of births rather than the ultimate size of the completed family. Even such a limited effect would nevertheless have a distinct and extended retarding influence on any indicator of aggregate fertility and on the rate of population growth, as well as a permanent effect on the size of the population at any future time. In a sense, then, even assertion of an effect entirely restricted to timing would be compatible with the claim that legalization of abortion was the "cause" of the observed short run decline in fertility.

Separating these timing and ultimate family size effects is inherently difficult, but inspection of age-specific fertility rates and statistics on the distribution of births by birth order,[44] which in general show a precipitous reduction of third and higher order births but little change in first and second births, as well as limited studies on women of completed fertility,[45] seem to support the conclusion that both the timing and the total number of births are changing in response to legalization of abortion.

By the time in life that third and higher order births are being postponed, the purely biological probabilities of conception are at the very least beginning their inevitable decline. The effect of declining fecundity is then to make "postponed" births marginally less probable in a purely biological sense, not to mention the cumulative life style arguments against reopening the family ledger.[46] A powerful a priori case can be built along this line suggesting some net positive (negative) completed fertility effect from almost any event that pushes higher order births forward (backward) in time.

Active Pronatalist Policies of the 1960s

We have noted that in each of these Eastern European countries there were conscious efforts to offset the aggregate effects on population growth of readily available, safe, and extremely inexpensive induced abortion. These counter-measures were diverse both in nature and in terms of the strength and determination with which they were employed. Specific policies ranged from "positive" incentive programs such as lengthened paid maternity leave, sharply increased level and progressivity of the system of family allowance payments, cash birth payments, preferential access to new apartments, and explicit new taxes on childless couples, to the extreme case of Romania where in late 1966 the abortion reform was almost completely revoked and divorce made more difficult to obtain. As indicated above, relatively limited administrative restrictions of abortion availability occurred in Czechoslovakia from 1962 to 1964 and in Bulgaria from 1967 to 1970. The unusual scope and power of the individual positive incentive programs and the striking variation in the combinations of policies employed in the individual countries invite detailed attention.

It is well to begin by stressing the prior existence in each of these countries of a complicated structure of programs and policies directly or indirectly intended to ease the financial strain on large families. As Berent indicates, the structure of the existing social welfare legislation seems to have aimed at redistribution of income in the direction of large families as a matter of equity and not as an explicit stimulus to high fertility.[47] As much as a quarter of disposable income is distributed through these social welfare funds, and the incidence of these payments varies closely with family size. In addition, important aspects of housing, price, and child care policy serve to underwrite or subsidize the costs of child rearing. While the existing structure of social welfare policies was clearly favorable to high fertility, it should be noted that the basic employment and economic development policies of these countries have stressed the improvement of the economic lot of the family through the labor force participation of the wife and are thus strongly detrimental to high fertility. It is within this institutional structure that the explicitly pronatalist policies of the 1960s were introduced, often working through the payment mechanism of the established welfare system or by reducing the existing institutional impediments to female labor force participation.

Hungary, unlike the other countries under study, has employed a thus far unbroken policy of relying exclusively on positive incentives. Beginning in the mid-1960s a series of programs were established with the explicit goal of raising aggregate birth rates and concentrating on stimulating second and third order births. In 1966 the level of monthly payments through the Hungarian family allowance system was raised more or less proportionally, as indicated in Table 9-10. At the same time family allowance coverage was extended to cover agricultural workers, although at considerably lower rates than for urban workers. In 1967 paid "post-maternity" leave of up to thirty-one months and reemployment guarantees were introduced for working mothers. This extended leave period began after the end of the normal five months of maternity leave at full salary and involved monthly payments of 600 Forints in urban areas and 500 in agricultural areas.[48] In 1970 these monthly payments were equalized for rural areas. Table 9-11 provides an indication of the relative magnitude of these

Table 9-10
Marginal Monthly Family Allowance Payments (A = early 1960s; B = late 1960s)

		Birth Order					
		1	2	3	4	5	More
Bulgaria							
A	leva	–	13	13	13	10	5
1969 [a]		5	15	35	5	5	5
Cash Birth Bonus		20	200	500	20	20	20
Czechoslovakia							
1957-59	Kcs.	70	100	140	180	220	220
1959-68 [b]		70	100	260	260	260	260
1968-present [c]		90	240	350	350	240	240
Hungary							
A	Forint	–	200	160	120	120	
1966		–	300	210	170	170	
Romania							
A	lei	100	100	100	100	100	100
B		130	130	130	130	130	130
Cash Birth Bonus [d]		–	–	1000	1000	1000	1000

a/ Prior to January 1, 1969, there was a maximum yearly income criterion for receipt of family allowances.

b/ These rates are for a family whose chief earner receives a monthly gross wage of less than 1400 Kcs. Rates for higher income levels are also progressive through the third child, but rise less rapidly than for this lowest income group.

c/ After the institution of the new schedule in July of 1968, the rates are no longer differentiated by income level.

d/ Prior to January 1, 1967, bonus payment applied to only tenth and higher births.

Source: J. Berent, "Causes of Fertility Decline in Eastern Europe and the Soviet Union," *Population Studies* 24, 2 (July 1970): 228, and Henry P. David, *Family Planning and Abortion in the Socialist Countries of Central and Eastern Europe* (New York: The Population Council, 1970): 65 and 173.

Table 9-11

Cumulative Family Allowance and Leave Payments as a Percentage of the Average Annual Wage (1967) in Hungary

	Birth Order				
	1	2	3	4	5
Family Allowance (1966)	–	16	27	36	45
Leave Payment [a]	32	32	32	32	32
Total [a]	32	48	59	68	77

[a] These figures refer to only the period in which the paid leave provision is in force. After the standard five-month maternity leave a maximum of thirty-one months of post-maternity leave in possible, contingent on the number of children in the family unit.

Source: Calculated based on figures cited in J. Berent, "Causes of Fertility Decline in Eastern Europe and the Soviet Union, *Population Studies* 24, 2 (July 1970): 288-289.

two programs, the combined leave and family allowance payments amounting to from 32 to 77 percent of the average wage in 1967. While the payment schedule for post-maternity leave is not cumulative, the total family allowance payment, which is zero for a one-child family, rises abruptly for the second child and less strikingly thereafter.

Appraisal of the unique and powerful set of positive pronatalist incentives invoked by the Hungarian government is difficult given the short period since implementation and the methodological difficulties of discriminating between changes in the timing of births and behavioral changes that will actually effect completed fertility.[49] In both 1967 and 1968 the number of births rose and the increase was especially marked among the working women who were eligible for the newly enacted post-maternity leave. But as Berent noted, the natality increase involved mostly first and second births, while fourth and higher order births continued to decline, at a somewhat reduced rate, suggesting the possibility that only timing and spacing were changing in response to the new incentives.[50]

In Czechoslovakia the first clearly pronatalist adjustment of the existing family allowance system came in 1959 when the high and (through the third child) sharply progressive rates indicated in Table 9-12 were instituted. Mention has already been made of the brief interlude of administrative restriction of abortion availability from 1962 to 1964. It is worth noting that in this one instance of administrative intervention, the Czech authorities imposed restrictions on the two groups most likely to suffer serious complications from induced abortion—women under sixteen years of age and/or women who had never carried a child to term. While this approach was medically inspired, at least in the first case it selected out the group most likely to seek illegal interruption in the absence of a governmentally-sanctioned alternative. Also in 1962 paid maternity leave was extended from eighteen to twenty-two weeks and the

Table 9-12

Cumulative Family Allowance as Percentage of Average Annual Wave in Czechoslovakia

	Birth Order				
	1	2	3	4	5
1959-1968 [a]	4	11	27	43	60
1968-present	6	21	42	58	74

[a] / Calculations are based on the payments received by families in the lowest income group, where the monthly gross wages of the chief earner are not more than 1400 Kcs.

Source: Based on figures cited in J. Berent, "Causes of Fertility Decline in Eastern Europe and the Soviet Union," *Population Studies* 24, 2 (July 1970): 288-289. Percentages for 1968 and after have been calculated by the author.

modest charge for abortion on "social" grounds which had been eliminated in 1960 was reinstated and made a function of income.[51] In 1964 the agricultural sector was included under the provisions of the 1959 family assistance system. Since no appreciable fertility upsurge was in evidence, except for the two year period of reduced abortion availability, further measures were undertaken in 1968. At this time the family allowance system was adjusted upward, with an especially large increase for the crucial second child,[52] cash maternity payments raised from 650 to 1000 Czech Crowns,[53] and maternity leave extended to twenty-six weeks. In 1970 in emulation of the apparently successful Hungarian example, paid post-maternity leave of up to a year was instituted, involving a monthly payment of 500 Kcs.

The institution of limitations on the availability of legal abortion in Bulgaria in 1967 has been considered in some detail above in the course of the discussion of urban-rural fertility. At the same time lump sum birth payments were raised (effective January 1, 1968) to the high levels indicated in Table 9-10 and the family allowance structure was adjusted, sharply increasing the payment for the third child and cutting in half the payments for fourth and fifth children as indicated in Table 9-13. While the Bulgarian birth rate did rise substantially in 1968 and slightly in 1969, the effects of the increased financial incentives cannot easily be separated from the fertility response to decreased abortion availability. Although no abortion data are available for these most recent years, the sharp fall in the number of live births in 1970, in concert with evidence of abandonment of the three-year-old restrictive abortion policy in that same year, suggest that the effect of the positive incentives was not overwhelming.

While similar in appearance to the Hungarian legislation, the Romanian operational practice of not requiring either application in advance through a medical commission or proof of identity seems to have generated an almost unbelievable level of legal abortion.[54] Intermittently available statistics suggest that 112,000 and 220,000 legal abortions were performed in Romania in 1958

Table 9-13

Cumulative Family Allowance and Other Maternity Payments as a Percentage of the Average Annual Wage (1968) in Bulgaria

	Birth Order				
	1	2	3	4	5
Family Allowance (1969)	6	24	66	72	78
Lump Sum Payment [a]	2	20	50	2	2
Total [a]	8	44	116	74	80

[a] The lump sum payment is not cumulative and refers only to the year following the individual birth.

Source: Calculated based on figures cited in J. Berent, "Causes of Fertility Decline in Eastern Europe and the Soviet Union," *Population Studies* 24, 2 (July 1970): 288-289; and Henry P. David, *Family Planning and Abortion in the Socialist Countries of Central and Eastern Europe* (New York: The Population Council, 1970): 65.

and 1959, respectively, and that by 1965 the number may have reached 1,115,000.[55] This figure suggests a ratio of four legal abortions for every live birth, far above the 1.4 figure recorded in Hungary in 1964, the .8 ratio for Bulgaria in 1967, or the .5 ratio in Czechoslovakia in 1968. Clearly, the Romanian populous had to come to depend almost entirely upon abortion as a means of birth control.

While the other countries which offered nearly equal ease of access to abortion generally developed various pecuniary incentives to attempt to offset the apparent resulting fertility decline, Romania delayed action of any sort until late 1966. When the ten-year-old reform legislation was precipitously revoked in October of 1966 the birth rate rose dramatically from the 13.7 level of the last three months of that year to 15.9, 22.8, and finally 39.3 in the succeeding three quarters.[56] After the passage of more than four years in which other means of birth control could presumably have been brought to bear, the Romanian birth rate is still at a level approximately five points above that which obtained in the year of the counter reform. Since some pronatalist policy adjustments were also finally made in 1966—including expansion of child care facilities and part-time employment opportunities for women, a 30 percent increase in monthly family allowances, as well as increased maternity grants for third children and severe restrictions on divorce,[57] it is difficult to determine how much of the upward jump in the birth rate should be attributed to the drastically curtailed availability of legal abortion.

Since illegal abortion obviously resurged after 1966, the decline in the number of legal abortions from the more than one million per year level of 1965 and 1966 to the figure of 52,000 reported by David and Wright[58] for 1967 is not the true net decline in the number of artificially terminated pregnancies. The unusually large number of "spontaneous" abortions, over 153,000, and a sharp rise in both overall maternal mortality and mortality specifically attributable to abortion in 1967 is evidence of this reality.[59] Nonetheless, attribution of all or even a significant proportion of the observed rise in the birth rate that remained years after the initial period of adjustment to the relatively modest program of positive incentives would certainly seem out of line with the "encouraging" but hardly spectacular experience of the other Eastern European countries.

Conclusion

In the absence of a fully determined causal model of fertility behavior, it is not possible to conclusively establish that alteration of abortion availability will always have large, permanent effects on fertility levels. The appropriateness of such a conclusion in the short run, however, is indisputable. The theoretical arguments offered above relating to the role of abortion reform in altering the costs of birth avoidance, and perhaps also the "desired family size" as operationally measured, suggest the likelihood of a significant long-term effect even if modern contraceptive techniques should come into more general usage. Both availability of abortion and institution of fertility-supporting incentive programs may predominantly influence the timing and spacing of births. But changes in the timing of births will inevitably have long-term effects on population growth rates, permanent effects on populations size at any given future time, and, at least in the case of influences which advance the date of the first birth, probable effects on levels of completed fertility irrespective of the degree of contraception sophistication. In principle these qualitative arguments would apply equally to the negative fertility effects of abortion availability and the positive influences of the various social incentives we have considered, even though in practice the magnitude of the responses to changes in abortion availability seem far more dramatic.

The overall empirical conclusion of this study is that there has been a remarkably coherent pattern of abortion and fertility changes in each of the countries we have considered in detail. In each case increased availability and use of legal abortion have been systematically associated with a sharply reduced number of live births, and indirect evidence has indicated a considerable decline in the practice of illegal abortion. This pattern may be clearly discerned in Hungary, Czechoslovakia, and Bulgaria in the period immediately after the implementation of the reforms of the mid-1950s; in Czechoslovakia after the termination of the moderate restrictions of the 1963 and 1964 period; and it may be anticipated in Bulgaria after the apparent elimination of the parallel restrictions of the 1968 to 1970 period.

Efforts to reduce the availability of legal induced abortion seem to be associated with increasing use of illicit means of securing interruption of pregnancy and, without visible exception, have been followed by an appropriately timed rise in the aggregate number of births. This relationship may be observed in Czechoslovakia during the 1963-1964 period of reduced abortion availability, in Bulgaria in the 1968-1970 period, and most markedly in Romania in the period following the precipitous revocation of that country's remarkably unrestricted and non-bureaucratic abortion system in October of 1966.

It is well known that the crude birth rate for Romania rose from 13.7 at the time of the abortion counter reform to slightly in excess of 39 per 1,000 three quarters later. It is of course also well known that there are other means by which to prevent parenthood. Reference to the yearly birth rates for Romania—beginning at 14.3 in the year of the counterreform and rising to a peak of 27 in the following year, with a fairly steady decline thereafter—confirms the considerable adaptability demonstrated by the Romanian population, but it is nonetheless remarkable that more than four years after the removal of the legal abortion alternative, and given other contraceptive possibilities and a well-established cultural propensity for illegal abortion, the Romanian birth rate remains more than 5 points above the level of 1966.

It is interesting to note that Romania, often heralded in the western press as the most "progressive" in outlook of the Eastern European countries,[60] is the only country in that group to adopt an entirely "administrative" and legalistic approach in order to stem the fertility decline generally thought to have resulted from the legalization of abortion. We noted that in Bulgaria, Czechoslovakia, and Hungary an extensive and remarkably powerful battery of financial and social incentives has been invoked in the explicit attempt to stimulate fertility. These have been predominantly "positive," non-coercive incentives which leave the fertility decision ultimately in the hands of the individual couple. In the case of Hungary this dependence on positive incentives has been unbroken in the fifteen years since the initial reform. This rejection of the temptation to regulate fertility behavior by ukase perhaps reflects the lessons learned in the largely unsuccessful attempt to suppress illegal abortion by "administrative" methods in the 1953-1954 period—the net failure of which set the stage for the gradual de facto liberalization that occurred in the two years before the formal implementation of the Hungarian reforms in mid-1956.

In both Bulgaria and Czechoslovakia there has been a single episode of recourse to administrative measures, but in general population policy has been dependent on a combination of positive financial incentives, improved child care, and "educational" programs. The most significant aspect of this program is the substantial magnitude of the cash benefits involved—reaching up to 100 percent of average yearly income per worker under certain relatively common circumstances. This is of course equivalent to the payment of a quasi-wage for child care during the early years of childhood, when the combined value of the benefits is at a maximum. There is here rather unambiguous evidence that women's labor force participation has at least been explicitly recognized as a major deterrent to fertility.[61]

Benefit payments of the magnitude exhibited in these Eastern European countries should serve to establish a fairly conclusive test of the power of financial pronatalist incentives—a test that the relatively trivial Canadian and French payments never could really provide. From an a priori theoretical perspective an economist would probably expect a definite, but not necessarily large, positive fertility response to such policies. It is, however, too early to offer an empirical conclusion, despite the existence of some positive natality signs in each of the three countries.[62] The difficulty of clearly distinguishing between relatively insignificant changes in timing or spacing and fertility changes that will truly affect completed family size is well known, and the problem will only be resolved by the passage of time.

What are the implications of this rich quasi-experimental experience for other times and other places? It is of course true that abortion is everywhere and plays a major role in fertility control in all of the low fertility, relatively developed countries.[63] The Eastern European experience seems to suggest that provision of safe, socially sanctioned, legal abortion will lead to rapid acceptance of abortion as a means of fertility control and induce a marked decline in the practice of illegal abortion with its associated high mortality and morbidity. Such immediate acceptance of induced abortion is surely in part the result of the low level of availability and use of modern methods of contraception and the high degree of interest in limiting family size in these countries.

But the extreme case of Romania clearly establishes the possibility that abortion may under certain circumstances be deemed to be a superior means of birth avoidance, by the public, as distinct from the medical profession, perhaps driving out of use alternative techniques, unless there is a vigorously implemented family planning program of the type apparently mounted in Poland.[64] It is clear that popular acceptance of abortion can spread very rapidly once legal and moral sanctions are removed and if high medical standards are obtained, thereby eliminating its somewhat sinister and dangerous association in the public mind. Learning behavior apparently proceeds rapidly, assisted by demonstration effects, as the progressive community acceptance of abortion makes it more and more an ordinary, unexceptional aspect of daily life. The one-time nature of the action and the implicit short time horizon required on the part of the user recommend abortion as a policy instrument having a rapid and definite effect on current fertility, requiring only the sure perception on the part of the individual couple that *this* child at *this* time is inappropriate. The requisite medical resources perhaps limit the usefulness of abortion liberalization as an element of population policy in the developing nations, yet the *net* burden on medical facilities might be less than anticipated.[65]

Once these patterns of mass dependence on legal abortion are established, however, they are difficult to reverse as a simple matter of governmental policy. The Czechoslovak restoration of 1965 and the apparently parallel Bulgarian action of 1970 testify to this, although the Romanian perseverance after the

1966 counterreform provides a contrary example. Once abortion has been legalized and widely utilized for a period of time, much of the inexplicit ethical and inertial resistance of individual women to this form of fertility control is removed, and future restrictive efforts are likely to foster a burgeoning illegal practice with great social and health costs.

Notes

1. J.M. Keynes, "The Economic Consequences of Declining Population," *Eugenics Review* 29, 1 (April 1937): 13-17; Alvin Hansen, "Economic Progress and Declining Population Growth," *The American Economic Review* 29 (March 1939): 1-15; and Joseph J. Spengler, "Population Movements, Employment, and Income," *Southern Economic Journal* 5, 2 (October 1938): 129-157, and "Population and Per Capita Income," *The Annals of the American Academy of Political and Social Science* 237 (January 1945): 182-192.

2. See Simon Kuznets, *Capital in the American Economy, Its Formation and Financing* (Princeton, N.J.: Princeton University Press, 1961); Richard Easterlin, *Population, Labor Force and Long Swings in Economic Growth* (New York: National Bureau of Economic Research, 1968); and Paul Demeny, "Investment Allocation and Population Growth," *Demography* 2 (1965): 203-232.

3. See Henry P. David, *Family Planning and Abortion in the Socialist Countries of Central and Eastern Europe* (New York: The Population Council, 1970), p. 44; and V.I. Lenin, *Sochinenia* 19 (Moscow: 1929): 206-207.

4. See M.G. Field, "The Re-legalization of Abortion in Soviet Russia," *The New England Journal of Medicine* 255, 9 (August 1956): 421-422.

5. For a more extensive treatment of the Soviet experience see Gordon Hyde, "Abortion and the Birth Rate in the USSR," *Journal of Biosocial Science* 2, 3 (July 1970): 283-292.

6. See Malcolm Potts, "Legal Abortion in Eastern Europe," *Eugenics Review* 59, 4 (December 1967): 232-249; and Christopher Tietze, "The Demographic Significance of Legal Abortion in Eastern Europe," *Demography* 1, 1 (1964): 119-125.

7. The legislative histories of induced abortion in the excluded countries vary. Albania has had no reform, while the German Democratic Republic underwent a limited liberalization in 1947, which was revoked in 1950, followed by partial reliberalization in 1965 and 1972. In Romania, where the reforms occurred in 1956, and where the guarantees of privacy were most complete, the popular response was even stronger than in Hungary. Unfortunate data gaps prevent systematic analysis of the Romanian case for the moment. This is particularly inconvenient in that Romania eventually wiped out the abortion reform law late in 1966 and thus offers a particularly interesting subject for

analysis. In the first four years after the abolition of the reform, the birth rate rose from the 1966 low of 14.3 to 27.4, 26.3, 23.3, and 21.1, respectively. In Poland the reform occurred in 1956, but particularly powerful religious opposition to abortion and a relatively effective family planning program have served to reduce the importance of legal abortion there.

8. The gross rate of reproduction (GRR) provides a measure of the number of female children that would be born to a representative woman during her fecund years, assuming that she lived her entire life subject to the age-specific birth frequencies that obtain for the entire female population in the given year for which the value of the index is calculated. The GRR ignores the possibility of mortality among women prior to the end of their fertile years. While subject to the further limitation of implicitly assuming indefinite continuation of the age-specific fertility pattern of one moment in time, the GRR is nonetheless a reasonably satisfactory indicator of the hypothetical consequences of that particular historical age-specific fertility structure for future population growth.

9. Net rates of reproduction, which embody more appropriate mortality assumptions for the female population, are always lower than the corresponding GRRs. For example, in 1962 the NRRs for Hungary and Bulgaria were .808 and .975, respectively. While a NRR of unity implies an eventually constant population size, the GRR calculated from the same age-specific fertility data will always show a value somewhat in excess of unity. Thus a GRR of 1.0 or less implies an even lower NRR and hence a negative intrinsic rate of population growth.

10. An unweighted average of the seventeen major Western European countries. In 1965, for example, only Belgium at 16.4, Luxembourg at 16.0, and Sweden at 15.9 had birth rates as low as or lower than Czechoslovakia, which had the highest birth rate of the countries presently under consideration.

11. The gross rate of reproduction in effect embodies an assumption that the age structure of fertile women is rectangular. While this eliminates the peculiarities of any specific national population, and is in some sense "neutral" in making comparisons between countries, real world population structures are not rectangular. An alternative is use of one particular country's age structure as a standard.

12. Changes in intrinsic fertility can be defined for our purposes as changes in age-specific birth frequencies. Observed crude birth rates necessarily reflect both shifts in the age-specific rates and changes in the population weights attached to the age-specific rates.

13. A.G. Volkov, "O nekotorykh prichinakh snizhenia koeffitsenta rozhdaemosti," in A.G. Volkov, ed., *izuchenie vosproizvodstva naselenia* (Moscow: 1968): 171-183; and J. Berent, "Causes of Fertility Decline in Eastern Europe and the Soviet Union," *Population Studies* 24, 1-2 (March and July 1970). The analysis offered here is original, but builds upon the three-way conceptual breakdown of the crude birth rate suggested by Volkov, p. 173, and

cited by Berent (March 1970): 38. Both Volkov and Berent cite historical levels for the values of the respective multiplicative terms but do not attempt to assay the magnitude of the effects of their changing values on the aggregate fertility measure.

14. The number of births occurring to women outside this range is inconsequential in the countries under study. For purposes of the ensuing analysis these births are treated as if they had fallen in the adjoining 15-19 year and 45-49 year age groups, respectively.

15. The year 1955 is a convenient point of reference for all of the countries concerned since the Soviet reforms occurred in December of 1955 and all of the other followed fairly soon thereafter. The Hungarian reforms occurred on June 3, 1956, the Bulgarian on April 27, 1956, the Romanian on September 25, 1957, and the Czech on December 19, 1957. In the Czech case the impact was felt much earlier since there had been almost a year and a half of debate in the newspapers and other media over the desirability of loosening abortion restrictions prior to actual legal change. Monthly figures on legal abortions and comments of professional observers suggest that the medical profession reacted to the changing climate of opinion and applied existing standards less rigorously in anticipation of the imminent legislative change. See C. Tietze, "Abortion in Europe," *American Journal of Public Health* 57, 11 (November 1967): 1930, footnote 40.

16. It is necessary to perform an additional calculation to break down the GFR term into its fertility and age structure components, the latter component having been identified by construction of a standardized general fertility rate, using 1955 population proportions as weights. The difference between the crude birth rates calculated with the observed GFR and those calculated with the standardized GFR is entirely the result of shifts in the age structure of women 15-49 years of age and should be subtracted from the total effect attributed to the B/W* term in order to isolate the pure fertility change.

17. Cited in David (n. 3): 166.

18. Ibid., 167.

19. Ibid., 163.

20. See Vladimír Srb, *Demografická Příručka* (Prague: Nakladatelství Svoboda, 1967): 118. "Other" abortions include both spontaneous abortions, some of which may have been illegally induced, and known cases of hospitalization for treatment of the effects of illegal interruptions.

21. See A. Černoch, "Les authorisations d'interruptions de grossesse en Tchécoslovaquie," *Gynaecologia* (Basel) 160 (1965): 293; and J. Lukás, "Abortion in Czechoslovakia," in *Sex and Human Relations* (Proceedings of the 1964 IPPF Conference, London), (New York: Excerpta Medica Foundation, 1965): 98. Both of these papers are cited by Potts (n. 6): 242-243.

22. See Potts (n. 6): 245.

23. For a detailed treatment of the standardization techniques and data on a

yearly basis, see R. McIntyre, "Economic Consequences of Abortion Reform in Eastern Europe" (unpublished paper), November, 1971.

24. See K.H. Mehlan, "Changing Patterns of Abortion in the Socialist Countries of Europe," *Family Planning News* 10, 10 (October 1969): 3. The revision of abortion laws seems to involve restriction of abortion "on demand" to women who (i) are 45 years of age or older, (ii) have three or more children, or (iii) have an established medical or eugenic reason for avoiding further births. All other women must now make application to a local panel of three physicians who are specifically enjoined to give weight to "social" arguments for termination of pregnancy. Abortion for women who have never borne a child is legal *only* on specified medical grounds, or in cases involving rape, incest, etc.

25. It has been assumed that these effects may be treated as additive and thus summed and subtracted from the changes in the crude fertility indicator to obtain a measure of the "pure" fertility change. To the extent that there is interaction between the "levels" of the analysis, this factor will generally tend to inflate the aggregate shift effect, thereby imparting a downward, and, for our purposes, a conservative bias to the estimates of the size of the "pure" fertility change.

26. Cited in Berent (n. 13), (July 1970): 277-278.

27. Berent (n. 13), (March 1970): 36.

28. See Hyde (n. 5): 285-286 and 291.

29. In part this is because of the general absence of penalties directed at the recipient of an illegal abortion. In many cases women will seek medical attention through legitimate channels after illegal abortion in order to guard against complications.

30. Even with perfect registration of illegal abortions this simple calculation would not be precise. It would still be necessary to take account of (i) the probability of occurrence of spontaneous abortion in the absence of intervention, (ii) the fact that an aborted pregnancy provides protection from the "next" pregnancy for only a fraction of the nine or more months associated with a normal pregnancy, and (iii) the high probability that some individuals will seek multiple abortions in a given twelve-month period.

31. For an interesting and appropriate analysis of patterns of transmission of abortion information in the United States in terms of a theory of "acquaintance networks," see N.H. Lee, *The Search for an Abortionist* (Chicago: University of Chicago Press, 1969). A discussion of the reasons for survival of a low level of illegal abortion in Hungary is provided by I. Hirschler, "Morbidity and Mortality from Abortion in Hungary, 1960-1967," in R.E. Hall, ed., *Abortion in a Changing World* vol. 2 (New York: Columbia University Press, 1970): 126-128.

32. Simple correlation coefficients for changes in these series for Bulgaria, Czechoslovakia, and Hungary are $-.79$, $-.78$, and $-.69$. A crude transformation of the data on births, in effect assuming an average six-month lag between

interruption and anticipated births, can be made by calculating $B_t^* = \frac{1}{2}(B_t + B_{t+1})$. Simple correlation of A_t and B_t^* yield coefficients of $-.84$, $-.76$, and $-.78$.

33. Cited in Berent (n. 13), (March 1970): 56.

34. Lukás (n. 21): 97

35. The simultaneous implementation of the broad pronatalist program discussed below and, perhaps, decreased care in the use of conventional contraceptive practices as well as further reduction in illegal abortion may explain this untidy experience.

36. David (n. 3): 69, reports evidence for 1970 that suggests a return to the permissive abortion standards of the mid-1960s for all women, regardless of marital status, who have had one or more children. Mention is made in contemporary Bulgarian sources of the serious need to stem the rising practice of illegal abortion.

37. As suggested by Berent (n. 13), (July 1970): 281-282. Henry P. David, "Abortion Legalization: The Romanian Experience," (a paper presented at The Population Association of America meeting, Washington, D.C., April, 1971), pp. 10-12, also seems to assert the essential immutability of "desired family size" in the face of alterations in the cost of birth prevention.

38. T. Paul Schultz, "An Economic Model of Family Planning and Fertility," *Journal of Political Economy* 77, 2 (March/April 1969): 162-166.

39. Ibid., 154.

40. Except with regard to the greater possibility of maintaining anonymity by seeking illegal abortion, which, however, carries along with it much greater risk of death or serious complications.

41. This latter influence will be felt according to the degree of perceived guilt or non-congruence associated with violations of formal legal or informal societal norms.

42. Potts (n. 6): 235-236; Chantel Blayo, "Fécondité, Contraception et Avortement en Europe de l'Est," *Population* (Paris) 25, 4 (July/August 1970): 842-844; and György Acsádi, "A Falusi és a Városi Családtervezés Közötti Különbsegek," *Demográfia* (Budapest) 12, 1-2 (1969): 47-64.

43. See Larry Bumpass and Charles Westoff, "The 'Perfect Contraceptive' Population," *Science* 169, 3951 (18 September 1970): 1177-1182.

44. See Berent (n. 13), (March 1970): 42, 50, and 53.

45. Ibid., 284-285.

46. Bumpass and Westoff (n. 43): 1180.

47. Berent (n. 13), (July 1970): 285. This discussion closely follows Berent's excellent exposition on pp. 285-292.

48. Ibid., p. 289, reports that in 1967 about 100,000 working women, or two-thirds of all working women who gave birth during the year, availed themselves of the extended leave provisions.

49. Both biological and psychological arguments could be offered to suggest

that in the absence of other changes, earlier acceptance of first and second births would increase the probability of additional births.

50. Berent (n. 13), (July 1970): 289.

51. David (n. 3): 165.

52. The second child is crucial from a policy perspective in a situation where it is deemed desirable to reverse the substantial and growing popularity of the one child family norm.

53. At the official exchange rate one Czech Crown (Kcs.) = $.139 (US), so 1000 Kcs. is roughly equivalent to $139.00.

54. See David (n. 3): 128. The fee for volitional terminations (not based on medical criteria) was only 30 lei or less than $2.00.

55. This figure was quoted by the Romanian publication *Scinteia*, on 27 October 1968, and cited in Blayo (n. 42): 831. This figure may well include both known illegal induced abortions and spontaneous abortions, which generally include a certain number of botched illegal abortions.

56. Even after revocation of the general abortion on demand system, induced abortions remained available to women who (i) were 45 years of age or older, (ii) were already "supporting" four or more children, or (iii) had established medical indications. See Henry P. David and N. Wright, "Abortion Legislation: The Romanian Experience," *Studies in Family Planning* 2, 10 (October 1971): 206.

57. As far as can be determined, the non-progressive structure of family allowance payments in Romania was not adjusted until late 1966. At that time the allowance paid for each child under fifteen was raised from about 100 to 130 lei per month. Maternity grants of 1,000 lei (about $55) previously made beginning with the tenth birth, began with the third birth after January 1, 1967. The new restrictions on divorce are quite exceptional, involving introduction of a large filing fee, ranging from 3,000 to 5,000 lei ($170 to $280) depending on income, and a compulsory six-month or one-year period of trial reconciliation contingent on whether there are children involved. David (n. 3): 129-130, reports a decline in the number of divorces granted from about 25,000 in 1966 to 48 in 1967, although undoubtedly a sharp rise will be observed in 1968. A perhaps coincidental decline in the crude marriage rate may also be observed at this time.

58. David and Wright (n. 56): 205-210.

59. Total maternal mortality in Romania rose from 235 in 1966 to 481 the following year. In part the rise is the result of the normal risks of child birth applied to a sharply increased number of births. Maternal deaths per 100,000 live births rose only slightly from 86 to 91. However, the number of abortion-related deaths rose from 83 in 1966 to 170 in 1967, and by 1969 amounted to 262. Although the total number of births had dropped off significantly by 1969, the rise in known abortion mortality was sufficient to hold total maternal mortality at 491. See World Health Organization, *World Health Statistics Report*, 1971, pp. 436-437.

60. This is perhaps often an inappropriate projection of certain foreign policy trends into the area of domestic social and economic policy.

61. Berent (n. 13), (July 1970): 289.

62. See for example, Vladimír Srb, "The 1969 Natality Upswing–the Fruit of Population Policy Measures," *Demosta* (Prague) 3, 4 (1970): 281-292.

63. See for example, C.V. Kiser, "Family Limitation in Europe: A Survey of Recent Studies," in C.V. Kiser, ed., *Research in Family Planning* (Princeton, N.J.: Princeton University Press, 1962): 235-242; A. Klinger, "Demographic Aspects of Abortion," paper presented at the *International Population Conference* vol. 2 (London: International Union for the Scientific Study of Population, 1969): 1153-1165; and Christopher Tietze and Sarah Lewitt, "Abortion," *Scientific American* 220, 1 (January 1969): 21-27.

64. The relatively powerful position of the Catholic church in Poland may well have been more crucial in inhibiting acceptance of abortion, although this must also have had some negative implications for family planning programs.

65. A special study of the recent liberalization of abortion legislation in India is currently being conducted by the Institute for Research in Law and Jurisprudence at the State University of New York at Buffalo.

Index

Abortion, 11; availability, 192; on demand, 213; history of, 210; illegal, 185; legalization in Eastern Europe, 183; liberalization, 199-202; and live births, 198; in U.S.S.R., 180

Access: and consumers, 50

Administration: and population programs, 5

Age: structure and births, 199; structure in Eastern Europe, 187; structure and fertility decline, 194; sex structure, 190; sex structure in China, 158

Aged, population, 184

AID (Agency for International Development), 129; and population control, 95

Aid, 110

Aird, J., 163

Albania, 185

Alberdi, 99

Alliance for Progress, 44

American Political Science Review, 4

Amoral familism, 110

Animal behavior, as in Ardney and Lorenz, 82

Anxiety: in Garland and Trudeau, 26

Approaches, aggregate, 21

Apter, D., 27

Ardrey, R., 82

Argentina, 100

Attitudes: antinatal, 132; in Wright, 137

Bachrach, P., 61

Banfield, E.C., 110

Baratz, M., 61

Bay, Christain, 22-25

Berelson, B., 6, 18, 46; coercion, 137

Belgium: birth rate, 211

Berent, J., 181; age structure, 187; birth rate, 212; fertility development, 196; social welfare legislation, 202

Bergman, E., 8; discussed by Nash, 71, 72

Biafra, 81

Big-family idea, 78

Bigotry, 53, 68

Birth: control and Chinese field workers, 162; order, 201; rate and age specifics, 211; crude rate, 94, 187, 188; crude rate and changes, 194; rate in Eastern Europe, 183; rate and incentives, 205

Blacks: in Wright, 140

Blake, J., 29, 110, 120

Bolivia, 100

Bounties: for sterilization, 25

Brazil, 100

Buck, J.L., 167

Bulgaria: abortion policy, 185, 199; historical data, 191

Burch, W., 26

Callahan, D., 25; ethical priorities, 30

Calhoun, J.B., density, 83

Camara, Msgr. Helder, 111

Canada: incentives, 209

Capital-labor ratios, 184

Catholic Church, 24; and abortion in Poland, 216; in Latin America, 101-103; in Wright, 148

Chandresekhar, S., 162

Chen, Pi-chao, 11

Child-care facility, 206

Child-survival ratios: in China, 164

Chile, 100

China, 12; economic socialist transition, 169-171; Family Revolution, 164-167; government attitude, 153; mass communication, 170, 171; public health network, 160-162; status of women, 167-169

Choplin, D., 98

Cialdini, R., 120

Clark, C., 19, 29

Clifford, W., 121

Coercion, 23, 113, 114; in Godwin, 129, 130; in Wright, 136

Colombia, 100

Commission on Population Growth and the American Future, 5, 41

Compulsory restraints, 20

Conference, 65; on Infant and Child Mortality and Fertility Behavior, 53

Congress, 73, 106

Consumers, 39, 49; in Ehrenreich, 66

Contraception: attitude toward, 144; need defined in Wright, 137; practices, 115; program, 10; technology, 51

Corporate wealth: in Clinton, 98

Corsely, G., 69

Costa Rica, 100

Cost structures: and abortion, 200

"Culture of poverty," 87

Cultural Revolution, 168

Custody: in China, 165

Czechoslovakia: abortion, 185, 188, 197; historical data, 191

Daly, H.E., 49

David, H.P., 206, 214; volitional termination, 215

Davis, Kingsley, 20, 65, 110

217

About the Contributors

Elihu Bergman is assistant director of the Harvard Center for Population Studies. His professional specialization has been the management of development programs in the U.S. and overseas. He has worked with The Ford Foundation, VISTA, Development and Resources Corporation, and the Agency for International Development. In 1971 Dr. Bergman received his Ph.D. in political science from the University of North Carolina at Chapel Hill, where his major interest was in the political analysis of population policy. Together with Professor Peter Bachrach, he is currently completing a book in that field entitled *Class and Power: The Formulation of American Population Policy* (D.C. Heath, forthcoming.)

Pi-chao Chen, associate professor of political science at Wayne State University, received his Ph.D. in 1966 from Princeton University. His major areas of interest are comparative politics, political demography, and demographic politics. Professor Chen's publications have appeared in *World Politics, Asian Survey, Population Studies,* and *Dévelopment et Civilisations.* Several of his monographs are to be published shortly.

Richard L. Clinton is assistant professor of political science at the University of North Carolina, Chapel Hill, where he earned his Ph.D. in 1971. His fields of special interest are Latin American politics, normative political theory, and the political implications of population change. In addition to articles in *The Journal of Inter-American Studies and World Affairs, Inter-American Economic Affairs, The Annals of the Southeastern Conference on Latin American Studies*, and *Alternatives* (Canada), he has contributed to several edited works and was co-editor, with William Flash and Kenneth Godwin, of *Political Science in Population Studies* (D.C. Heath, 1972).

Moye W. Freymann is director of the Carolina Population Center at the University of North Carolina, Chapel Hill. He received his M.D. from John Hopkins University in 1948 and, after public health experience in Iran and India, completed his Dr. P.H. at Harvard in 1960. He has contributed chapters to a large number of books and reports.

Steven Garland is a doctoral candidate in political science at the University of North Carolina at Chapel Hill. In addition to his population policy research in Puerto Rico, he is currently involved in an intensive experiment designed to test the principles of humanistic anarchism.

R. Kenneth Godwin, assistant professor of political science at Oregon State University, received his Ph.D. from the University of North Carolina at Chapel

Hill in 1971. His research interests and publications are in the fields of Latin American politics and comparative political behavior, particularly the problems encountered in devising survey instruments and interpreting survey data. Professor Godwin was a contributor to and co-editor, with Richard Clinton and William Flash, of *Political Science in Population Studies* (D.C. Heath, 1972).

Robert J. McIntyre, assistant professor of economics at Pennsylvania State University, received his Ph.D. from the University of North Carolina at Chapel Hill in 1972. His major research interests are in the areas of European economic history, the economic analysis of fertility, the demographic effects of abortion, and comparative economic systems.

A.E. Keir Nash is associate professor, vice-chairman of political science, and president of the AAUP chapter at the University of California, Santa Barbara. Receiving his Ph.Ð. from Harvard in 1967, he served during 1970-71 as director of political research of the National Commission on Population Growth and the American Future, in which capacity he edited the Commission research volume, *Governance and Population* (Washington, D.C.: Government Printing Office, 1972). He is the senior author of *Oil Pollution and the Public Interest* (Berkeley, 1972), and his writings have appeared in numerous journals, including the *American Political Science Review*, the *Journal of American History*, the *Virginia Law Review*, and *Mercurio* (Italy).

Robert Trudeau, assistant professor of political science at Providence College in Providence, R.I., earned his Ph.D. from the University of North Carolina in 1971. His fields of interest include Latin American politics, normative political theory, and political development. He has done field research in Costa Rica and currently is conducting research into population policy processes in Puerto Rico. From 1964 to 1966 Dr. Trudeau served as a Peace Corps Volunteer in Honduras.

Gerald C. Wright, Jr., assistant professor of political science at Florida Atlantic University, was awarded his Ph.D. in 1972 by the University of North Carolina at Chapel Hill. His principal interests lie in the linkages between mass political behavior and public policy.